D1064518

To Steal a Book Is an Elegant Offense
Intellectual Property Law in Chinese Civilization

Studies in East Asian Law,
Harvard University

To Steal a Book Is an Elegant Offense

Intellectual Property Law in Chinese Civilization

William P. Alford

Stanford University Press,
Stanford, California
1995

Studies in East Asian Law, Harvard University

The Harvard Law School, in cooperation with the John King Fairbank Center for East Asian Research, the Harvard-Yenching Institute, and scholars from other institutions, conducts a program of training and research designed to further scholarly understanding of the legal systems of China, Japan, Korea, and other jurisdictions in East Asia. In conjunction with this program, a series of publications was established in 1967.

Stanford University Press   Stanford, California
© 1995 by the Board of Trustees of the Leland Stanford Junior University
Printed in the United States of America

CIP data appear at the end of the book

Stanford University Press publications are distributed exclusively by Stanford University Press within the United States, Canada, and Mexico; they are distributed exclusively by Cambridge University Press throughout the rest of the world.

This study is dedicated to Daniel Shen Alford and his four grandparents. May he lead as worthy a life as they have.

Acknowledgments

I know no better way to preface a study on intellectual property than to recognize the contributions of others. Such acknowledgment must begin in this case with an expression of my deep gratitude to the law firm of O'Melveny & Myers, which, in but one of its many contributions to the public weal, provided support that helped launch this project. In selecting me through an international competition as the first recipient of a grant to commemorate its centennial, O'Melveny & Myers provided me with the equivalent of a research sabbatical. During that period and since, I have been able to interview public and private decision makers, as well as victims and perpetrators of infringement; pour through musty archival materials here and abroad; traverse back alleys in search of "pirates"; and through more conventional means carry out the bulk of the research that forms the basis of this book. I am no less appreciative of the wise counsel that Warren Christopher, who was formerly the firm's managing partner, and Howard Chao, Gary Horlick, the late Richard Sherwood, John Stamper, Ko-Yung Tung, and others at O'Melveny & Myers offered, all the while remaining mindful of my need for scholarly independence.

I also feel very thankful for the generosity of many others. The late Professor Melville Nimmer was an inspiration. Although Mel was a preeminent scholar of copyright, he always found time to help younger colleagues and, in this and many other ways, exemplified how one might gracefully blend professional excellence with kindness. The deans under whom I have been fortunate enough to have worked—Dean Robert Clark of the Harvard Law School and Dean Susan Westerberg Prager and Professor Carole Goldberg-Ambrose of the UCLA School of Law—did exactly what good deans should do, providing the heartfelt scholarly encouragement and the much appreciated material support necessary to carry out such a project. Christine Cervenak, Jau-yuan Hwang, Margot Landman, Ouyang Jehng, Peter Lin, Liang Zhiping, Mark Ramseyer, Arthur Rosett, Shen Yuanyuan, Frank Upham, Lloyd Weinreb, Yin Xiong, and Yu Xingzhong generously and insightfully reviewed part or all of the manuscript during its many drafts.

My teacher Jerome Cohen and sinological colleagues, including Randle Edwards, James Feinerman, Sharon Hom, Andrew Hsieh, Philip Huang, William Jones, Natalie Lichtenstein, Stanley Lubman, Hugh Scogin, Karen Turner, Susan Weld, and Margaret Woo, with patience and good humor all added substantially to my understanding of law in China. Chang Wejen, Susan Cherniack, Eddy Harrison, David Ben Kay, Lawrence Liu, Michael Moser, Julia Murray, Shao Chiung-hui, and Mark Sidel kindly shared with me a variety of materials on intellectual property in China. Muriel Bell, Peter Dreyer, and John Feneron of the Stanford University Press were kind, helpful, and highly literate editors. Han Deyun, Peter Neumann, and Franklin Zee proved to be exceptional research assistants, unearthing a wealth of valuable information. Cheryl Frost, Margaret Kiever, Susan Salvato, Melissa Smith, Deborah Soares, and Kathryn Ying pored through my almost illegible drafts with extraordinary care and patience.

Apart from those named above, I am also indebted to the scores of individuals I interviewed in the United States and abroad. Many spoke to me on the condition that I preserve their anonymity. As a result, data gleaned from my interviews are cited by date and place, rather than by interviewee.

Additionally, I would like to thank, among other institutions, the Harvard Law School and its East Asian Legal Studies Program; the Harvard Law Library; the Harvard-Yenching Library; the library of Harvard's John King Fairbank Center for East Asia Research; the Chiang Ching-kuo Foundation for International Scholarly Exchange; the Dean's Fund at the UCLA School of Law; the International Studies and Overseas Program at UCLA; the Research Committee of the Academic Senate at UCLA; the Law Library and Rudolph Oriental Collection at UCLA; the ministries of the Interior and Justice of the Republic of China; the Academia Sinica; the National Library of the People's Republic of China;

the State Copyright Administration of the People's Republic of China; the Intellectual Property Center of the People's University of China; the China Council for the Promotion of International Trade; China Patent Agents (H.K.) Ltd.; Baker & McKenzie; Lee & Li; Paul, Weiss, Rifkind, Wharton & Garrison; International Business Machines Corporation (Japan); Lockheed Corporation; Universal/ MCA; the Office of the United States Trade Representative; the United States Patent and Trademark Office; the Copyright Office of the United States; and the U.S. embassies in Beijing and Seoul.

I would also like to thank those institutions of higher learning at which I was able to present papers drawn from the material that makes up this book. They include the University of Arizona College of Law, the Boston College Law School, Case Western Reserve University, the Columbia University School of Law, the University of Connecticut School of Law, Harvard Law School, Lewis and Clark College Northwestern School of Law, National Taiwan University, and Washington University, St. Louis. I am also grateful to the *Journal of Chinese Law*, which published an earlier version of chapter 2 in volume 7, no. 1 (1993).

Finally, I wish to thank my parents, Hyman and Rose Alford, my wife, Shen Yuanyuan, and my dearest friend, Jonathan Kempner, for all they have done and continue to do.

I have rendered Chinese names and terms in pinyin romanization, except where it would be confusing to do so (e.g., Taipei). All translations are mine unless otherwise indicated.

Notwithstanding the generous support provided me by so many persons and institutions, I remain responsible for the opinions expressed and errors contained in this work.

W.P.A

Contents

Illustration from a 1985 pamphlet by the Jilin sheng gongshang xingzheng guanliju (State Administration for Industry and Commerce of Jilin Province), *Zhonghua renmin gongheguo shangbiaofa tushi* (An Illustrated Explanation of the Trademark Law of the People's Republic of China). The accompanying text reads, "Article 40: Those who pass off someone else's registered trademark, by means including the unauthorized making or selling of items bearing that trademark, besides being required to compensate the person whose trademark has been infringed and being subject to punishment by [an administrative] fine, may if directly responsible be charged by the legal organs with criminal responsibility in accordance with the law." The man standing behind the bench is identified as the presiding judge.

To Steal a Book Is an Elegant Offense
Intellectual Property Law in Chinese Civilization

One

Introduction

To steal a book is an elegant offense.
Chinese saying of unknown provenance

Although scholars both East and West credit the Chinese with having contributed paper, movable type, and ink to humankind, China has yet to develop comprehensive protection for what is created when one applies inked type to paper.[1] To be sure, this has not been for a lack of effort in promulgating formal legal protections for intellectual property. In recent years, both the People's Republic of China (PRC) and the Republic of China (ROC) have taken major steps designed to bring their copyright and other intellectual property laws into close conformity with the expectations of the U.S. government, which had threatened to impose hundreds of millions of dollars in trade sanctions on each in response to what Washington termed their cavalier attitudes toward such American property.[2] These developments notwithstanding, protection for intellectual property remains closer to rhetoric than reality on the Chinese mainland, and problems persist across the Taiwan Straits.

This book considers why intellectual property law, and in particular copyright, has never taken hold in China. For purposes of this study, intellectual property is defined principally to encompass copyright, patent, and trademark,[3] although other less significant forms will at times be addressed. *Copyright* is intended to protect original literary, artistic, and musical works, with the focus of protection being the expression of an idea, rather than the idea itself. State acknowledgment of such rights, at least in the West, dates from the Enlightenment and is grounded in the United States in Article I, section 8, clause 8 of the Constitution.[4] In today's world, copyright is typically said to encompass the exclusive rights to reproduce, distribute, display, perform, or prepare derivative versions of the work in question. A *patent* is a limited-term monopoly granted by government to the inventor of a novel, nonobvious, and useful product, manufacturing process, machine, chemical composition, design, or plant in exchange for public disclosure of the pertinent innovation. Considered by historians to have emanated, at least in the West, from fifteenth-century Venice, patents, too, have constitutional grounding in the United States.[5] In this study, a *trademark* is a word or symbol that identifies the source of goods (or services in the case of a servicemark). Unlike copyright and patent, trademark protection does not have a constitutional basis; rather, it emerged in Anglo-American jurisprudence from the common law, although in the United States and elsewhere trademarks are now protected statutorily.

At its core, this study advances four broad propositions. The first is that, contrary to the assertions of Chinese scholars[6] and the expectations of Western theorists,[7] imperial China did not develop a sustained indigenous counterpart to intellectual property law, in significant measure because of the character of Chinese political culture. Second, initial attempts to introduce European and American intellectual property law to China at the turn of this century were unsuccessful because they failed to consider the relevance of such models for China and instead presumed that foreign pressure would suffice to induce ready adoption and widespread adherence to such laws. Third, in an unwitting reprise of the early twentieth century, current attempts to establish intellectual property law, particularly on the Chinese mainland, have been deeply flawed in their failure to address the difficulties of reconciling legal values, institutions, and forms generated in the West with the legacy of China's past and the constraints imposed by its present circumstances. The book's final proposition is that although the United States has used what diplomatic leverage it has with the PRC and the ROC as liberally with regard to intellectual property concerns as to virtually any other issue, the effort has been problematic, notwithstanding the conclusion of much-trumpeted bilateral agreements.[8] American policy regarding intellectual property law has been based on fundamental misconceptions about the nature of legal development and is therefore in need of major reformulation.

This study is divided into five parts, following the introductory comments in this chapter. Chapter 2 examines whether there was in China any indigenous protection for intellectual property before the introduction of Western notions of such law in the late nineteenth and early twentieth centuries. There is evidence of restrictions on the unauthorized reproduction of certain books, symbols, and products, but this should not be seen as constituting what we in the United States now typically understand intellectual property law to be, for their goal was not the protection of property or other private interests.[9] After a brief review of the received wisdom on the growth of such law, chapter 2 then considers why Chinese civilization, which was for centuries the world's most advanced scientifically and technologically, and which by any standard has long been one of the most sophisticated culturally, did not generate more comprehensive protection for its rich bounty of scientific, technological, and artistic creation. In doing so, it suggests a need for recasting the terms in which the imperial Chinese legal tradition has conventionally been characterized.

Chapter 3 delves into early efforts to introduce foreign notions of intellectual property law in China. Its first section takes the negotiation and attempted implementation of commercial treaties between China and the United Kingdom and the United States at the turn of this century as a focal point for exploring ill-fated foreign efforts to impose intellectual property law on the Chinese. The second section assesses similarly unsuccessful efforts undertaken a generation later, by the Nationalist Chinese government, to transplant to China intellectual property law from abroad with scant alteration. Throughout, the chapter emphasizes the problems inherent in utilizing bodies of law and legal institutions generated in one society as a model for legal development in a second and seemingly quite different setting.

Chapter 4 examines the varied experience of the PRC with regard to intellectual property law. During the early years of the PRC, China's new leaders instituted measures for the regulation of intellectual property that, although inspired by Marxism, resonated with elements of the Chinese past that they were attempting to repudiate. By the 1980's, however, this approach was discredited and the PRC instead made unprecedented efforts to develop "socialist" trademark, patent, and copyright laws with "Chinese characteristics." The chapter explores the rationale for this endeavor, the nature of the laws generated, and the manner of their implementation, while arguing that this example provides broader insight into the character of the wider law reform launched soon after the end of the Cultural Revolution in 1976.

Chapter 5 addresses the situation of the ROC during its tenure on Taiwan. It begins by examining the disparity throughout much of this period between the formal law and Taiwan's reputation as the most celebrated center internationally for the piracy of intellectual property. The chapter then considers recent efforts to revise the ROC's intellectual property laws in view of both the pressure brought to bear on its government by the United States and the extraordinary political, economic, social, and technological changes under way in the island republic.

The book's sixth and final chapter critically examines American policy designed to spur the growth of intellectual property law in China, concluding with a discussion of ways in which the effort to foster respect for such property rights depends on the expansion of broader political and economic rights in China.

Such a study is not without substantial difficulty on many levels— beginning with the inquiry that lies at its heart. The very act of examining intellectual property law with reference to China entails a reliance—explicit or otherwise—on definitions of intellectual property derived from Western settings. In this reliance, one must avoid construing the path that intellectual property law in the United States or other jurisdictions has followed as providing a "normal" or inevitable course against which Chinese developments are to be evaluated.[10] Indeed, even on the two sides of the English Channel, intellectual property law developed in markedly different ways, just as there remain divergent opinions within and among the major industrialized democracies on a number of important dimensions of this area of the law[11]—including the central question of whether intellectual property law is effective in its stated goal of spurring inventiveness and creativity.[12] In considering the unauthorized use abroad of American intellectual property,[13] it is also important to guard against overstating either the extent of protection that the relevant U.S. laws are intended to provide even within our own borders[14] or the degree to which we actually have adhered to such laws here. Neither copyright, patent, trademark, nor any other intellectual property laws create absolute rights in this country. The control that each is intended to provide is qualified, in terms of public use (as in the fair use of copyrighted materials) and of duration (as in the seventeen-year non-renewable term of a patent), among other reasons. And as Charles Dickens, Anthony Trollope, and many others learned the hard way, the United States did not grant even formal protection for foreign copyrighted materials until 1891—by which time we had passed through what arguably might be termed our period as a developing country.[15] Nor has the United States ceased to be both a producer of and market for a myriad of infringing items.[16] How many among us can honestly claim never to have employed photocopying, videotaping, or audio recording equipment in an unlawful fashion—if, indeed, we even know what the law currently provides in such areas?[17]

The need to guard against extrapolating normality from the West dictates further precautions. First, such seemingly neutral modes of inquiry as economic analysis, wherever they come from on the political spectrum, may be more particularistic historically and culturally than is generally imagined. Thus, for example, the early Marxist belief that capitalism must precede socialism assumed that "Oriental despotism" precluded the "living fossil" (Marx's affectionate name for China) from being in the vanguard of nations on the path to communism.[18] Nor is such ethnocentricity limited to the left, as evidenced by the fact that much of mainstream economic theory in this country for long essentially presumed that the measure of state intervention evident in the economies of Japan and the so-called Little Dragons (Hong Kong, Singapore, South Korea, and Taiwan) constituted a virtually insurmountable impediment to the very prosperity that these jurisdictions now enjoy.[19]

Seeming neutrality must also be questioned with respect to the use of language. The use by different societies of common terminology does not necessarily ensure that such terms will carry the same meaning in each setting.[20] Indeed, meaning may vary for different reasons, ranging from the process of absorption of one society's vocabulary and concepts into another to a conscious effort to suggest a higher measure of adherence to international norms than may be warranted.

Similar caution is called for with respect to more avowedly cultural explanations. The recognition that cultural factors, however broadly defined, are by their very nature less conducive to "hard" proof than their economic counterparts is no excuse for being conclusory. Just as economically deterministic analyses run the risk of being unidimensional, so do approaches rooted in portrayals of culture as essentially impervious to change, whether from within or beyond the society being examined. Moreover, we must remain mindful that at no time is any society's culture monolithic, given class, gender, ethnic, regional, and other differences.

A second major difficulty lies in the fact that although there is a great deal of writing about intellectual property law and related issues in the United States, much of it aspires to do little more than describe doctrine. As a result, it generally fails to provide a strong historical or conceptual home base from which one can compare issues of intellectual property protection in different societies. Even the most ambitious articles often fall short—typically by premising discussion on unstated (and, one fears, unwarranted) assumptions about the genesis or impact of such law,[21] or by failing to adequately address the question of why this particular form of property warrants treatment different from its tangible counterparts.[22]

The difficulties of researching intellectual property law are hardly confined to the relative sparsity of writing contemplating its underlying rationale and broader implications, for at the opposite end of the spectrum, there are all too few attempts to portray its operation in any systematic fashion. Most such efforts are either anecdotal or uncritically dependent on data provided by trade associations and other interested parties, since those engaged in pirating intellectual property have not been considerate enough to compile statistics for academic researchers. Moreover, the intangible nature of intellectual property complicates detection of its unlawful appropriation, particularly given modern technology, and the public, even in countries considered vigilant about protecting rights in such property, remains more tolerant of its infringement than of virtually any other form of illegal activity.[23] Indeed, victims are frequently hesitant to acknowledge infringement, fearing that the value of their intellectual property may be diminished and the receptivity of certain host governments to their operations may be impaired.

Further impediments exist to exploring the area of intellectual property law on either side of the Taiwan Straits. Ironically, although the PRC is engaged in a historically unprecedented effort to develop a legal system suitable for a society encompassing elements of Confucianism, communism, and capitalism, scholarship on contemporary Chinese law places too much emphasis on the exegesis of code provisions. Chinese and foreign scholars alike generally slight both the processes through which such rules are formed and the ways in which these rules operate in society. And if misdirected attention characterizes a goodly portion of the scholarly writing on the PRC, academic inattention has been the problem besetting the ROC, for that jurisdiction's remarkable efforts at transforming its political and legal life in recent years remain far too modestly chronicled beyond the Chinese world.

Finally, there are difficulties generated by the reluctance of informants to provide evidence of behavior that might be construed abroad as illicit, immoral, or improper and that might affect bilateral relations with the United States and other technology-exporting nations or complicate efforts to accede to the General Agreement on Tariffs and Trade (GATT).[24] In the PRC, these concerns are intensified by the government's faith that a significant influx of foreign technology will enable China to compensate rapidly for time lost to the chaos of the Cultural Revolution years[25] and its concomitant determination to portray the climate for technology transfer and foreign investment as favorably as possible. Accentuating the complexity of the task confronting foreign sinologists are the highly sensitive involvement of the government of the PRC in the media, both as infringer and as censor,[26] and the existence of a multitiered body of law, important elements of which have not routinely been disclosed to foreigners (or most Chinese, for that matter), even if their interests are involved.[27]

Given these conceptual and practical difficulties, one might well question the soundness of inquiring about a "Western" subject in an "Eastern" context. For those skeptical about undertaking such an inquiry for its own sake, an additional answer is provided by the fact that both the PRC and the ROC are using Western models of intellectual property law and claiming benefits that normally accrue to jurisdictions that comply with the major international intellectual property conventions, all of which are basically derived from the experience of Western nations.[28] And, if further justification is desired, perhaps it may be found in the experience of the purveyors and purchasers of infringing items, whose daily activities remind us that East and West are inextricably linked in matters of intellectual property.[29]

Two

Don't Stop Thinking About . . . Yesterday: Why There Was No Indigenous Counterpart to Intellectual Property Law in Imperial China

> The Master [Confucius] said: I transmit rather than
> create; I believe in and love the Ancients.
>
> *The Analects of Confucius*, bk. 7, ch. 1

The notion that copyright arose soon after the advent of printing enjoys wide currency in the scholarly world. Chinese historians date copyright from the rise of printing during the Tang Dynasty (A.D. 618–906),[1] while Western theorists of economic development contend that the inexpensive dissemination of texts necessitated the formal legal protection that copyright is intended to provide.[2] In short, the conventional wisdom among "intellectual property scholars . . . [is] that copyright emerged with the invention of printing," as Zheng Chengsi and Michael Pendleton declare in their recent monograph on copyright in the PRC.[3]

This chapter takes issue with the received wisdom, at least as concerns imperial China (221 B.C.–A.D. 1911). After first endeavoring to delineate an appropriate scope for inquiring into imperial Chinese legal history, it explores Chinese efforts to regulate the reproduction of literary and other creation and innovation prior to the twentieth century. Finding neither a formal nor an informal counterpart to copyright or other major forms of intellectual property law, this chapter then considers why imperial China did not respond to the introduction of printing and other major technological advances in the manner that both Chinese and Western scholars would have us believe.

Sinologists have long characterized Chinese law from the first imperial dynasty, the Qin (221–206 B.C.), through the last dynasty, the Qing (A.D. 1644–1911), as "overwhelmingly penal in emphasis," in the words of Derk Bodde and Clarence Morris, authors of the best-known Western work on Chinese legal history.[4] Focusing on the imperial codes that were promulgated during each dynasty, such as the *Da Qing lü li* (Laws of the Great Qing Dynasty),[5] the conventional wisdom holds that the "positive law," in Joseph Needham's words, was confined to "purely penal (criminal) purposes."[6] As a consequence, the "civil law remained extremely underdeveloped," and the concerns typically addressed through it in the modern West were instead the domain of village and clan elders acting pursuant to custom.[7]

The foregoing image requires serious reconsideration. The emphasis on public, positive law and the dichotomy between civil and criminal law so deeply ingrained in contemporary Western society have led to a mischaracterization of the role and nature of imperial Chinese law. The Chinese neither saw public, positive law as the defining focus of social order nor divided it into distinct categories of civil and criminal. Rather, traditional Chinese thought arrayed the various instruments through which the state might be administered and social harmony maintained into a hierarchy ranging downward in desirability from heavenly reason (*tianli*), the way (*tao*), morality (*de*), ritual propriety (*li*), custom (*xixu*), community compacts (*xiang yue*), and family rules (*jia cheng*) to the formal written law of the state.[8] Public, positive law was meant to buttress, rather than supersede, the more desirable means of guiding society and was to be resorted to only when these other means failed to elicit appropriate behavior.

Far from being indifferent to the concerns we now address through civil law, the imperial Chinese state accorded them great prominence, paying particular attention to the family, which was both a social and economic unit. As befits an agrarian state self-consciously organized along the model of an extended family, the standards embodied in its various norms from heavenly reason down to public, positive law focused to a very substantial degree on matters encompassed in the "modern West" under the rubric of civil law. The inattention of both Chinese and foreign legal historians to the more ethereal of these precepts and the veritable fixation of such scholars on the written law's penalties has obscured the very concerns those penalties were designed to promote and, in so doing, prevented us from fully appreciating their true significance.[9] We must not lose sight of the fact that more than half of the ten most serious offenses (the Ten Abominations, or *shi e*)[10] under imperial Chinese law consisted of misdeeds involving the family. Impiety toward one's senior relatives, for example, carried far greater repercussions than the murder of a stranger. Indeed, in view of the weight imperial codes gave such matters, one might well argue that the Chinese state had a singular concern with one of the core foci of our civil law.

The idea that the state's reliance on family heads and village elders to enforce local customs expressed an imperial Chinese indifference to what we call civil law also needs revision. The state's reliance on family heads, village elders, and guild leaders to apply local custom—as embodied in family rules [*jia cheng*],[11] guild charters (*hang zhang*),[12] and other less formal expressions of such practices—should instead be seen as akin to a controlled delegation of authority. It was reminiscent of, if far less formal than, tax farming, pursuant to which local private merchants were crucial to the collection of state revenues.[13] As such, it ingeniously allowed the state's influence to reach far further than would otherwise have been the case, given the range of dialects and customs, poor communications infrastructure, and persistent budgetary problems that by the late Qing provided no more than a single local representative of the emperor (known as the district magistrate) for every 200,000 subjects.[14]

The suggestion that the imperial state's reliance on family, village, and guild leaders to administer local custom was a sign of state concern for, rather than indifference to, family and economic matters seems less radical if one appreciates that in making their decisions, such leaders were likely to have been applying basic values consistent with those that the state's official representatives would have employed had they been more directly involved.[15] The delegation of authority "required continuing adherence to the social guidelines set down in the Four Books [which were among the great Chinese Classics],"[16] in the words of the historian Ray Huang.[17] The emphasis in the family or guild on the acceptance of one's position in the hierarchy (be it as a child or as an apprentice),[18] and on the performance of those obligations that went with each position, had clear parallels vis-à-vis the state. So it was, for example, that local magistrates were known as the *fumu guan*—or "father/mother official"—of the populace.[19] As Confucius observed in the *Analects* when questioned about the fact that he was not then in public service, "be filial, only be filial [towards your parents] and friendly towards your brothers, and you will be contributing to government."[20]

Further evidence that family, village, and guild leaders were acting as responsible, albeit informal, delegates of the state emerges from the consistent patterns of interaction between them and their local magistrates throughout the imperial era. The state charged clan and guild leaders with a range of tax collection and related obligations and also held them responsible for the conduct of their members.[21] Indeed, in some instances, magistrates went so far as to require the certification of guild chiefs and to review the rules that such leaders drafted.[22] The heads of these family and economic units were also able to refer difficult cases to their local magistrates—particularly if they involved challenges to clan or guild rules, or to the authority of their senior members.[23] Conversely, magistrates, who appear to have been confronted with many more legal matters than the conventional wisdom would have us believe, were quick to dispatch appropriate cases back to the leaders of such units—especially as administrative regulations penalized these officials if they had formally to resolve more than a modest number of cases.[24]

In view of the foregoing, study of legal regulation in imperial China should thus not be limited to the penal sanctions in dynastic codes. It must, at a minimum, also address the remainder of imperial China's public, positive law; means other than public, positive law through which the state directly endeavored to maintain social order; the ways in which the populace sought to invoke the state's authority; and the elaborate and varied fabric of indirect ordering through family, village, and guild.

Considering the full scope of their legal history, the Chinese were not indifferent to the unauthorized reproduction of texts and other items. There is evidence from before the establishment of the Zhou dynasty in 1122 B.C. of interest in the ways in which commodities were identified,[25] concern from the Qin era with the distribution of

written materials,[26] and attention from the Han dynasty (206 B.C.–
A.D. 220) to barring the unauthorized reproduction of the Classics.[27]
Nonetheless, it is with the advent of printing during the Tang period
that one first finds substantial, sustained efforts to regulate publication and republication.[28] What appears to have been one of the
earliest such measures was issued in A.D. 835 by the Wenzong Emperor in the form of an edict, which, as was routine, became a part
of the Tang code.[29] The decree prohibited the unauthorized reproduction by persons of calendars, almanacs, and related items that
might be used for prognostication, which, it observed, were being
copied in great quantity in the Southwest and distributed throughout China. Far from being arcane, questions of time and astronomy
were central to the emperor's assertion that he was the link between
human and natural events—and so were to be tightly controlled by
court astronomers, while works regarding prognostication were of
concern because they might be used to predict the dynasty's down-
fall. This initial ban on the pirating of officially promulgated works
soon expanded. Before its collapse, the Tang dynasty also prohibited
the unauthorized copying and distribution of state legal pronouncements[30] and official histories, and the reproduction, distribution, or
possession of "devilish books and talks" (yaoshu yaoyan) and most
works on Buddhism and Daoism.[31] Unfortunately, evidence as to
the effectiveness of these various provisions is scant.

Spurred by advances in printing technology and a relative rise in
literacy, the early years of the Song dynasty (A.D. 960–1279) saw
a marked increase in the production of printed materials by both
the Imperial College (or Directorate of Education, as guozijian has
variously been translated) and "private" persons, many of whom,
in fact, were government officers carrying on sideline activities.[32]
Concerned about the proliferation of undesirable printed materials,
in 1009, the Zhenzong Emperor ordered private printers to submit
works they would publish to local officials for prepublication review
and registration.[33]

The principal goal of prepublication review was to halt the private reproduction of materials that were either subject to exclusive
state control or heterodox. By the Song, the former category included both those items covered in Tang Wenzong's edict of 835 and
authorized versions of the Classics (which were only to be reproduced under the auspices of the Imperial College), model answers to

imperial civil service examinations, maps, and materials concerning the inner workings of government, politics, and military affairs.[34] Pornography, broadly defined, and writings using the names of members or ancestors of the imperial family in "inappropriate" literary styles or that were "not beneficial to scholars" were also deemed heterodox.[35]

The penalties crafted by the state to enforce the prepublication review system underscored its objectives. Persons failing to obtain official approval prior to printing works that were neither subject to exclusive state control nor banned altogether might suffer one hundred blows with a heavy bamboo cane and the destruction of their printing blocks. Those who reproduced controlled or prohibited items risked far greater punishment.[36] The unauthorized reproduction of astronomical charts, for example, called for a 3,000-li (i.e., approximately 500-mile) exile. This was a severe penalty, indeed, given that one would not only be sent off to a desolate border region but largely be cut off from one's family, ancestral burial grounds, and linguistic and cultural home base.

One interesting by-product of the Song's prepublication review system was that persons who obtained its approval appear at times to have included in works they printed notices of such state action in an effort to combat unauthorized reproduction. Typical of these was a notice contained in a twelfth-century Sichuan work of history stating, "This book has been printed by the family of Secretary Cheng of Meishan[,] who have registered it with the government. No one is permitted to reprint it."[37] Unfortunately for the Cheng family and others similarly situated, the same laws that so carefully and stringently penalized unauthorized reproduction of the Classics and banned the heterodox neither explicitly forbade the pirating of more mundane works nor set forth sanctions for so doing. There is some evidence of printers of the innocuous seeking the assistance of local officials to combat unauthorized use of their works and even of signs being posted to that effect—but these efforts appear scattered,[38] ad hoc, and may well have been attributable to the fact that, as with Secretary Cheng, private printers and local officials were often one and the same. Indeed, by the late Song era, the dynasty appears to have had difficulty in securing enforcement of the ban on unauthorized reprinting of works intended to be under exclusive state control.[39]

The Song's imperial successors, and especially the Ming

(A.D. 1368–1644), endeavored to strengthen state control of publication, although relatively few changes were made to the formal structure of regulation until the Qing.[40] Each post-Song dynastic code specifically forbade the unauthorized republication of governmental works on astronomy, the civil service examinations, and other materials long considered sensitive. Additionally, each contained provisions banning "devilish books." These provisions were supplemented periodically by special decrees—as may be seen, for example, in the Hongwu Emperor's (1368–92) orders that all works disparaging the newly founded Ming dynasty even indirectly through the use of homophonic puns be eliminated,[41] and in the Qianlong Emperor's (1736–96) famous decree of 1774 requiring that all literature be reviewed so that any books containing heterodox ideas could be destroyed.[42]

Notwithstanding the Ming dynasty's goal of exercising more control over publication, the formal prepublication review system developed by the Song appears to have lost much of its vitality. Efforts were made during the mid and late Ming to revitalize official control, principally at the local level, but seem not to have been particularly successful, judging from extensive accounts of the unauthorized reproduction and alteration of texts for commercial reasons.[43] As a consequence, Qing rulers moved to strengthen this function of local officials, going so far in 1778 as to direct the reinstitution of a strict system of local prepublication review.[44]

This high degree of state interest in the control of publication was not mirrored with respect to the unauthorized reproduction of that which we now protect through trademark or patent. Although prior to the twentieth century, the Chinese state oversaw matters of commerce and industry more closely than has typically been recognized,[45] it did not develop comprehensive, centrally promulgated, formal legal protection for either proprietary symbols or inventions.

The dynastic codes did, through elaborate sumptuary laws, restrict the use of certain symbols associated with either the imperial family (such as the five-clawed dragon) or officialdom.[46] They also barred the imitation of marks used by the ceramists of Jingdezhen and others making goods for exclusive imperial use,[47] and made it illegal for certain craftspersons to send information about their work out of China.[48] These prohibitions did not, however, presage a broader pattern of centralized legal regulation.

The absence of direct imperial legal regulation of trademarks and inventions did not wholly bar the development of concern for its protection against unauthorized use. Northern Song (960–1127) records reveal that a family named Liu of Jinan, Shandong, used a mark containing both a drawing of a white rabbit and an accompanying legend to extol the virtues of its sewing needles.[49] Nor were the Lius and their white rabbit alone. Guild regulations, clan rules, and other sources indicate that producers of tea, silk, cloth, paper, and medicines, among other products, from at least the Song period onward, sought to maintain the brand names and symbols they had developed by marking their goods, by declaring that others could not use the marks involved, and by registering them with guilds and at times, local officials.[50] Additionally, some—such as the producers of the celebrated Tongren Temple line of medicines—sought to maintain the confidentiality of their manufacturing process by employing only family members or eunuchs, or by keeping vital parts of the process secret from nonfamily employees.[51]

The same documents that yield data regarding efforts to protect proprietary marks and processes also, however, indicate the great difficulty of doing so.[52] There appears to have been massive counterfeiting of well-known brand names and marks, as well as extensive attempts to imitate secret manufacturing processes—often with questionable results. Merchants and producers endeavored to deal with these problems both directly and through guild and comparable organizations, but when all else failed—as appears often to have been the case—they turned to local officialdom. Help was sought from local officials, not on the basis of any code provision specifically outlawing such imitating, but instead by imploring these "father-mother" figures to prevent unfairness and deception.[53] Thus, for example, sericulturists whose "trade-marked" silk in the Shanghai area had been improperly copied were able in 1856 to seek the assistance of their district magistrates, who ordered the infringers to stop.[54] Such appeals, however, do not appear to have been large in number, even taking account of the anecdotal nature of the evidence available. Nor do they appear often to have been successful in bringing the objectionable activity to an end.

Although the characterization of imperial Chinese law as wholly penal obscures the degree to which such law addressed civil matters, it does not follow that intellectual property law existed in China centuries before it arose in the West. Virtually all known examples of efforts by the state to provide protection for what we now term intellectual property in China prior to the twentieth century seem to have been directed overwhelmingly toward sustaining imperial power. These official efforts were only tangentially, if at all, concerned either with the creation or maintenance of property interests of persons or entities other than the state or with the promotion of authorship or inventiveness. This is perhaps most obvious with respect to provisions of the dynastic codes barring ordinary people from reproducing symbols, such as the five-clawed dragon, associated with the throne or officialdom. It is also evident in the fact that although the Tang and later dynasties went to considerable lengths to restrict the unauthorized reproduction of government materials and to ensure the accuracy of those it licensed, they seem to have been unconcerned about the pirating or improper editing of other works. Indeed, it is more accurate to think of prepublication review and the other restrictions on reprinting described above, together with the absolute ban on heterodox materials, as part of a larger framework for controlling the dissemination of ideas, rather than as the building blocks of a system of intellectual property rights, whether for printers, booksellers, authors, or anyone else.

Only the efforts of printers, booksellers, and other guilds or merchants to establish their particular monopolies seem to presage the notion that persons or entities other than the state might enjoy an interest in intangible property akin to the protection provided for tangible personal property or real property throughout much of imperial Chinese history.[55] Even this limited interest appears to have been tolerated by the state and its local representatives chiefly because it advanced other objectives. It is no coincidence that official expressions of concern about unauthorized copying often focused either on the textual distortions and errors contained in pirated editions of the classics, dynastic histories, and other orthodox works or on the fact that persons responsible for such editions were disrupting local peace by violating monopolies granted to local officials or influential gentry in their districts. Similarly, it is not unduly cynical to view the state's implicit and occasionally explicit support for guild efforts to protect trade names and marks as aimed at the preservation of social harmony by maintaining commercial order and reducing instances of deception of the populace.

The Chinese were obviously not alone in linking state interest with the protection of what we term intellectual property. In both the common and civil law worlds, the idea of limiting the unauthorized copying of books was originally prompted not by a belief that writings were the property of their authors, but by a desire to give printers an incentive not to publish heterodox materials.[56] Similarly, the early history of patent law in the West owes far more to the state's desire to strengthen itself than to an acknowledgment of any inherent property interest of the inventor.[57] Thus, for example, the English throne awarded patents to foreigners who introduced new products or processes to the British isles, even if those persons were not themselves responsible for the innovation in question.[58]

But the seventeenth and eighteenth centuries witnessed the development of an approach toward intellectual property in Europe that had no counterpart in imperial Chinese history. Simply stated, there developed in England and on the Continent the notion that authors and inventors had a property interest in their creations that could be defended against the state.[59] Society, growing numbers of Europeans came to believe, would benefit by providing incentives to engage in such work and disseminate the results. China, by contrast, continued to regulate this area predominantly in terms of how best to maintain the state's authority.

To take heed of this distinction is not to suggest that the Chinese ought to have followed the same course as the West.[60] Rather, it is to ponder why a civilization that for centuries paid particular attention to the regulation of publication, that for long was a world leader in science and technology, and that celebrated at least certain types of innovation,[61] did not provide more comprehensive protection for its rich bounty of creation.

Neither Chinese nor foreign scholars of intellectual property law contribute much to such an inquiry. The former, for example, typically treat imperial efforts to control the dissemination of ideas as constituting copyright, and so end the inquiry there.[62] They see little need to consider why—if China had copyright from the Tang dynasty—enforcement appears to have been negligible, subsequent foreign efforts to foster such laws were unavailing, and other forms of intellectual property law were not forthcoming in a sustained fashion. Foreign scholars also provide scant assistance. Surprisingly few of the Western scholars who write about intellectual property have endeavored to analyze the development of such law in the West, let alone elsewhere. Instead, most recent scholarly writing touching on such development either consists chiefly of historical narrative[63] or portrays intellectual property law solely in terms of economic development—as a concomitant of industrialization in general or as a response to particular technological breakthroughs.[64]

Clearly, economic and technological factors should not be ignored in the effort to understand why the imperial Chinese state did not provide systematic protection for the fruits of innovation and creation. China may well have been as generally prosperous and as technologically advanced as any area in the world from the seventh through the twelfth centuries.[65] Nonetheless, being preindustrial, China had little in the way of the inexpensive mass production that some scholars see as an impetus to establish intellectual property law.[66] So it was, for example, that although in China printing had been invented by the Tang and movable type by the Song,[67] "methods suitable for the mass printing of [materials such as] newspapers" were to originate in the West, and then centuries later.[68] Moreover, the fact that no more than 20 percent of Chinese were literate even by the early twentieth century[69] and the possibility that the absence of the corporate form may have impeded the type of capital formation needed for large-scale commercial innovation[70] may also help us understand why few actors, other than persons such as the Chengs and Lius, seem to have been concerned with protecting intellectual property.

These economic and technological considerations notwithstanding, it is to political culture that we must turn for the principal explanation as to why there were no indigenous counterparts to contemporary ideas of intellectual property law throughout imperial Chinese history.[71] Lying at the core of traditional Chinese society's treatment of intellectual property was the dominant Confucian vision of the nature of civilization and of the constitutive role played therein by a shared and still vital past.[72] That vision saw civilization as defined by a paradigmatic set of relationships, each bearing reciprocal, although not necessarily equal, responsibilities and expectations, which the parties were morally bound to fulfill. Typically, individuals found themselves in a number of such relationships—the most important of which were those between ruler and subject, father and son, and husband and wife.[73] Only through encountering the past—

which provided unique insight into the essence of one's own character, relationships with other human beings, and interaction with nature—could individuals, guided by nurturing leaders, understand how properly to adhere to those relationships of which they were a part.[74]

The dual functions of the past—as the instrument through which individual moral development was to be attained and the yardstick against which the content of the relationships constituting society was to be measured—posed a dilemma. The indispensability of the past for personal moral growth dictated that there be broad access to the common heritage of all Chinese. Nonetheless, the responsibility of senior members of relationships for the nurturing of their juniors[75]—together with the fact that reference to the past, far more than public, positive law or religion, defined the limits of proper behavior in what were, after all, unequal relationships—demanded more controlled access. Both functions, however, militated against thinking of the fruits of intellectual endeavor as private property.

The relationship of ruler and ruled exemplified the power of the past, while also illustrating the rationale for providing measured access to it. The notion of the Chinese people as a family, with the ruler as parent, is one that has had great and enduring currency since preimperial times.[76] In that capacity, the ruler had a fiducial obligation to provide for both the spiritual and physical well-being of the populace, who, in turn, were expected to be loyal and productive. Although the Chinese early on had a far more sophisticated formal legal system than has typically been recognized at home or abroad, the very nature of this relationship was such that public, positive law could serve neither as the primary instrument for ensuring that the people genuinely understood what was expected of them nor as a means for encouraging rulers to discharge their responsibilities in a suitable fashion. As Confucius indicated in the *Analects*, "Lead the people with governmental measures and regulate them by law and punishments, and they will avoid wrong-doing, but will have no sense of honor and shame. Lead them by virtue and regulate them by the rules of propriety [*li*] and they will have a sense of shame and, moreover, set themselves right."[77]

The standards meant to govern the ruler-subject relationship—virtue and the rules of propriety—derived their content and legitimacy chiefly from the common heritage of the Chinese people, rather than from any action, whether political, legal, or otherwise, of contemporaneous figures, including the ruler himself. Indeed, much the same point might be made with respect to the entire moral ethos that underlay Chinese civilization.[78] Nowhere is this more apparent than with the *li*—the "rites" that defined morality and propriety. Having evolved from a set of rituals into a code of conduct well before the time of Confucius, the *li* at once embodied and expressed the most profound insights and experience of the so-called Ancients who had established society and compiled the Classics.[79] As such, the *li* fostered a mutually reinforcing personal and social ordering that linked the present simultaneously with that which came before and that which was to follow.

This sense of the power of the past was also manifested in the concept of the rectification of names (*zhengming*), which Confucius indicated would be the "first measure" he would advise a ruler to institute on assuming power.[80] In essence, it involved the expectation that current rulers would carry out their responsibilities in a manner consistent with the moral standards set by their most worthy predecessors. The idea of the Mandate of Heaven (*tianming*) embodied a similar expectation. It, in effect, provided that rulers failing to discharge their responsibilities in keeping with such standards—which had their genesis in preimperial days[81] and, presumably, were known in general form to all[82]—might lose the Mandate and, with it, their claim to rule.[83] In short, a shared past defined the limits of legitimate power in the present.

Given the potential validating—and invalidating[84]—force of the past, those with or aspiring to power sought to cloak themselves in the past while also tailoring it to suit their particular needs. The desire to draw on the legitimating capacity of the past is evident in the degree to which the basic structure, forms, and images of imperial governance persisted, even as their content may have changed throughout two millennia of growth, upheaval, and violent transitions of power. Indeed, even rebels seeking to dislodge those in power consistently structured the alternatives they proposed so as to gain legitimacy from the past.[85]

The power of the past was also to be seen in the reliance of Chinese rulers from the Sui (A.D. 581–618) onward for thirteen centuries on the world's first civil service.[86] At least in theory, from its earliest days, officials were to be identified through an examination system that viewed knowledge of the past—both in terms of the questions asked and the manner in which they were to be answered—as evidencing the attributes needed to resolve the problems of the present.[87] This, in turn, greatly influenced the character of education. After all, a thorough immersion in the Classics would surely do more for the development of character, and, with it, the ability to serve in government effectively, than would more technical training. The latter, by its very nature, had little to say about morality and therefore, could be left to those whose virtue had not developed to the point at which they could benefit fully from a classical education.[88]

The legal system displayed this same concern with deriving legitimacy through association with the past. Thus, the basic conceptual and classificatory framework for the imperial code continued largely unchanged from its preimperial precursors through the Sui dynasty, during which it was modified only in part.[89] This revision, in turn, set the basic format for imperial codes through to the end of the imperial era, with the result that "30 to 40 percent of the statutes in the Ch'ing Code [operative until the twentieth century] go back unchanged to the T'ang Code of 653."[90] Once again, as was the case with the structure of government and, as we shall see, with literature and the arts, this unswerving employment of the past ought not to mask the fact of enormous change, but should instead highlight the context within which that change occurred. After all, the remaining 60 to 70 percent of the statutes in the Ch'ing (i.e., Qing) Code did change, while even the 30 to 40 percent that remained unchanged on the face of it were in fact transformed through an extensive additional body of law, including an ever-evolving array of substatutes.[91]

Contrary to what one might initially expect, the imperial Chinese legal system did not adhere to a formal system of binding precedent, although, in fact, magistrates and other officials involved with the law did draw on compilations of prior cases as they reached and sought to justify their decisions.[92] But on reflection, the absence of binding precedent may actually have connoted an even greater embracing of the past—as the Confucian morality and wisdom of the ages that officials were assumed to have cultivated in preparing for and taking the imperial examinations were surely seen as a truer and more historically valid guide for making decisions than any set of rules formulated or cases resolved by one's predecessors in office.[93]

Use of the past to mold the present also took a darker form. Early on, the Chinese came to recognize that those who controlled the compilation of history, the interpretation of its lessons, and the characterization of the current dynasty for historical purposes wielded great influence. This led to the establishment by the Han and emulation by subsequent dynasties of elaborate state historiographic offices that engaged in the world's most systematic continuous gathering of historical data prior to the twentieth century.[94] But, less positively, it also lay behind repeated attempts throughout imperial history to shape the content of the historical record. Small wonder, then, that, in an ominous foreshadowing of future efforts at such control, the Han subjected the epochal historian Pan Gu (A.D. 32–92) to an extended imprisonment for engaging in unsanctioned historical work.[95] Nor ought it to be surprising that rulers from Qin Shihuang in the earliest years of the first imperial dynasty[96] to Qianlong[97] in the ebbing years of the last should endeavor to eradicate all they deemed heterodox. As Li Si, China's first prime minister and advisor to Qin Shihuang, is reported to have said, "Anyone referring to the past to criticize the present should, together with all members of his family, be put to death."[98]

As important as the acquisition and maintenance of imperial power may have been, there was more to efforts to regulate intellectual endeavors than the desire to buttress such claims. Coinciding with and obviously reinforcing these secular concerns was the idea of the ruler as fiduciary. In that capacity, the ruler had not only the authority but also a responsibility to ascertain how best to nurture the populace. Central to that responsibility was the need to determine which knowledge warranted dissemination and which ought to be circumscribed in the best interests of the commonwealth. The ruler's parentlike position enhanced the legitimacy of imperial efforts to control the flow of ideas and suggests that there was a greater coherence to such regulation than scholars have typically assumed.[99]

"Lacking," as Thomas Metzger has put it "John Stuart Mill's optimistic view that good doctrines would emerge victorious out of a free marketplace of ideas, Chinese political philosophers since Mencius and Xunzi have instead emphasized the human tendency to become deluded through the interplay of 'false' and 'correct' doctrine."[100] In his role as fiduciary, the ruler had an affirmative obligation to filter out and destroy harmful knowledge—such as that

found in "devilish books and talks," which might contain porno-
graphic as well as politically and religiously suspect materials—
rather than permit it to delude his charges. By the same token, there
were certain types of information, such as that contained in maps,
calendars, and astronomical texts, for which the emperor and his
officials alone had legitimate use in their fiduciary capacity. Conversely, the spread of other knowledge, such as that embodied in
the Classics, might benefit society (and, not coincidentally, enhance
the imperial position), justifying assistance to persons having the
Imperial College's permission to reprint approved versions of such
works, especially in order to stem the production of "butchered
summaries" and otherwise inaccurate copies. And, finally, there was
further knowledge—neither orthodox, heterodox, nor official—
that the imperial government did not endeavor directly to protect,
bar, or otherwise regulate, with the result that its treatment varied
widely according to local circumstance.

The throne's efforts to define and supervise the realm of acceptable ideas were not as avowedly totalitarian as they might initially
seem, given that the shared past that placed a premium on such control perforce harbored a collective memory of the outer limits of
power.[101] Nonetheless, the state's emphasis clearly was focused far
more on political order and stability than on issues of ownership
and private interests. This did not preclude state support for persons seeking to prevent others from infringing on their monopoly
over the reproduction of certain materials and symbols. Through
its prepublication review procedures, the state protected the monopoly of printers to whom it had entrusted reproduction of authorized versions of certain materials, such as the Classics. So, too,
as has been discussed above, the state, both directly through local
magistrates and indirectly through its tacit delegation to specified
local groups of considerable responsibility in the commercial area,
supported guilds, families, and others in their efforts to maintain
the integrity of their trade names and marks. But in each instance,
this protection emerged from, and was ultimately to be defined by,
the state's interest in preserving imperial power and fostering social
harmony.

The rationale for imperial Chinese protection of intellectual property dictated the character of that protection. Neither formal nor
informal bodies of law vested guilds, families, and others seeking

to preserve their monopoly over particular items with "rights" that might be invoked to vindicate their claims against the state or against others throughout China. Nor was the provision of state assistance, whether direct or indirect, merely a matter of privilege. In keeping with the tenor of the fiducial bond underlying the relationship between ruler and ruled, there existed among civilized persons expectations as to what was appropriate and fair, as well as a sense that an appeal to one's magistrate or other representatives of the state might be warranted in the event those expectations went unfulfilled. So it was that printers charged with responsibility for printing certain texts or guilds that had developed particular medicines might seek official assistance against persons appropriating what fairness and custom dictated was theirs, and that officials on occasion responded in the interests of fairness and the maintenance of harmony.[102]

The content of expectations concerning the appropriateness of individuals and groups exercising control over the expression of particular ideas derived, in turn, from the critical role that the shared past played in the Confucian understanding of both individual moral and collective social development. Simply stated, the need to interact with the past sharply curtailed the extent to which it was proper for anyone other than persons acting in a fiducial capacity to restrict access to its expressions.

The power of the past and its consequences for possession of the fruits of intellectual endeavor are well captured in the passage in the *Analects* in which Confucius indicates, "The Master [i.e., Confucius himself] said: 'I transmit rather than create; I believe in and love the Ancients.' "[103] The essence of human understanding had long since been discerned by those who had gone before and, in particular, by the sage rulers collectively referred to as the Ancients, who lived in a distant, idealized "golden age."[104] To avail themselves of that understanding in order to guide their own behavior, subsequent generations had to interact with the past in a sufficiently thorough manner so as to be able to transmit it.[105] Yet, as Confucius demonstrated in undertaking to edit the Classics and to comment on them in the *Analects*, transmission, far from being a passive endeavor, entailed selection and adaptation if it was to be meaningful to oneself, one's contemporaries, and one's successors.[106]

This sense of the past's compelling pertinence, and of intellectual endeavor as the medium through which interaction with and transmission of it was possible, permeated virtually all facets of Chinese civilization. As the noted scholar of Chinese literature Stephen Owen has observed, in the Chinese literary tradition "the experience of the past roughly corresponds to and carries the same force as the attention to meaning or truth in the Western tradition." [107] Thus, in classical Chinese literature, the past survives and warrants consideration, not merely as an obvious foil for contemporary activity,[108] but, more important, because "the Confucian imperative insists that in encountering the ancients, we ourselves must be changed [for] we discover in the ancients not mere means but the embodiment of values." [109]

The process of transformative engagement with the past was, in turn, made possible through reliance in Chinese literature, and especially classical Chinese poetry, on a common body of allusion and reference, commencing with the classics and built up over time. To be sure, as T. S. Eliot has observed, all poetry [110]—and, one might add, all literature—draws on and therefore owes an obligation to the past. And yet this use of shared imagery in Chinese literature is distinguishable from its seeming counterparts elsewhere. In Joseph Levenson's words, "to cite the Classics was the very method of universal speech," [111] to a further-reaching and more enduring degree than even the Bible in the Judeo-Christian world or the Koran in Islam. As the "very method of universal speech," such allusion and reference, in effect, constituted a sophisticated cultural shorthand that was potentially accessible, at least in theory, throughout the civilized (i.e., sinicized) world, facilitating access from the present to the past or, for that matter, the future.

To speak of the relative omnipresence of the past and the existence of a unique, shared intellectual vocabulary is not to suggest that classical Chinese poetry was lacking in originality, any more than it is to dismiss transmission as only a mechanical process. Rather it is to underscore the context within which originality arose and was expressed and, in so doing, to heed what the fourteenth-century poet Gao Bing (1350–1423) termed "innovation within the bounds of orthodoxy." [112] Indeed, over time, Chinese poets and literary theorists have expressed a myriad of views as to the very question of what constituted appropriate interaction with the past. Some, such as the influential late Ming advocate of a return to antiquity (*fu gu*) Li Mengyang (1472–1529), argued for a fairly literal following of the past, saying that "prose (*wen*) must be like that of the Qin or the Han, and poetry (*shi*) must be like that of the High Tang."[113] "This," they contended, "was justified because the rules used by the ancients were not invented by them, but really created by Nature . . . [so that] when we imitate the ancients, we are not imitating them but really imitating the natural law of things."[114] Others, such as Yuan Zhongdao (1570–1624) of the *gongan* school, took a very different view, suggesting that in their desire to "imitate words and lines" of earlier literature, Li Mengyang and his colleagues missed the more essential "meaning and flavor" (*yiwei*) animating the great poetry of the Tang.[115] But what united such disparate views—and indeed, classical literature more broadly—was the need to address in so central a fashion the past and approaches to it.

Poetry, of course, was but one literary form in which this concern was evidenced. In the much-prized discipline of history, the model, not only for the standard dynastic histories (*zheng shi*), compiled for almost two millennia, but for "history writing of all kinds," was, in the words of the historiographer Edward Pulleyblank, "a patchwork of excerpts, often abridged but otherwise unaltered, from [the historian's] . . . sources, with any personal comment or judgement kept clearly separate." This structure, suggests Pulleyblank, grew out of the belief that "the work of the historian was to compile a set of documents which would speak for themselves rather than to make an imaginative reconstruction of past events." As was the case with the transmission of the Ancients by Confucius himself, or the heavy employment of allusion and references to the classics in poetry and other literary forms, this manner of historical inquiry should not be construed as connoting a lack of originality. As Pulleyblank observes, "the selection and arrangement of [the historian's] . . . material called for the exercise of critical judgement, and conclusions about the causes of events or the characters of historical persons could be expressed separately in the appropriate place."[116]

The concern with the past evidenced in classical poetry and literature was mirrored in Chinese painting and calligraphy. As with poetry, "engagement with the past validated the present"[117] by posing "the resource of [the] past to renew . . . life repeatedly in the recurrent present."[118] For many, the artistic process itself, accordingly, was understood as a type of spiritual exercise through which one's moral sense might be both expressed and enhanced.[119]

This was particularly true for the literati (*wenren*), who in theory, if not always in practice, subscribed to the famed Song artist Mi Fu's (1051–1107) belief that "in matters of calligraphy and painting, one is not to discuss price. The gentleman is hard to capture by money."[120]

Although later in its genesis and less catholic in its force, a common vocabulary emerged in painting and calligraphy that facilitated communication across time and space.[121] As was the case with literature, there was much debate among both artists and theorists[122] as to the most appropriate way in which to relate to the past. Some, such as the "orthodox school" of the early Qing, saw a "lineage" in painting, parallel to "the succession of Confucian philosophers from Confucius himself down to Wang Yang-ming in the Ming dynasty," to which they advocated fairly literal adherence, at least as a departure point.[123] As Wu Li (1632–1718) put it, "to paint without taking the Sung and Yuan masters as one's basis is like playing chess on an empty chessboard, without pieces."[124] Others took a far more expansive view, contending that latter-day painting should be less literal and should, instead, strive to capture the ideas that animated earlier work.[125] Still others felt a need to address the past as a precondition to expressing their own vision. As the Qing artist Dao-ji, or Shi-tao, (1642–1708) wrote:

> Painters of recent times have all appropriated the styles of the old masters . . .
>
> In the broadest sense, there is only a single method [of painting], and when one has attained that method, one no longer pursues false methods. Seizing on it, one can call it one's own method.[126]

Again, as with poetry, however much artists and scholars may have been divided as to the best stance toward and use of the past, they were at one in their focus on it.

Given the extent to which "interaction with the past is one of the distinctive modes of intellectual and imaginative endeavor in traditional Chinese culture,"[127] the replication of particular concrete manifestations of such an endeavor by persons other than those who first gave them form never carried, in the words of the distinguished art historian and curator Wen Fong, the "dark connotations . . . it does in the West."[128] Nor, as was often the case in the West, was such use accepted grudgingly and then only because it served as a vehicle through which apprentices and students developed their technical expertise, demonstrated erudition, or even endorsed particular values, although each of these phenomena also existed in imperial China.[129] On the contrary, in the Chinese context, such use was at once both more affirmative and more essential. It evidenced the user's comprehension of and devotion to the core of civilization itself, while offering individuals the possibility of demonstrating originality within the context of those forms and so distinguishing their present from the past.

In view of the foregoing, there was what Wen Fong has termed a "general attitude of tolerance, or indeed receptivity, shown on the part of the great Chinese painters towards the forging of their own works."[130] Such copying, in effect, bore witness to the quality of the work copied and to its creator's degree of understanding and civility. Thus, Shen Zhou (1427–1509) is reported to have responded to the suggestions that he put a stop to the forging of his work by remarking, in comments that were not considered exceptional, "if my poems and paintings, which are only small efforts to me, should prove to be of some aid to the forgers, what is there for me to grudge about?"[131] Much the same might be said of literature, where the Confucian disdain for commerce fostered an ideal, even if not always realized in practice, that true scholars wrote for edification and moral renewal rather than profit. Or, as it was expressed so compactly in a famed Chinese aphorism, "Genuine scholars let the later world discover their work [rather than promulgate and profit from it themselves]." If, after all, even the characters constituting the Chinese language itself, as the famed Song statesman Wang Anshi (1021–86) observed, "actually came from nature . . . and were not created by human beings, but merely imitated by them . . . from configurations of nature,"[132] on what basis could anyone exclude others from the common heritage of all civilized persons?

Three

Learning the Law at Gunpoint: The Turn-of-the-Century Introduction of Western Notions of Intellectual Property

> We possess all things. I set no value on objects strange or ingenious, and have no use for your country's manufactures.
>
> The Qianlong Emperor to King George III
> of England, October 3, 1793

In his famous dismissal of King George's proposal to establish official diplomatic and trade relations, the Qianlong Emperor (1736–96) gave voice to his dynasty's long-standing indifference to foreign objects, manufactures, and ideas.[1] Yet well before the Qing fell, that indifference was to change substantially,[2] and with that change came the Chinese state's first formal legal measures concerned with systematically protecting "ingenious" objects. This chapter commences by examining early Chinese-Western legal interaction, both as a prelude to a more specific discussion of intellectual property law and for the broader lessons it imparts regarding Chinese foreign relations during the late imperial period. It then explores initial efforts, first by foreigners and later by self-styled Chinese reformers, to introduce "modern" ideas of intellectual property law into the land "possess[ing] all things," before concluding with a consideration of why these early law reform efforts failed to meet expectations.

The Qianlong Emperor could be dismissive of King George's proposal because the Middle Kingdom already had in place gener-

ous provisions for dealing with the *waiyi*, or "outer barbarians"—
the term the Qing used to refer to all Europeans and North Americans.[3] As R. Randle Edwards has artfully demonstrated,[4] the Qing
not only perpetuated the basic framework that the Ming dynasty had
established for regulating *huawairen* (literally "persons outside Chinese civilization") but, under Qianlong himself, expressly adopted
a policy of "deferring to barbarian wishes" (*fuxun yiqing*) that made
special concessions to those unruly foreigners from the West.[5] From
1744 onward, foreigners were permitted to reside for part of the year
in designated enclaves in Canton and Macao and do business with
licensed Chinese intermediaries, known as the *hong*.[6] At the same
time, in an effort to accommodate foreign ways, responsibility for
all foreign disruptions of harmony in those enclaves, save for homicides of Chinese, was delegated through the *hong* merchants to the
barbarians' leaders,[7] who persisted in maintaining what seemed to
Chinese officialdom to be rather minute distinctions (e.g., British,
French, American, etc.).[8]

Although Chinese officials believed that they were making considerable concessions to the distant barbarians, Western merchants
and their governments were not content with this early regulatory
framework. They objected strenuously to the application of Chinese
law to foreigners accused either of murdering Chinese or of committing other crimes beyond Canton and Macao. In the words of representatives of the British East India Company, "Chinese laws . . .
are not only arbitrary and corruptly administered, but founded on a
system in many respects incompatible with European ideas of equity
or justice."[9] These perceived differences in fundamental values surfaced in a series of incidents, running from the case of the *Lady
Hughes* in 1784[10] to the outbreak of the Opium War in 1839, in which
Western authorities construed the application of Chinese law and
legal procedures as denying even the rudiments of fairness, while
Chinese officials reacted to these expressions of foreign concern as
constituting unwarranted interference in Chinese affairs.

Foreign concern about Chinese law was not, however, limited
to cases of homicide and other serious disruptions of harmony.
Long before King George III's proposal of 1793 to expand relations,
English and other foreign merchants had expressed their displeasure
with what had come to be known as the Canton, or *hong*, system,
which, they argued, constrained trade and subjected them to the ex-

actions of the *hong* merchants.[11] By the beginning of the nineteenth century, with the Chinese little interested in British "objects strange or ingenious," British and other merchants began to engage in blatantly illegal sales of significant quantities of Indian opium, creating a market for imports where foreign manufactures had failed.[12] These sales multiplied rapidly, and by the late 1820's, after years of enjoying a surplus in its trade with Britain and other *waiyi* nations, "China experienced an unfavorable balance of trade virtually for the first time in its history."[13]

The Qing government deplored opium's debilitating effects on the populace of South China and dire impact on the economy.[14] Initially, it addressed the problem by underscoring the fundamental illegality of opium sales under Chinese law and by taking measures directed at both Chinese and foreigners to enhance enforcement. When these measures proved unavailing, particularly with respect to foreign merchants, Lin Zexu, the imperial commissioner charged with the responsibility for stamping out the opium problem, turned to a different type of law—namely, what the "outer barbarians" called international law. His foreign audience, however, paid no more heed to appeals to the Swiss jurist Emerich de Vattel's *Le droit des gens* of 1758 than it had to the Qing code,[15] leading Lin to make a final and desperate plea on moral grounds to Queen Victoria. In an extraordinarily poignant letter, he implored her to bar British merchants from engaging in an activity that she clearly would not tolerate in England—but failed to receive even the courtesy of a response.[16]

In the ensuing Opium War (1839–42), the far better equipped British inflicted a sharp defeat on the Chinese forces and extracted extensive diplomatic concessions as well. Western merchants and missionaries were granted access to the Chinese interior under the Treaty of Nanking of 1842 and comparable treaties concluded during the next twenty years with the United States and other nations seeking to enjoy similar privileges through most-favored-nation status.[17] Furthermore, in direct response to complaints about Chinese justice, these treaties also required that foreigners accused of crimes against Chinese subjects be tried according to their own nation's law by representatives of their home government resident in China.[18] Although originally limited to the criminal sphere, over the second half of the nineteenth century, an increasing number of foreigners and Chinese converts to Christianity managed to have civil cases and even criminal matters involving Chinese defendants heard either by foreign consular representatives or by the Mixed Court established to handle judicial affairs in the foreign-run International Settlement of Shanghai.[19]

Notwithstanding abundant scholarship on the political import of extraterritoriality, relatively little attention has been devoted to what that system meant for Chinese drawn into it. In effect, extraterritoriality mandated that Chinese seeking redress against foreigners avail themselves, essentially without assistance,[20] of a legal order the fundamental principles of which were alien to the Chinese legal tradition. Chinese were accustomed to a legal culture that relied in both its formal and informal dimensions on authority figures to find the truth through "inquisitorial means." Extraterritoriality instead confronted them with an adversarial system in which disputants were required to argue for their version of the truth before a judge from the foreign party's nation,[21] who was unlikely either to know the Chinese language or to be fully conversant with Chinese practices. Even when the Chinese had access to substantive foreign statutory and case law that was to be applied—which one doubts was often the case[22]—these materials typically were only available in a foreign language and may have had precedential or other meaning that was not readily evident to persons unfamiliar with Western ideas of legality. Compounding these difficulties in the instance of the United States, for example, was the fact that if the consular officials acting as judges (who rarely had any legal training)[23] erred, appeal had to be taken within the continental United States.[24] This effectively foreclosed recourse to higher courts for the Chinese, particularly after the Chinese Exclusion Act of 1882 excluded virtually all Chinese from entering the United States.[25] Ironically, this system, imposed by Westerners because of the injustices Chinese law supposedly perpetrated on foreigners, perpetrated many of the same injustices on the Chinese, leaving them with few victories and much skepticism regarding Western justice.[26]

Issues of intellectual property were not of consequence in Chinese economic and legal interaction with the West prior to the Opium War or in the first decades thereafter.[27] There was little foreign investment in China, and trade was confined to items such as opium, tea, and raw silk, sold as bulk commodities, rather than under brand names. To be sure, there were periodic allegations of inferior grades of tea being passed off as their more costly counterparts from Longjing and elsewhere, but these were cast chiefly in terms of consumer fraud.[28]

As foreign economic involvement in China expanded, however, during the latter part of the nineteenth century, charges of the unauthorized use of foreign trade names and trademarks began to arise.[29] At first, these seem chiefly to have taken the form of the improper use by Chinese merchants of the names of Western businesses in order either to avoid paying the *likin* (internal tax) to which Chinese, but not foreigners, were subject or to secure internal transit permits.[30] So it was that David Sassoon and Sons Co., a British firm, found itself locked in legal battle in 1884 with the Chinese firm of Wong Gan Ying, which it charged had improperly done business under the name of a foreign enterprise.[31] And so it also was that complaints were lodged in 1897 against Chinese opium processors in Swatow—not for having produced opium, but for having sold their product under a British trade name, presumably to benefit from the hesitancy of local Chinese officials to enforce the law stringently against foreigners.[32]

By the turn of the century, intellectual property problems began to multiply as Chinese entrepreneurs sought to take advantage of the popularity of imports—and of items produced in foreign-owned local factories. Operating in an atmosphere of unprecedented international attention to intellectual property—in the aftermath of the formation in 1883 of International Union for the Protection of Industrial Property (the Paris Convention), which deals with patent and trademark, the promulgation in 1886 of International Union for the Protection of Literary and Artistic Property (the Berne Convention), which addresses copyright, and what the famed patent scholar Fritz Machlup has termed the revival of such law in the West[33]—foreign merchants expected that the integrity of trademarks that they had duly registered at home would be maintained in China.[34] In holding such expectations, they seemed little concerned that China was not a party to either convention or any other treaty concerning intellectual property, and was therefore under no formal legal obligation to respond to foreign allegations of unauthorized trademark use either by Chinese or by other foreigners. Nor did they appear fully to appreciate the difficulties of rendering Western-language trademarks and trade names in Chinese so as to preserve the identity of the original mark, while creating a mark that would be felicitous in the Chinese context.[35] In any event, it was evident by century's end that a range of foreign trademarks were, at least in the eyes of their holders, increasingly being abused.

Although stirred by the promise of a market of "four hundred million customers,"[36] foreign merchants did not endeavor in any concerted fashion to redress their grievances concerning trademarks through the Chinese legal system. In large measure, this mirrored the general disdain of foreigners for a system with which they had little familiarity and for which they had even less respect.[37] To be sure, Chinese law offered scant formal protection for intellectual property through the end of the nineteenth century. Article 153 of the Qing code required commercial "agents" to avoid setting "unjust" prices for their merchandise, Article 154 sought to punish those who realize an exorbitant profit through "monopoly" or other undue influence, and Article 156 prohibited manufacturers from representing certain goods as being of higher quality than they were.[38] There is no evidence, however, that these broad prohibitions were regularly used to address trademark issues. Subsequent attempts by the Qing government during the 100-Day Reform of 1898 to issue laws governing the press,[39] the importation of advanced technology, and inventions similarly failed to impress foreigners as providing meaningful protection. Nor did Western business regard the recognition, through imperial edicts promulgated during the last years of the century, of printers' monopolies over approximately twenty types of texts as any more effective.[40] And while members of some Chinese guilds were able to maintain the integrity of their own brand names or to prevail on local officials to assist them in preventing others from copying the cigarettes, wine, medicines, and other products for which they had become famous,[41] these protections were localized and, in any event, unavailable to foreigners.

Believing there to be little point in turning to the Chinese, foreign merchants instead appealed to the local representatives of their home governments for assistance. By century's end, foreign consulates began to register marks belonging to their nationals and to convey those registrations to the Imperial Maritime Customs Service,[42] which the foreign treaty powers had established in 1854 and since controlled. But these measures proved unavailing, in part for want of effective enforcement powers, particularly beyond the foreign settlements in Shanghai and the other major treaty ports,[43] and in part because of the overall breakdown of civil order resulting from the so-called Boxer Uprising of 1900.[44] As a consequence, the British Foreign Office endeavored initially to address the trademark issue and other commercial issues in the negotiation of the protocol concluding the Boxer Uprising. That negotiation, however, soon proved overly complex and interwoven with those the Chinese were conducting with the other treaty powers. As a result, the Foreign Office instead resolved to negotiate a free-standing commercial treaty, notwithstanding the contention of some China hands that Britain's failure to impose the terms it desired as a part of Boxer Protocol meant that the "right of China to have a will of its own is recognized."[45]

The negotiations that ensued, first with the British and soon thereafter with the Americans and Japanese, were not confined to intellectual property. The treaty powers were eager to establish what they deemed a suitable environment for conducting international business. They pressed the Chinese to eliminate the *likin*, which was seen as encumbering foreign efforts to reach the market of 400 million;[46] to adopt a uniform national currency;[47] and to develop laws governing mining and joint-venture enterprises, as well as intellectual property. If such concessions were forthcoming, it was suggested, they would instruct the Imperial Maritime Customs to institute new tariffs and again ban opium,[48] and they might even be "prepared to relinquish extra-territoriality when satisfied that the state of the Chinese law, the arrangements for their administration and other considerations [so] warrant."[49] The Chinese negotiating team, which was headed by the noted entrepreneur-turned-official Sheng Xuanhuai[50] and included representatives of the newly formed Ministry of Foreign Affairs and foreign consultants drawn from the Maritime Customs, was scarcely in a position to resist entering into such discussions.[51]

Trademark protection was the centerpiece of the intellectual property issues addressed in commercial agreements that the Chinese accordingly concluded with Britain, the United States, and Japan. In essence, the Chinese government undertook, in the words of the British treaty, to "afford protection to British trade-marks against infringement, imitation, or colourable imitation by Chinese subjects." [52] Reflecting the interest of Chinese negotiators in under-scoring China's sovereign equality as a first step in breaking down extraterritoriality, and the ironic belief of some Chinese officials that a market of "200 million" existed in the West and Japan for their products, [53] China agreed to grant foreigners this protection "in order to secure such protection [abroad] . . . for its subjects." [54]

Given that China did not at this time have a national trademark law, the treaties left open the question of how to afford protection to foreign marks. The Mackay Treaty of 1902 with Britain provided that the Chinese government would establish offices "under control of the Imperial Maritime Customs Service where foreign trade-marks may be registered on payment of a reasonable fee," [55] but none of the treaties required registration, specified who might exercise the privilege of registration with respect to which marks, or enumerated the benefits of registration. What, after all, was a "British trade-mark," particularly in view of the fact that use, rather than registration, sufficed to provide exclusive right to a mark in Britain? [56] Might a Chinese subject seek to register in China a mark used in Britain? Might a British subject seek to register in China a mark used there, but not in Britain? Who, in short, were to be holders and how might they protect their marks in China, absent registration—or, for that matter, with it?

China's 1903 treaty with the United States premised protection on registration, which was to be sought "by the proper authorities of the United States," but neither it nor Japan's contemporaneous treaty provided answers to the types of questions raised above in connection with the Mackay Treaty. Nor did these treaties specify where or under what circumstances such registration was to occur, other than to indicate that registration would take place "at such offices as the Chinese government will establish for such purpose, on payment of a reasonable fee, after due investigation by the Chinese authorities, and in compliance with reasonable regulations." [57]

The provisions of these early agreements concerning forms of intellectual property other than trademarks were somewhat more specific but still left vital questions unanswered. Thus, the treaty of 1903 between the United States and China, which, curiously, was the only one of the three to discuss patents, stated that China would provide a limited term of patent protection "to citizens of the United States on all their patents issued by the United States, in respect of articles the sale of which is lawful in China, which do not infringe on previous inventions of Chinese subjects, in the same manner as patents are to be issued to subjects of China."[58] But the treaty also indicated that such protection would only commence after the Chinese government had established a patent office and adopted a patent law, without setting a date for establishing such an agency or providing interim protection. Similarly, the American treaty provided that in return for the United States granting Chinese subjects "the benefits of its copyright laws,"[59] the Chinese government would "give full protection, *in the same way and manner and subject to the same conditions upon which it agrees to protect trade-marks*, to all citizens of the United States" (emphasis added) with respect to materials "especially prepared for the use and education of the Chinese people."[60] Other works were not entitled even to this uncertain level of protection, although their authors had a "right" to "due process of law" if their works were "calculated to injure the well-being of China"— whatever these undefined terms might mean.

The vagueness and variation of those provisions of the turn-of-the-century commercial treaties dealing with intellectual property was not without consequence, as is borne out most graphically in the case of trademarks. To comply with obligations undertaken in the treaties, China's Ministry of Foreign Affairs "invited" the Maritime Customs to prepare a draft trademark law.[61] Working closely with British consular officials and merchants, a Maritime Customs team headed by a British deputy inspector-general generated a draft trademark law that bore more than a passing resemblance to British law, while otherwise responding to British interests.[62] This was most evident in the draft's provision that foreign marks used in China were entitled to protection, even if not registered, either in China or abroad. Similarly, taking account of the fact that British merchants might not be able to produce registration certificates for marks used in Britain, the drafting committee determined early on that persons who chose to register foreign marks in China need not prove prior foreign registration.[63] In specifying the body to receive and act on registration applications, the committee selected the Imperial Maritime Customs itself, through which British influence ran deeply, rather than an entity more directly under Chinese control.

The draft prepared by the Imperial Maritime Customs at the

request of the Ministry of Foreign Affairs did not meet with approval from China's fledgling Ministry of Commerce, which had been founded in 1903 with a multifaceted mission, including responsibility for developing a modern body of commercial law, reducing China's growing dependence on foreign goods, fostering exports, and improving the lot of Chinese merchants selling abroad.[64] Objections to the Customs draft centered on the issues of registration, treatment of foreign-owned marks, and administrative responsibility and jurisdiction, judging from a superseding draft soon thereafter developed by a Ministry of Commerce team working with Japanese advisors.[65] Departing largely from the Anglo-American model employed by the Customs team, the Commerce draft declared in its very first article that anyone, "no matter whether Chinese or foreigner, who desires to have the exclusive use of a trade-mark must first register the same."[66] As a concession to foreign interests, applicants would be granted a six-month priority period, commencing with the establishment of the Chinese trademark office, in which they might register marks for which "various [Chinese] officials may have issued proclamations giving protection"[67] or that had been registered abroad before the opening of the Chinese trademark office. In the future, this period of priority for foreign registered marks was to be reduced to four months. Registration was to be denied, however, to any mark that imitated official seals, "destroy[ed] respect for rank, . . . [did] injury to the Customs of the country and . . . deceive[d] the people" or was identical to one that had been in public use, albeit not registered, in China for two or more years.[68]

No less important were the changes the Ministry of Commerce draft proposed making in the administration and jurisdiction of the trademark law. Citing the fact that the American and Japanese treaties did not specify which agency was to take responsibility for trademark administration and dismissing the Mackay Treaty's reference to the Imperial Maritime Customs on the grounds that it had not yet been established when negotiations with the British were being conducted, the ministry took the position that it should establish a single national trademark office in Beijing, which might have branch offices in Shanghai and Tianjin for the express purpose of facilitating registration.[69] Far from doing away with extraterritoriality, the draft provided that cases of infringement involving Chinese and foreigners were to be tried by officials of the defendant's government, with representatives of the plaintiff's government present. Thorough though it was, the ministry's draft evoked concern from the British, who saw it as giving advantage to the Japanese, while failing to stem counterfeiting of their trademarks by the Chinese or other foreigners.[70] But the German, French, Swiss, and other European governments reacted even more strenuously. The Ministry of Commerce's draft, in their minds, made undue concessions both to Anglo-American jurisprudence—as evidenced, for example, in the provision of de facto protection to unregistered marks that had been in use for more than two years in China—and to the Japanese, who had been accorded a unique advisory role in the drafting process.[71] Compounding these problems, the Europeans contended, were lack of timely notice of the draft's proposed changes and China's inadequate preparation for the administration of any such laws.

As a consequence, the civil law powers took the lead, soon to be followed by the British and Americans, in pressing the Chinese to set aside the Ministry of Commerce draft, pending its revision with expanded foreign "assistance."[72] Toward that end, the treaty powers formed a committee to elicit merchant reaction and "advise" the Chinese. Within months, the committee developed a series of proposed amendments to the draft. One of the most notable of these, reflecting a compromise between the Anglo-American and Continental lawyers, recommended that marks in use prior to the turn-of-the-century treaties be protected even in the absence of registration, but that those introduced thereafter be protected only if registered. Additionally, in an effort to keep the Chinese authorities from developing too much independence, the committee and other interested foreign parties called on the Chinese to recognize without examination any mark duly registered by a treaty power and to involve the foreign powers more intimately in China's trademark law drafting process by using more Western advisors and employing the Imperial Maritime Customs for at least some registration purposes.[73]

Notwithstanding its weak bargaining position, the Chinese government not only sought to stand firm in the face of increasing foreign pressure but strove to turn the situation to its advantage.

Reminding the treaty powers that the imperial government had followed Western advice in studying foreign trademark law prior to enacting its own, Chinese officials responded to the diplomatic committee's proposed changes by accentuating the great variations among the trademark laws of the treaty powers.[74] They further observed that allowing either foreign consular officials or local Chinese magistrates to resolve particular cases was certain to cause confusion, as "it is impossible that they should be familiar with all the affairs of the Trademark Office and the circumstances attaching to any action which may be brought." Accordingly, "so that equitable decisions may be obtained, and that the interests of both Chinese and foreigners may be protected," it was necessary, contended the Ministry of Commerce, that there be a "centralization of all authority" for trademark infringement cases in a system of Chinese courts to be established under its auspices.[75]

Although Chinese officials reminded the foreign diplomatic community that the centralization of authority over all trademark disputes was in keeping with those provisions of the turn-of-the-century commercial treaties promising to relinquish extraterritorial privileges when the Chinese legal system was "modernized," none of the treaty powers responded favorably to this Chinese proposal.[76] Britain and the United States, among others, made concerted efforts to persuade the Chinese to alter their position, arguing that the proposed system discriminated against their nationals and, in any event, was premature, given the West's view of the quality of the Chinese legal system.[77] With the foreign powers refusing to approve the proposed Chinese regulations and the Chinese refusing to substitute a draft more in keeping with their wishes, a stalemate ensued. The Chinese central government in turn relied on this deadlock as a rationale for not promulgating a permanent trademark law for two decades, with the result that the protection promised by the turn-of-the-century treaties was not available until 1923, and then more in name than fact.[78]

Similar situations obtained with respect to the development of patent and copyright laws and the relevant administrative agencies. Thus, although the Chinese had committed themselves in 1903 to provide patent protection for certain American inventions, more than two decades passed before foreigners received even the nominal protection first accorded Chinese nationals in 1912, which itself produced fewer than 1,000 patents over its first thirty years.[79] Nor did protection prove any more readily forthcoming with regard to copyright, even taking account of the fairly limited scope of the pertinent provisions of the American and Japanese commercial treaties. In 1906, 1907, and 1908, the Qing government issued laws on printing and newspapers, but the registration systems they provided were aimed at controlling printers, with the result that these laws ultimately treated Chinese and foreign authors equally by protecting neither.[80] For years, the Chinese resisted pressure from the United States and other treaty powers to promulgate legislation implementing their treaty obligations. Because the turn-of-the-century treaties specified that copyright protection was to be accorded in the "same way and manner and subject to the same conditions" as trademark protection, the Chinese government contended, it was premature to issue a copyright law until the trademark law "goes into force and proves acceptable and effective."[81] And when, in 1910, the Chinese finally did succumb and issue a "provisional and experimental copyright act . . . [that gave] certain very limited exclusive rights to Chinese authors,"[82] it neither "purport[ed] to put the above treaty provisions into effect" nor, according to a leading practitioner, gave "any protection" to foreigners.[83]

Finding little solace in Chinese legislative efforts and desiring, in any event, to maintain extraterritoriality,[84] Britain, the United States, and other treaty powers sought instead directly to protect their intellectual property against infringement in China by nationals of other treaty powers.[85] Accordingly, late in 1905, the major treaty powers commenced negotiation of a series of bilateral agreements amongst themselves designed to provide reciprocal protection.[86] These provided, for example, that an American national who had registered a trademark in Italy might bring an action before the Italian Consular Court in China against a person subject to the jurisdiction of that court. Notwithstanding ongoing allegations against Japanese merchants, these bilateral agreements soon significantly eased the problem of infringement among the treaty powers' nationals.

The treaty powers' problems with infringement by the Chinese were not so easily ameliorated. On the contrary, these problems multiplied during the period between the conclusion of the Mackay Treaty and the promulgation in the late 1920's of the first Chinese laws designed to implement the promises made by the turn-of-the-century treaties regarding intellectual property.[87] Increased industrialization enhanced the capacity of Chinese enterprises to copy foreign intellectual property,[88] while the spread of literacy through the *baihua* (vernacular) movement[89] and the growth of a sizable urban elite provided pirates with ever-greater incentives. Infringement of items from textbooks to tobacco products was rampant, judging from the accounts of diplomats, merchants, and local governmental organs.[90] In the words of Norwood Allman, who served as U.S. consul in Shanghai and was an assessor in the Mixed Courts prior to establishing his own law practice in China, "it is undoubted that there is now [1924] widespread unauthorized reproduction in China of foreign patented articles."[91]

Typical of the problems were the experiences of the famed American publisher of G. & C. Merriam, which invested heavily in the preparation of a bilingual version of *Webster's Dictionary* that it hoped to introduce to China.[92] Even before bringing its dictionary onto the Chinese market, Merriam discovered that the Commercial Press in Shanghai had already begun to distribute its own Chinese language version of *Webster's*. Merriam accordingly brought suit in 1923 against the Commercial Press before the Shanghai Mixed Court, invoking both the copyright and trademark provisions of the treaty of 1903 between the United States and China. Counsel for the Commercial Press offered an array of arguments, ranging from reliance on the literal meaning of the 1903 treaty's limited copyright provisions to lavishing praise on the Press for its patriotism in making foreign knowledge available. In the end, the court found that the dictionary did not fall within the limited class of American works entitled to copyright protection, but rejected the Commercial Press's contention that its use of a seal virtually identical to *Webster's* was no more than an unintentional coincidence. As a consequence, the court imposed a moderate fine (of 1,500 *liang* of silver) on the Commercial Press but did nothing to halt its continued publication of its version of *Webster's*—albeit without the identifying seal.[93]

Unable to secure uniform national intellectual property laws, foreign parties in China sought whatever alternative protection they could find. A number registered their trademarks, patents, and copyrights with the Maritime Customs, for although such registration had no legal effect before 1923, many foreign holders assumed that it might serve as proof of their long-standing ownership interest should they later seek to invoke the assistance of Chinese courts or officials in combating infringement.[94] Others sought to generate such proof through registration with their consulates, notwithstanding the fact that consuls were able to do little more than bring diplomatic pressure to bear within their own consular districts. Still, others, particularly in Shanghai and a small number of additional areas with a strong foreign presence, were successful in persuading local Chinese officials to exercise their discretionary powers to take action, at least on occasion, against infringers. Thus, the expatriate Shanghai *North China Daily News* reported with great praise the issuance during the summer of 1907 by the local *daotai* (circuit intendant) of proclamations designed to "prohibit further copying of patterns by Chinese" of "cigarettes manufactured by the British-American Tobacco Company (Limited) . . . and also . . . the soaps for which Messrs. A. E. Burkill & Sons are the sole agents."[95] The records of the Shanghai Mixed Court reveal instances, such as a 1915 case concerning the trademark Vaseline, in which the court came to the assistance of foreign trademark holders on equitable grounds, in the absence of a trademark law.[96]

The specter of foreign intervention that provided foreign holders of intellectual property with sporadic protection was, of course, essentially unavailable for their Chinese counterparts. Histories of major publishers and other enterprises, author's diaries, handbooks for the conduct of business, governmental records, and a host of other documents vividly portray the difficulty faced by Chinese with potentially marketable intellectual property—whose ranks were growing by virtue of the expansion of the middle class and technological change.[97] This was evidenced, for example, in the problems encountered by the "new breed of commercial writers" who arose as "the urban readership emerged and the facility of rapid printing became clear," only to find their attempts to earn a living from their prose thwarted by the fact that "copyrights existed but were unenforceable."[98]

Typical of the plight of Chinese authors was the experience of the novelist Xu Zhenya with his highly popular work *Yuli hun* (Jade Garden Spirit). Having initially published it in serial form beginning in 1912 in a periodical known as the *Minquan bao* (People's Rights Journal), Xu was dismayed to discover his tale of romance republished and sold at considerable profit by the People's Rights Publishing Section, which was affiliated with the journal. Eager to realize some of that profit, but unable to make headway with the publisher, Xu contended, in the words of a leading chronicler of the literature of that era, "that the new, Western thing known as the 'legal copyright' should remain with the author."[99] When his efforts at persuasion proved unavailing, Xu took the publisher to court under China's fledgling copyright law and prevailed, only to find the pirating of his celebrated love story to have spread still further in the interim. Exasperated, Xu finally chose to give away or sell at cost copies of the book in order both to strike back at the printers who had blithely pirated his work and to draw attention to his situation. Nor did Xu's ability to protect his own work improve markedly even after he formed his own publishing company, judging from the fact that although "some have even estimated a total circulation [for his next major novel] of over a million, . . . Xu . . . probably sold only a few tens of thousands."[100]

Western diplomats and merchants involved in these early attempts to implant "modern" intellectual property law in China attributed their failure to what they characterized as the inability of the Chinese to understand such law. As the U.S. consul general in Shanghai wrote to his ambassador in 1904, "The Chinese seem to have confused a trademark with a patent."[101] "You will remember," he added, "that in our negotiation of the [1903] Treaty, it seemed nearly impossible to explain to them the difference between a trademark and a patent." Nor were the Americans alone in such sentiments, judging from the reservations that the Germans and others expressed about the Ministry of Commerce's desire to centralize authority over trademark registration and infringement.[102]

Foreign assumptions as to why early efforts to foster "modern" intellectual property law in China proved so difficult were accurate in some measure. Notwithstanding the amassing by Shen Jiaben[103] and Wu Tingfang[104] of data regarding foreign legal systems and the subsequent utilization by the Chinese government of British, Japanese, and other foreign advisors,[105] it is evident that in the early twentieth century, Chinese officials in both the capital and the provinces had not thoroughly addressed the implications for China of intellectual property law. This is borne out, for example, by the tenor of early Ministry of Commerce memorials concerning such protection.[106] After noting that the United States, Japan, and other nations with patent laws attained high levels of economic success, these memorials suggest that China, too, might wish to adopt comparable measures. They fail, however, to indicate how such law— which they rightly declared to be without precedent in Chinese history[107]—was to be successfully absorbed, or even to take note of the plethora of practical difficulties confronting these and other aspects of the turn-of-the-century law reform effort. These memorials, in effect, equate the promulgation of such law with its implementation, whether in China or abroad.

Provincial and local officials were no more sophisticated about such matters. This was evidenced, for instance, by the rules regarding patents issued in 1906 by the Jiangnan Bureau of Commerce.[108] In an unconscious reprise of early patent law in the West, those rules, *inter alia,* provided for the issuance of what were described as patents to Chinese for imitation, rather than innovation. Such rewards were to be granted to those who imitated Western methods for producing paper, extracting oil, and other valuable industrial processes—with the length of the patent to vary according to the importance of what was appropriated from abroad.

These difficulties notwithstanding, it is important neither to overstate the incomprehensibility of Chinese intellectual property law in the late Qing and early Republican eras nor to assume that this was the sole reason Chinese of this period failed to embrace such laws more vigorously. The same documents that reflect a lack of familiarity on the part of Ministry of Commerce officials with many facets of intellectual property law and a naiveté about what the adoption of such law would entail also evidence both an appreciation that economically successful nations had patent laws and the perception that trademarks might help foster commerce. As a consequence, these same Ministry of Commerce materials call on Chinese negotiators to secure reciprocal protection abroad for Chinese marks in order to build up foreign markets for Chinese products, as well as to maintain China's sovereign honor.[109] It is also apparent that Chinese representatives clearly understood copyright well enough to negotiate a limit of China's promise of protection to materials "especially prepared for the use and education of the Chinese people," so that "Chinese subjects shall be at liberty to make, print, and sell original translations into Chinese of any [other] works written or of maps compiled by a citizen of the United States."[110] The inclusion of that limitation should not be attributed solely to the possibility that U.S. negotiators may have been interested in seeing American ideas disseminated in China, given the vigor with which Chinese authorities sought to uphold the right of their nationals under the treaty of 1903 to reproduce and translate virtually all American books.[111]

An awareness of at least some forms of marketable intellectual property extended beyond official circles. As printing and manufacturing technologies grew in sophistication, a modest number of authors and entrepreneurs joined guild members in efforts to prevent others from making unauthorized use of their creations,[112] although such awareness could hardly be described as widespread. Chinese nationals, particularly in Shanghai, showed some degree of familiarity with brand names in commercial boycotts staged in 1905 against American goods[113] to protest the passage of legislation designed to exclude Chinese from the United States in contravention of the Burlingame Treaty,[114] and in 1919 to express Chinese anger over Japanese expansionism.[115] Amidst a background of complaints about the difficulty of preserving any semblance of intellectual property in China, a small number of foreign observers suggested that the Chinese displayed some regard for trademarks.[116]

Questions of understanding of intellectual property law were, of course, not the only factors at play. Skepticism at the highest levels of the Chinese state seems to have impaired the late Qing law reform in general—which even with genuine support would have been extremely difficult to effectuate. To be sure, Shen Jiaben and others pleaded forcefully for legal reform, contending that without it China might well not survive in a competitive world filled with nations no longer burdened, as was China, with what he described as an antiquated legal system.[117] Nonetheless, the Empress Dowager Cixi and her most influential advisors, especially in the years immediately following the Boxer Uprising, regarded law reform as, at best, an unfortunate short-term expedient needed to calm the restive masses and appease the treaty powers before Qing power could be reasserted in its proper form.[118] And most important, as had been the case throughout imperial Chinese history, the government's interest in the publication remained focused on the control of ideas and the maintenance of order, rather than on the protection of private property interests or the nurturing of a marketplace of ideas.[119] As a consequence, elements of reform that Shen and his colleagues saw as essential—such as the abolition of many of the sharp status differences found in the Qing code in favor of a "modern" criminal code stressing equality—were either rejected or accepted in so watered-down a fashion as to dilute the very purpose of their adoption.[120]

Even those dimensions of the law reform effort that enjoyed sufficient support to be adopted largely as proposed faced immense difficulty—as was the case with the first Chinese company law, which in 1901 introduced the idea of limited liability and took a highly supportive approach toward entrepreneurial endeavor.[121] That law presumed that newly organized mechanisms for dispute resolution, such as chambers of commerce under the auspices of which arbitration acceptable to both Chinese and foreigners might be held, would rapidly be established.[122] And yet, owing to the weakness of the central government by the early twentieth century, little effort was devoted either to training individuals who might administer these new rules and institutions or to educating merchants and the broader populace as to their meaning and implications.

If anything, the problems that plagued the initial law reform efforts of the late Qing regime intensified during the final years of the dynasty and the early years of the Republic, preceding the consolidation of power by the Guomindang in the late 1920's. By the time of the ascension of the three-year-old Emperor Puyi to the throne in 1908, the Qing regime was in such disarray, and its ability to govern so deeply impaired by its own corruption, surging Han objections to Manchu rule, and the corrosive effects of China's semicolonial status,[123] that even proponents of further law reform recognized the relative futility of their undertakings. Nor were those who strove to take up the Qing dynasty's mantle in the first two decades following the 1911 revolution better able to attain success. Although attempts were made by various groups during this interregnum to build on the law reform work of the Qing, their motivation typically seems to have been legitimation rather than genuine legal reform. This was perhaps most graphically exemplified in 1915 by the early Republican President Yuan Shikai, who endeavored to restore the monarchy with himself as emperor. Eager to ease this blatant betrayal of the Republic he was serving, Yuan adopted the reign name of Hongxian (Great Constitutional) Emperor in the belief that this would demonstrate his self-professed abiding commitment to the rule of law.[124] In any event, conditions throughout this era were hardly propitious for legal reform.

As if the foregoing were not problematic enough, the very manner in which the treaty powers sought in this context to introduce intellectual property law into China appears, ironically, to have been a major factor impairing its reception. Apart from the essentially self-serving advice provided by a small core of British, Japanese, American, and other foreign advisors largely involved in legislative drafting and general legal counseling, it appears that the treaty powers made no substantial efforts to show the Chinese government why intellectual property law might be of benefit to China, to assist in the training of Chinese officials with responsibility in this field, or to educate the Chinese populace as to its rationale.[125] Nor does there appear to have been any serious attempt either to enlist the support of Chinese holders of commercially valuable intellectual property for the building of such law or to take account of Chinese circumstances, save for the copyright provisions of the U.S. and Japanese treaties. Instead, what was good for each treaty power was deemed by nationals of that particular treaty power, perforce, to be good for China.

Unhappy at being forced to negotiate the turn-of-the-century commercial treaties, Chinese officials initially assumed that adoption of the legal and other "reforms" called for in those agreements— including intellectual property law—would, at least, hasten the end of the much-detested extraterritoriality. They therefore moved to add the trappings of such laws to satisfy the treaty powers.[126] When it soon thereafter became apparent that these powers were in no hurry to fulfill their treaties' commitment to relinquish extraterritorial privileges, the initial limited Chinese willingness to legislate in this area largely dissipated. This was replaced, as has been depicted above, by efforts to employ intellectual property law itself as a tool in the struggle to ward off the foreign powers. As a consequence, U.S. Ambassador Rockhill's observation that "as China has no copyright laws and grants no protection to her own people, it would avail Americans little to be placed upon the same footing with them" remained as true two decades after the conclusion of the turn-of-the-century treaties as when he first uttered it in 1906.[127]

If the turmoil of the first two decades following collapse of the Qing dynasty was an impediment to efforts to formulate a sound new legal order, the brief interlude of relative stability enjoyed during the Nanjing government's early years hardly provided more auspicious circumstances. Wrapping themselves in the mantle of the Guofu (Father of the Nation), Sun Yatsen (1866–1925),[128] the Guomindang took power in 1928 after having turned bloodily against the Communists,[129] with whom it had uncomfortably been allied in efforts to stop warlordism and reunite China during the late 1920's. With the outbreak in Manchuria in 1931 of what was to become World War II, and with its own efforts to eradicate Chinese communism, the Guomindang, too, proved unable to escape the cycle of violence and realize a sustained period of peace.

The violent birth of its regime notwithstanding, the Guomindang soon sought a thorough transformation of the Chinese government in order to lay the foundation both for ending the disorder that had long afflicted China and for convincing the treaty powers that extraterritoriality was no longer justified.[130] Building on Sun's vision of a government of five branches, the Guomindang in its early years in power elaborated what it described as a modern government for a new China.[131] And so doing, the Guomindang developed and promulgated what its legal advisors—many of whom were foreign-trained—believed would be a fitting formal legal structure.[132]

The development of laws regulating creative and inventive endeavor was a key element of the effort to foster a new legal system. The first such measure, promulgated shortly after the Guomindang took power in 1928, was the Copyright Law.[133] Borrowing heavily from the German example, as filtered through the Japanese, this law provided that authors were entitled on registration with the Ministry of Internal Affairs to protection for books, music, photographs, designs, sculpture, and other technical, literary, and artistic works. In the case of Chinese nationals, this protection, which encompassed moral as well as economic rights, was to run for the life of the author plus thirty years. For foreigners, on the other hand, it was limited to ten years [134] and was available, as its implementing regulations specified, only for works "useful for [the] Chinese" created by persons "whose country recognizes that Chinese people are entitled to enjoy author's rights in that country." Although specific translations were to be protected, the right to translate a work copyrighted in a foreign country was not. Holders whose rights were being infringed might bring civil actions seeking damages or an injunction against further improper publication or might endeavor to have Chinese and foreigners alike prosecuted in Chinese courts.

In vesting the Ministry of Internal Affairs with registration authority, the law also provided that the ministry might "refuse to register [a work] in one of the following cases: (1) the work obviously goes against the doctrines of the Guomindang or (2) the release of the work is prohibited by other laws." [135] These restrictions were amplified in the Publication Law promulgated two years later and its implementing regulations,[136] only to be further expanded after the commencement of World War II.[137] Published works were not to contain anything, according to Article 19 of the Publication Law, "intended to . . . undermine the Guomindang or violate the Three People's Principles" of Dr. Sun Yatsen, "to overthrow the Nationalist Government or to damage the interests of the Republic of China," to "destroy public order," or to "impair good customs and habits." [138] To ensure that these prohibitions were met, books, newspapers and other works were not to be released in the event that the work "involved doctrines and affairs of the Guomindang" unless the Ministry of Internal Affairs or the Central Propaganda Department of the Guomindang granted a permit.[139] Such a permit, in turn, was a prerequisite to obtaining a copyright, although the prospect of not being able to secure rights for works of this type must have seemed a minor penalty in view of the Publication Law's provision that persons releasing such works without a permit might be subject to imprisonment, fines, the seizure of their publications, and the destruction of their type.[140]

Although less intimately interwoven in the fabric of political life, the trademark and patent measures promulgated by the Nationalist government during its years in Nanjing were not without their notable provisions. Protection for trademarks required registration with the central government, which had authority, under the Trademark Law issued in 1930 and amended in 1935, to bar marks that it deemed prejudicial to public order or that utilized the portrait or name of Dr. Sun Yatsen, the plum blossom, or other signs evocative of the national government or the Guomindang party.[141] Registration carried a term of twenty years, contingent on initial use of the mark in China within a year of its registration and continuing local use thereafter. Nonresident aliens were eligible to obtain registration for their marks through the use of Chinese agents, provided that their home nations offered comparable protection to China, and subject to the law's stipulation that if a mark had been used before registration was sought, the party using the mark first in China was entitled to registration even over parties who had previously registered it abroad. And as was the case with copyright, infringement cases were to be tried in Chinese courts, irrespective of the nationality of the defendants.

Protection for Chinese, if not foreign, inventions was set forth in the Measures to Encourage Industrial Arts promulgated in 1932.[142] These measures, in turn, were supplemented by the Nationalist government in 1949 with the introduction of a patent law prepared five years earlier in which, in the words of a foreign skeptic, "practically every known provision of patent law is incorporated." The legal regime envisioned offered patent protection, save for chemicals, foods, and pharmaceuticals, to Chinese as well as for foreigners, provided that their own nations reciprocated such protection.[143] Patent protection was not to be absolute, but rather was contingent on the requirement that the invention be worked within a three-year period or be subject to a compulsory license. Once again, the Chinese courts were to be the arbiter of infringement, which could be the subject of civil or criminal actions.

These elaborate efforts at "modernizing" the law notwithstanding, there appears, from accounts of Chinese and foreign observers alike, to have been little change in Chinese practice during the Nationalist government's two decades in power on the mainland.[144] Thus, for example, after noting in his 1969 study of book pirating in Taiwan that there was in the 1928 Copyright Law "no concern manifest . . . for the international aspects of protection," David Kaser remarks that "protection of any kind for literary property was so seldom recognized as deserving of attention in China that very, very few cases of alleged violation went to litigation; precedents, although not unknown, were rare."[145] Similar sentiments have been expressed by commentators as varied as Shen Ren'gan, the first head of the PRC's State Copyright Administration, who has declared that "despite laws promulgated by the Guomindang government, it was impossible . . . to assure the author's justifiable rights and interests,"[146] and Professor He Defen of National Taiwan University, who is a leading authority on copyright.[147] Nor does the situation appear to have been appreciably different with respect to trademarks or patents. "When . . . there is a case of infringement [of trademark] . . . the local courts do not take the opinion of the [National Trademark] Bureau into consideration," two British China hands of the 1930's typically noted; rather, the courts reached decisions irrespective of the existence of duly registered trademarks.[148] In the words of a sympathetic 1945 report by a subcommittee of the National Foreign Trade Council, based in New York, "adoption of suitable statutes relating to Patents, Trademarks and Copyrights will not be enough [i]f China is to derive any real benefit. . . . No matter how sound a law may be, it is of no value if it is not enforced."[149]

Clearly, the disruption occasioned by the invasion of Manchuria in 1931, Chiang Kai-shek's ongoing campaign to eradicate the Communists, further Japanese aggression, and the Chinese civil war that followed greatly impaired efforts to infuse life into the laws on intellectual property promulgated during the Nationalists' first two decades. Yet, more fundamentally, these laws failed to achieve their stated objectives because they presumed a legal structure, and indeed, a legal consciousness, that did not then exist in China and, most likely, could not have flourished there at that time. Structurally, each of these laws granted rights only to those persons who had registered their intellectual property with the appropriate governmental agencies and further specified that such rights were to be enforced through recourse to the nation's court system. Such a registration requirement may have made sense in the foreign context from which it was borrowed. It was, however, far less appropriate for China in the early twentieth century, given that, in the words of Chiang Kai-shek himself, "when something arrives at a government office it is *yamenized*—all reform projects are handled lackadaisically, negligently, and inefficiently,"[150] and given the virtual absence of personnel trained to administer such a registration system.[151]

Much the same point could be made regarding the notion of vindicating one's rights through the courts. Of China's 2,000 counties (*xian*), which had an average population of over 200,000, little more than 10 percent had as much as a single district court,[152] and many such courts were staffed by judges and lawyers of decidedly limited training and expertise. Nor was the situation much better even after another decade of efforts at law reform. In 1946 China still had only 479 courts, many of which were still not staffed by professional jurists.[153] So it was that the Harvard-trained political scientist Qian

Duansheng was able to conclude during the last years of the Nanjing era that "in draftsmanship the codes are, on the whole, well
done. If they have not been duly enforced, it is . . . because of the
inaccessibility of the courts, the incompetence of the judges, and,
especially, the interference of authorities other than the judicial in
the administration of justice." [154] Beneath these structural problems,
however, there were even more basic matters of legal consciousness
at play. From its inception, the Nationalist government justified the
slow pace at which it introduced constitutional reform by reference
to Sun Yatsen's theory of "tutelage." Sun's theory suggested that
the Chinese people were historically so ill-prepared for democracy
that only controlled movement in that direction under firm control
of the Guomindang, taking account of the time needed for mass
education, could succeed in transforming China. Nonetheless, in a
manner typical of Republican law reform in general, the lawyers and
officials involved in preparing the trademark, patent, and copyright
measures of this era drafted them as if their audience consisted of
other urban sophisticates as versed as they were in foreign ways.
There appears to have been scant recognition in these laws, and scant
acknowledgment in their application, that the overwhelming majority of their fellow Chinese citizens were unfamiliar not only with
the niceties of "modern" intellectual property but with the very idea
of vindicating rights through active involvement in a formal legal
process meant to be adversarial in nature.

Nor were problems of legal consciousness the exclusive province
of the 90 percent of China's populace who dwelt in the countryside.
The urbane lawyers and others involved in preparing Republican
China's modern legal codes seem not to have appreciated that the
idea of a strong, independent legal system, which underlay the laws
they drafted, was profoundly at odds with the self-perceived mission of the government they served. For all the new codes it put on
the books, the Nationalist government quite simply had little use for
the formalities of law when they interfered with its political agenda.
It was, for example, no coincidence that of more than 69,000 officials against whom charges of corruption were made to the central
government's Control Yuan during the notoriously freewheeling
years between 1931 and 1937, only 268 were found guilty and fewer
than 60 received any sort of punishment. [155] Copyright laws might
speak of the importance of preserving an author's rights, but these

were automatically to give way in the face of what was taken to be an unquestionable need to control the flow of ideas. The Nationalist government, in short, heeded only too well the January 1924 statement of the Guomindang Congress that "democratic rights . . . must not be carelessly bestowed." [156]

Four

Squaring Circles: Intellectual Property Law with Chinese Characteristics for a Socialist Commodity Economy

> Is it necessary for a steel worker to put his name on a
> steel ingot that he produces in the course of his duty? If
> not, why should a member of the intelligentsia enjoy
> the privilege of putting his name on what he produces?
> Popular saying in China during the
> Cultural Revolution (1966–76)

Although the founders of the PRC excoriated their Nationalist pre-decessors for being enamored of foreign ideas and practices,[1] they, too, looked abroad in developing law for their "New China."[2] Years before the invalidation in 1949 of the entire corpus of Republican law,[3] the Chinese Communist party drew extensively on the example provided by the USSR as it formed model "soviets" in the Chinese countryside and began to articulate a legal system.[4] With the establishment of a Chinese people's republic on October 1, 1949, such efforts to learn from abroad intensified.

In the area of intellectual property law, the Soviet model proved more accessible to China than those used by the Guomindang.[5] In large measure this was because of the ways in which the values that underlay the Soviet model reflected traditional Chinese attitudes toward intellectual property. This was especially the case with regard to the belief that in inventing or creating, individuals were engaged in social activities that drew on a repository of knowledge that belonged to all members of society. As the young Marx wrote in 1844:

Even when I carry out scientific work, an activity which I can seldom conduct in direct association with other men, I perform a social, because human, act. It is not only the material of my activity—such as the language itself which the thinker uses—which is given to me as a social product. My own existence is a social activity. For this reason, what I myself produce, I produce for society, and with the consciousness of acting as a social being.[6]

To be sure, Marx's views on the social nature of language and of invention, and Confucius's concept of the transmission of culture arose from very different ideological foundations. Nonetheless, because each school of thought in its own way saw intellectual creation as fundamentally a product of the larger society from which it emerged, neither elaborated a strong rationale for treating it as establishing private ownership interests.

The Soviet example also evoked the Chinese tradition in its approach to the dissemination of knowledge. There are, of course, many differences between Marxism-Leninism, with its ultimate goal of a classless society, and Confucianism, with its belief in the necessity of hierarchy.[7] Nonetheless, each clearly envisioned that it was wholly appropriate—indeed, necessary—to control the flow of ideas to the populace. Moreover, each believed that this control was to be exercised by a very small group of persons for the benefit of society as a whole. In this respect, too, the Soviet case was far more compatible with both the objectives of the Beijing leadership and the broader Chinese context than were the models Republican China had used, which presumed the existence of a marketplace of ideas in a manner neither acceptable to the leadership of the Chinese Communist party nor previously witnessed in the Middle Kingdom.

The cornerstone of the PRC's early efforts at regulating intellectual property, the Provisional Regulations on the Protection of Invention Rights and Patent Rights of August 11, 1950, followed the Soviet model in establishing a "two-track" system.[8] The preferred track provided for the granting by the state of certificates of invention to select inventors. These certificates entitled persons or entities responsible for worthy advances to recognition and monetary rewards tied to the savings realized from their inventions, while vesting in the state the right to exploit and disseminate those inventions. Alternatively, the state might issue patents vesting inventors with ownership and fundamental control, thereby entitling them to receive whatever royalties might be negotiated.[9]

Unlike the USSR, the PRC did not craft its two-track system in order to calm the anxieties of Western multinational enterprise.[10] Rather, this division resulted chiefly from the Chinese Communist party's inwardly focused policy of national reconstruction and was designed to garner technology needed by the state while calming the anxieties of Chinese intellectuals and holders of substantial private property, whose participation was needed to rebuild the country.[11] Inventions made by workers outside their course of employment, by individuals in private enterprises, or by foreigners resident in China might qualify, at the inventor's choice, for either a certificate of invention or a patent, with the latter vesting control over the invention's future use, including the right to extract royalties. New inventions were to be state property, however, if they were made in the course of employment in state-owned enterprises, concerned national security, or "affected the welfare of the great majority of the people," such as advances in agricultural and stock species or pharmaceuticals.[12] Those responsible for such innovations were eligible for inventor's certificates, but did not enjoy any ongoing property interest in their inventions. Accordingly, the state could determine whether and how their creations could thereafter be used by other Chinese entities without prior approval or the payment of a licensing fee.

As initially promulgated, the Inventions Regulations sought to preserve as much discretion as possible for the state. Thus, for example, they empowered the principal administering and enforcement body, the Central Bureau of Technological Management of the Finance and Economic Committee of the General Administration of Commerce, both to set terms of protection for patents and certificates of invention for periods of from three to fifteen years and to establish the rates at which holders of certificates were to be rewarded. Further control was to be exercised through provisions of the regulations that required the working of patents within two years and forbade the transfer of patent rights without the Central Bureau's permission. Subsequent supplementary measures, culminating in the 1954 Decision on Encouraging Inventions, Technical Improvements, and Rationalization Proposals Concerning Production, preserved the Central Bureau's discretion on term, but specified a fixed table of monetary rewards for certificates tied to production savings realized by use of the invention.[13]

Notwithstanding the relatively greater attention focused on inventions, issues of trademark and payments for publication were also addressed during the PRC's formative years. In 1950, the Chinese government promulgated the Procedures for Dealing with Trademarks Registered at the Trademark Office of the Former Guomindang Government and the Provisional Regulations on Trademark Registration. The former invalidated all registrations by the Nationalist government, while the latter provided for the establishment of a new registration-based trademark system.[14] Registration, which was available for specified foreign marks, seems to have been instituted largely to provide holders among the so-called national bourgeoisie with the opportunity to seek at least nominal protection for their marks.[15] Relatively few holders, bourgeois or otherwise, however, sought to avail themselves of this opportunity—whether because registration was not required, the entities administering this law were unproven, intellectual property law remained unfamiliar, or anxiety still ran high as to the political consequences of asserting such property interests.

No comparable provisional regulations were promulgated with respect to copyright during the early years of the PRC—or, for that matter, for years thereafter. But, even apart from the state's efforts to assert control over the content of what was published, the topic of relations between authors and publishers was hardly neglected even in the early years of the PRC. Chinese officials and scholars closely studied the Soviet example, which at least in theory provided that authors were entitled to fixed "basic payments" for their work, based predominantly on the number of copies printed, which the Chinese termed *gaofei*, and had the right to prevent unauthorized alteration of their work.[16] Enjoyment of each right, however, was dependent on approval by the state—which, in any event, controlled all authorized publishing outlets.

Building on the Soviet example, the PRC first approached the question of remunerating authors as part of its broader effort to spur the intelligentsia to meet the vast scientific and intellectual needs of a state ravaged by decades of revolution and war, while simultaneously maintaining careful administrative control over "publication work" generally. The initial official pronouncements concerning such payments appear to have been made in five resolutions passed by the so-called First State Publications Conference, held in Beijing in October 1950 under the auspices of the Ministry of Culture. These resolutions, which did not have the force of law, but were clearly understood to express official policy, stipulated that "publishing circles should respect the rights both of authors and of [other] publishers: acts such as the unauthorized reproduction, plagiarism, and distortion [of texts] are prohibited." [17] They also set forth broad guidelines meant to shape relations between authors and publishing houses. Central among these was the indication that "the author's remuneration shall, in theory, be based on the nature of the work [with scientific works valued more highly than those in the humanities], the quality and quantity of [Chinese] characters, and the print-run of the work." [18]

Reinforcement for the general principles enunciated in the Five Resolutions came in the early 1950's with the promulgation by the State Administration of Publication and other organs of a series of pronouncements designed to regulate the publishing industry more closely. Most prominent were the 1952 Rules on the Editorial Organization and Work System of State Publishing Entities, which called on the leadership of such organs to form "contracts" with authors. [19] These contracts, which were more akin to confirmations of relationships authorized by the state plan than freely negotiated arm's-length agreements, followed the Soviet model and concerned the submission of manuscripts, publication, and payment. [20] Additional formal efforts to address various aspects of these issues were made during the 1950's through a series of official pronouncements, including stipulations directed to "correction of the phenomenon of reprinting books at will," general regulations regarding publishing, rules on the remuneration due authors of works on literature and the social sciences, [21] and sets of classified draft regulations that were never officially promulgated concerning the rights of foreign and Chinese authors. [22] Throughout all this, the standard for remuneration set out in the resolutions issued in 1950 continued in force.

The difficulties of assessing the efficacy of any intellectual property law regime are intensified with respect to the PRC, particularly prior to the opening of the late 1970's. Nonetheless, there is reason to believe that notwithstanding efforts to appeal to intellectuals and others in the national bourgeoisie, the rules developed in the early years of the PRC failed to respond to the changing Chinese political circumstances of the 1950's. Thus, even with attempts in 1954 to rationalize the reward structure for inventions, only six certificates of invention and four patents were issued through 1958.[23] At the same time, there appears to have been much "copying and applying [of] the technology, techniques, and products developed in more advanced countries, without paying any royalties."[24] Similarly, in the trademark area, there was through the 1950's an "increasing use of unauthorized trademarks."[25] Moreover, according to a leading Chinese authority, by "1956, the great majority of [China's] capitalist and commercial enterprises [had] completed their socialist transformation . . . [so that] the administration of the trademark law was looked upon as only a matter of supervision over the quality of goods, and the question of protection of the exclusive right to use the trademark ceased to exist."[26] As for publication, the infringement of clearly identified proprietary works continued apace, even by state enterprises such as *Xinhua* (the New China News Agency), which was the only entity authorized to distribute books. Nor did the publishing contracts called for in the 1952 rules on editorial organization appear to exercise much deterrence—which ought not to be surprising in view of the absence at that time in China of both a basic contract law and effective means of legal redress for righting civil wrongs.[27]

By the early 1960's, efforts were under way to recast the preliminary framework governing patents, trademarks, and payments for authors that had developed during the first years of the PRC. These attempts were prompted not so much by the relative ineffectuality of the earlier rules as by overarching political considerations. Both the Anti-Rightist Movement of 1957 and the Great Leap Forward of 1958–60 raised doubts about the appropriateness of material incentives for those engaged in inventive, creative, and commercial activity.[28] Moreover, the so-called Socialist Education Campaign, launched in 1962, advocated the restoration of ideological purity by eradicating various "anti-socialist" tendencies said to have arisen during the 1950's, including the use of material incentives. As a consequence, in what became known as the struggle between "redness" and "expertise," scientists and other intellectuals were berated for placing professional development ahead of the Communist party's objectives and were accordingly required to devote substantially more time than before to political study and manual labor.[29]

Reflecting the political tenor of the times, China's fledgling intellectual property laws were amended during this period to reduce their stated concern with property rights and their reliance on material incentives. On November 3, 1963, the State Council[30] supplanted the Provisional Regulations on the Protection of Invention and Patent Rights with two sets of permanent regulations— the Regulations to Encourage Inventions and the Regulations to Encourage Improvements in Technology.[31] Although not a single patent appears to have been issued during the preceding six years, these new sets of regulations struck patent protection from the law and specified that henceforth inventions and improvements in technology were to be the exclusive property of the state.[32] Indeed, even the system of certificates of inventions, which had not established property rights but only entitled inventors to receive payments tied to the savings realized from their work, was discontinued.

In place of the prior system of patents and certificates of invention, the regulations promulgated in 1963, in the words of the principal Communist party newspaper, *Renmin ribao* (People's Daily), sought to "encourage scientists and technicians, as well as staffers and workers generally, to make inventions and technical improvements" by declaring individuals and entities responsible for such advances to be eligible for both "material" and "honorary" awards.[33] Consistent, however, with the notion that "in giving awards, politics should be in command, extensive ideological work carried out, and the principle of combining honorary awards with material awards maintained," the material awards provided by the new regulations called for far lower payments than the previous schedules of rewards, which had been tied to a fixed scale of "bonuses." This new monetary recognition was to be complemented by a set of honorary rewards, ranging from exhortational certificates and banners to application of one's name to the invention made and free trips to workers' resorts.[34] Even with cutbacks in material incentives, there were, according to the *Guangming ribao* (Enlightenment Daily),[35] still "people thinking seriously of fame and wealth for themselves . . . [who looked] upon knowledge and technique as their private property, made a monopoly of their technical knowledge and refused to exchange their experiences in research. Having in mind the 'cornering of the market,' they are unwilling to disseminate their talent and skills." [36]

The retrenchment was not limited to inventive activity. On April 10, 1963, the State Council replaced the Provisional Regulations on Trademark Registration with Regulations Governing the Control of Trademarks. [37] Unlike the Provisional Regulations, under which exclusive rights in marks could be obtained, the new regulations made no mention of "rights" or of "exclusive use." Instead, their declared purpose was "strengthening the control of trademarks and making enterprises guarantee [baozheng] and improve the quality of their products" [38]—objectives not otherwise easily attainable in a society that lacked significant consumer protection law and relied heavily on planning rather than market forces. In keeping with this emphasis, the new regulations and their implementing rules required that all trademarks be registered, that registration applications contain statements of the quality of the subject products, and that the General Administration of Commerce assume oversight responsibility. The General Administration, as a result, was to have the authority both to receive complaints about goods that failed to meet their supposed standards and, where such complaints proved accurate, to cancel registrations. [39]

There were, of course, no comprehensive promulgated provisional copyright regulations to be revised. But in keeping with the move to curtail such "rights," the move that had commenced in the late 1950's to reduce gaofei intensified. [40] In March 1961, the Ministry of Culture issued a circular specifying that the prior practice of remunerating authors in part according to the number of books printed or reprinted was to be eliminated. [41] In its place, authors were to receive more modest payments, based on the number of characters a work contained and its "quality." The criteria for the determination of "quality" were left unspecified, but they presumably mirrored the Communist party's political agenda.

As substantial as was the redirection of Chinese intellectual property law of the early 1960's, it paled in significance relative to the changes wrought by the so-called Great Proletarian Cultural Revolution, which commenced in 1966. [42] In the effort fundamentally to reshape Chinese society, the realm of acceptable discourse was even more sharply curtailed than had previously been the case. [43] Thus, for example, from 1966 to 1971, all theater was banned save for eight model revolutionary "operas."[44] Concomitantly, the professional endeavors of virtually all scientists, writers, and other intellectuals were disrupted, and large numbers of them were sent to the countryside, imprisoned, or subjected to physical abuse. The formal legal system was denounced as following a "black line" and being inherently and hopelessly reactionary,[45] while many informal dispute resolution processes were either abandoned or politicized to a point of ineffectuality.[46]

In this climate, even the revised framework of the early 1960's for the regulation of intellectual property was not immune from attack. Not only did the state cease the reduced payments authorized by the 1963 Regulations on Inventions,[47] but individuals increasingly proved unwilling to acknowledge their personal role in inventive activity. A *Xinhua* release of October 1966 declared, for example:

In China's major inventions, it is impossible in many cases to establish who are the inventors, because the combined effort of so many people and so many units are involved, and no one claims the credit. No one has come forward, for example, to claim an award or any patent rights for any important discoveries and inventions made during the past six years by the people of the Daqing oil field.[48]

Efforts to maintain the compulsory trademark registration system established in 1963, which had led to the granting of some 2,000 to 3,000 marks a year, ground to a halt. Moreover, the very idea of trademarking goods, even to assure quality for consumers, was lambasted as a concession to a commodity economy and, as such, improper for the new China.[49] Indeed, as Mark Sidel indicates, "thousands of similar and dissimilar goods" were sold under such ideologically pure, but non–identifying labels as "Red Flag," "East Wind," and "Worker-Peasant-Soldier," with the result that quality varied widely, massive unauthorized copying occurred, and consumer confusion was rampant.[50]

With acceptable discourse greatly narrowed, many authors found their works regarded as no longer suitable for distribution,[51] making contractual protection irrelevant. Those authors whose works were deemed worthy of publication were unable to secure protection in any case, since the state itself freely reproduced or tolerated the reproduction of such works without obtaining the permission of the author or original publisher, providing any remuneration, or, in some instances, even acknowledging authorship.[52] As was asked during the Cultural Revolution, "Is it necessary for a steel worker to put his name on a steel ingot that he produces in the course of his duty? If not, why should a member of the intelligentsia enjoy the privilege of putting his name on what he produces?"[53]

The Cultural Revolution is said not to have ended until the arrest of the Gang of Four in the autumn of 1976, but by 1975 Zhou Enlai, Deng Xiaoping, Hua Guofeng, and others in the leadership who were disturbed by the slow pace of China's developmental efforts had already begun to call for a program of "Four Modernizations" aimed at enabling China to reach world-class strength in agriculture, industry, science and technology, and military matters by the end of the century.[54] By 1977, these objectives took center stage as Deng and others who had earlier been purged for taking a "pragmatic" approach to building Chinese socialism in the late twentieth century assumed power.

Believing the promotion of scientific and other intellectual work to be crucial if the nation were to make up for the decade of development and training lost to the Cultural Revolution,[55] China's new leadership launched a series of measures designed to enhance the position of intellectuals and facilitate their endeavors.[56] Part of this undertaking—which included a revitalization of higher education, the reinstitution of academic examinations for university entrance, and the delivery of florid speeches praising the role of intellectuals in socialist reconstruction[57]—was directed toward intellectual property law. In keeping with the approach taken generally toward rebuilding China's self-decimated legal system,[58] efforts were made from 1977 on to restore the broad framework for the regulation of intellectual property that had been in place prior to the Cultural Revolution. Thus, with respect to science, the Chinese government in 1978 reissued the 1963 regulations that provided both monetary and honorific rewards for inventors.[59] A year later the state issued Regulations for the Reward and Encouragement of Natural Sciences, which essentially sought to extend to the natural sciences the basic principles laid down in the 1963 regulations.[60]

Similar efforts to return to the status quo ante of 1963 were made concerning trademarks. The newly reconstituted State General Administration for Industry and Commerce (SAIC), the China Council for the Promotion of International Trade (CCPIT)[61] and other organs once again relied on the Trademark Regulations of 1963.[62] No less important, these organizations strove to reestablish both China's system of internal trademark regulation and its international trademark relations, each of which had suffered during the Cultural Revolution.[63] In regard to copyright, the issuance in 1977 by the State Administration of Publication of the Trial Circular Concerning Basic and Supplemental Payments for News Publications revived,[64] at least in name, the levels of compensation to which authors had been entitled before the Cultural Revolution. Soon thereafter, these were superseded by the Provisional Regulations on Basic Payments for Books, which called for the granting of payments at a level consistent with those made prior to the Great Leap Forward.[65]

With these measures in place, the United States and the PRC were able in 1979 to conclude a trade agreement, said by the Carter administration to satisfy the requirements of the 1974 Trade Act for pacts with socialist nations.[66] Under the agreement, each side indicated that it "recognize[d] the importance of effective protection of patents, trademarks, and copyrights"[67] and pledged itself to "take appropriate measures under [its] . . . laws and regulations and with due regard to international practice" to accord protection to the works of citizens of the other nation.[68]

Having reestablished as interim measures the broad outlines of the pre–Cultural Revolution systems for inventive activity and the labeling of products, the leadership set in motion processes designed to generate the legal framework needed to undergird the scientific, technological, and economic advances that they hoped China would make. In 1978, the State Science and Technology Commission, which was reestablished that year at the supraministerial level to oversee "general policy for scientific and technological development," was directed to work up long-range policy on inventions.[69] A year later, the SAIC was charged with similar responsibility for trademarks, and in the early 1980's, a special copyright committee was formed.[70]

The task confronting these various entities was a daunting one. Individuals lacking direct experience in intellectual property, as that discipline was understood beyond the socialist bloc, were asked to devise rules capable of nurturing an economy undergoing a dynamic and essentially unprecedented transition without transgressing the Communist party's uncertain and oft-shifting political line. In so doing, they could not avoid, at least implicitly, confronting fundamental and difficult questions about the character and direction of Chinese socialism and, indeed, about the sources of ingenuity and motivation more generally.

The debates concerning the drafting of a patent law, which were among the most intense concerning economic legislation during the first decade following Mao Zedong's death, illustrated both the complexity of this particular undertaking and the tensions that characterized Chinese law reform efforts of this era.

Proponents of a patent law protective of ownership interests placed primary emphasis on its likely salutary economic effects,[71] arguing that China needed to smash the "iron rice bowl" (*tie fanwan*) mentality of the Cultural Revolution that rewarded all equally, irrespective of the quality of their work, and that was now seen as having stifled initiative and held back the nation.[72] This could only be accomplished, they contended, by adopting a system that provided meaningful material incentives. By permitting those who had so contributed to reap the fruits of their labors, a patent law would also, it was suggested, allow China's most innovative organizations to accumulate additional capital and strengthen their management, which would spur further inventive activity and help make up for time lost to the Cultural Revolution.[73] Establishment of a patent regime, requiring that patents be openly published in a systematic fashion, might also create a greater interchange of information among Chinese scientists. This interchange would likely provide fuller access to technical advances than had been possible when scientists feared that disclosure might jeopardize whatever modest rewards were available.[74]

Although stressing domestic considerations, proponents of a patent system did not ignore the benefits that might accrue to China internationally. They recognized that the early years of the "open" policy had not resulted in the transfer to China of foreign technology of the quality and quantity desired by the leadership.[75] Aware that foreign anxiety over the absence of an effective framework for intellectual property protection was one principal reason for this shortfall,[76] scholars and officials, including such well-known figures as Zhang Youyu and Ren Jianxin,[77] contended both in domestic publications and in media aimed toward foreign distribution that China needed to institute a patent system "to import advanced technology for acceleration of the four modernizations."[78] Such a system would not only allay foreigners's fears about the disposition in China of their technology, but might also make it possible for China to participate in international exchanges of patent application information, thereby expanding the range of data available to Chinese scientists.[79]

Apart from fostering the transfer to China of sorely needed foreign technology, those in favor of a patent system further contended that it would also generate other benefits internationally. Given, as one proponent put it, that approximately 150 other nations, including many socialist and developing nations, already had patent laws, the establishment of law in this area would serve to reassure even those potential foreign investors unconcerned about technology transfer that China was serious about constructing a legal system conducive to international business, while also generally enhancing China's image among the family of nations.[80] Adoption of a patent law meeting international standards would also enable China to adhere to the Paris Convention and so attain better protection abroad for Chinese technology.[81] Leading Chinese publications were suggesting that the failure to obtain patent protection abroad for Chinese advances had already resulted in the appropriation of Chinese inventions by foreigners.[82] And, reflecting the optimism felt by many in leadership and scientific circles about the pace of Chinese technological development, it was argued that the need for protection abroad of Chinese scientific advances was likely to become far more intense in the years ahead.[83]

Many nonetheless strongly opposed adoption of a patent system as intrinsically antithetical to socialist principles and inherently corrupting.[84] The granting of such private property rights, they argued, might harm national development by giving a few individuals control of important technologies, enabling them either to profit unjustifiably or to deny access to vital information altogether.

Opponents of a patent system also expressed concern about the Western "literary-industrial complex," which some believed might patent so broadly in China as to stifle the development of indigenous science and so leave the nation dependent on the outside world economically, scientifically, and militarily. It would be foolhardy, they argued, to risk draining China's limited foreign exchange reserves to pay royalties—especially when much of the same technology could be acquired at no cost, albeit without authorization. In addition, some contended, the openness a patent system provided might even enable foreign entities to make off with the latest Chinese innovations.[85]

Given how sharply the lines of debate were drawn, it took no less a personage than Deng Xiaoping to determine that China should adopt a patent law intended to endow inventors with rights in their innovations without undercutting their responsibilities to the state.[86] With this decision, the drafting committee turned its attention to the question of how to construct such a law. Resuming efforts under way even prior to the committee's formal initiation to identify the full range of options, delegations were dispatched to major industrial nations with differing patent systems (including the United States, West Germany, and Japan); to socialist states believed by the Chinese to be relatively prosperous (such as Romania and Yugoslavia); and to the principal international bodies concerned with intellectual property issues (including the World Intellectual Property Organization [WIPO] and the United Nations Education, Science and Cultural Organization).[87] The full patent laws of some 35 jurisdictions were translated and those of more than 100 other nations summarized, while the legislation and practice of the Nationalist Chinese, both on the mainland prior to 1949 and on Taiwan since, were carefully, if quietly, scrutinized, as was the experience of Hong Kong.[88] Nor was attention solely directed externally, as the committee "solicited the views of cadres in factories, scientific research institutes, universities and government agencies."[89] In the end, the drafting committee spent more than five years, during which it went through some 20 drafts prior to finally producing a bill—only to have the National People's Congress (NPC) take the unusual step of amending the legislation before it passed the Patent Law on March 12, 1984.[90]

The Patent Law's passage was widely heralded, both at home and abroad, as signaling the dawn of a new era in Chinese economic and legal development.[91] In celebrating the creation of a novel property right, however, Chinese commentators eager to spur the infusion of technology and foreign observers flush with the sense that China had at last come to see the world their way failed adequately to heed the degree to which the law's drafters had taken seriously Deng Xiaoping's injunction and carefully qualified the very rights they were establishing. As was the case with respect to Chinese law reform in general, far too many individuals, consciously or otherwise, sub-scribed to a unitary vision of legality, presuming that adoption of a particular legal form in China would yield results there comparable to those produced by similarly denominated laws in the industrial-ized world. Consequently, they were oblivious both to the ways in which that form had been altered to meet Chinese objectives and to the further challenges that the Middle Kingdom's historical legacy and current conditions would pose.

In fact, in the Patent Law, as with much of the body of law produced throughout the 1980's, the PRC sought to articulate a "socialist legality with Chinese characteristics" that strove to adapt foreign legality to Chinese circumstances and so was a less drastic departure from prior practice than has generally been assumed. New rights, drawn principally from foreign models, were to be estab-lished, but their scope was to be sufficiently circumscribed so as not to conflict with the national interest as understood by central authorities who had just begun to scale back their role in the indus-trial sector and had little intention of doing so in the political arena. Stated differently, as concerned both Chinese and foreigners, there was rather less than met the eye to the rights proffered in the new Patent Law—even as that law accorded each separate treatment, in so doing exemplifying yet another prominent feature of Chinese legality from imperial days through the initial post–Cultural Revo-lution law reforms.

Although the 1984 law provided for the granting of "patent rights" to persons or entities with "invention-creations" meeting the requisite standards of novelty, inventiveness, and practicality, it nonetheless reflected uneasiness at the introduction of a form of private property fundamentally new to China. The law and its concurrently issued regulations were structured, albeit subtly, so as to confine its seemingly broad grant of rights within tolerable bounds—on the one hand making it difficult for individuals to secure rights through which they might extract monopoly rents, while on the other holding forth the promise of material rewards in order to spur individuals to be innovative. This was most readily apparent in the law's direction of Chinese away from invention patents, with their fifteen-year term, and either toward utility model patents, which offered lesser rights and a five-year term, or toward monetary rewards in lieu of any grant of rights.[92] Article 6 of the new law specified that only entities could apply for patents in "service invention-creations," which were defined broadly elsewhere to encompass anything made on or in relation to one's job, using materials or data from one's work unit (*danwei*), or within a year of leaving one's unit.[93] Given the centrality in the mid 1980's of one's *danwei*—which typically provided housing, welfare benefits, and a social context, as well as employment, for industrial workers[94]—and given the difficulty at that time of independently securing sophisticated equipment or sizable capital, this effectively precluded Chinese nationals from securing invention patents in their own names.[95] Instead, persons responsible for "service invention-creations" were to receive a "money prize" from their unit, while individuals carrying out inventive activity apart from their *danwei* might apply for a utility model or alternatively forgo seeking such rights in favor of a monetary reward under the 1963 Inventions Regulations, which had been reissued for this purpose in 1982.[96]

The limits on rights potentially available to Chinese were also evident elsewhere in the Patent Law. Article 29, for example, provided foreigners who had filed patent applications abroad with a twelve-month priority period within which to seek protection in China, but made no similar concession for Chinese. The law's provisions on compulsory licensing similarly disadvantaged Chinese. Article 14 vested the State Council and provincial governments with the authority to compel state entities to license patents they held, subject only to the requirement that such a step be taken "in accordance with the state plan" and that a fee, to be determined by the state, be paid. The situation for collectives or individuals was hardly any better, as Article 14 empowered pertinent governmental units to order the licensing of any patent they might own of "great significance to the interests of the state or to the public interest . . . [that might be in] need of spreading and application." Patents owned by foreigners or by Sino-foreign joint ventures, on the other hand, were to be subject to compulsory licensing only if the patentee failed within three years of receiving the patent to "make the patented product, or use the patented process in China, or otherwise to authorize other persons" to do so.[97]

On its face, the Patent Law ironically gave the appearance of reprising treaty port days in granting greater legal privileges to foreigners and their local partners than to other Chinese. Arguably, this concession can be explained as emanating from the leadership's belief that foreigners would not transfer advanced technology to China were their rights as circumscribed as those accorded Chinese. Nonetheless, this bifurcation, and others created in the course of law reform, not only ran counter to the state's professed move away from a planned economy toward one in which domestic and foreign interests would presumably be competing on an economic basis, but also threatened to entrench the latter over the former, coming as they did at a highly formative stage in the growth of a Chinese market.[98]

Closer scrutiny of the Patent Law and its implementing regulations reveals, however, that while spared certain of the disadvantages their Chinese counterparts may have faced, would-be foreign patentees suffered others largely peculiar to their situation and shared still others with their local brethren. Thus, for example, although the exclusion from patent coverage of chemical, pharmaceutical, or alimentary inventions by Article 25 nominally applied equally to everyone, in fact, foreigners had by far the most to lose in these areas, in which, typically, inventive steps were relatively easy to discern and copy, and in which, therefore, legal protection has been particularly valuable, according to empirical studies conducted in an American setting.[99] Much the same point might be made with regard to Article 11 of the 1984 law, which in failing to protect process patents (which address the processes through which products are made) effectively foreclosed the possibility of halting the importation into China of products made in third countries that do not protect processes, while sharply reducing the likelihood of discerning infringement within China. A similar logic applied with respect to the limitation in Article 45 of the term for invention patents to 10 years, which worked to the particular disadvantage of foreign parties, given that their applications, as the law presumed (and practice has borne out) typically concerned technology of far greater value than their Chinese counterparts. And the law's requirement, in Article 19, that Chinese and foreigners alike work through authorized patent agents was less evenhanded than it may have appeared, given the relative unfamiliarity of most foreigners with the Chinese scene (and their concomitant greater reliance on agents whose independence, especially as regards infringement issues, remains to be proven).[100] Moreover, unlike their Chinese counterparts, who were free to choose from among thousands of agents, foreigners were limited initially to one and then subsequently to less than a handful of agencies.

Whatever singular difficulties patentees from both China and abroad had to face, each was also confronted with the conundrum of rights carrying little in the way of legal remedies. In a manner typical of the first decade of post–Cultural Revolution law reform from the Constitution down, the Patent Law of 1984 had far more to say about the rights being provided than about the means through which individuals might vindicate them. To be sure, the law, at Article 60, provides that patentees seeking to protect their rights might "directly institute legal proceedings in [or take appeals to] the people's court." Nonetheless, its overall thrust is toward a largely unbounded administrative resolution of problems—in a manner more in keeping with the model of a centrally directed economy than much of the publicity surrounding the promulgation of the Patent Law would have led one to believe. Thus, for example, Article 65 of the law provides that "where any person usurps" the rights or interests of another, "he shall be subject to disciplinary sanction by the entity to which he belongs or the competent authority at the higher level." Neither Article 65 nor any other provision of Chinese law, however, either clearly articulates procedures pursuant to which administrative resolutions of this type are to be reached or indicates how such entities and authorities, which presumably are not versed in the intricacies of patent doctrine, are to address the very types of questions for which the Patent Law elsewhere requires the use of authorized patent agents. Without denigrating the value of non-litigious modes of dispute resolution, one is hard put to imagine that in the China of the mid 1980's—with its limited labor mobility and institutional rivalries—individuals would strenuously assert their rights either against their superiors before their common employer or against outside infringers when adjudicatory authority was vested with the unit for which the accused worked.

If Article 65 is a particular constraint on remedies potentially available for Chinese, there is scant comfort for foreigners in the Patent Law's remaining remedies. In a manner reminiscent of PRC approaches toward legality, at least through the mid 1980's, the Patent Law largely limits itself to administrative or criminal remedies, each of which leaves principal remedial powers in the hands of officialdom. Little is provided in the way of civil remedies, which, presumably, would vest more discretion with patentees. Thus, the law authorizes the Patent Office to order infringers to "stop the infringing act and to compensate for the damage" and calls for the prosecution, under the Criminal Law, of any person who "passes off the patent of another," while its implementing regulations specify the scope of administrative fines.[101] As ill defined as these provisions are, and as uncertain as the enforcement of such administrative orders may be, the Patent Law offers no explicit counterpart on the civil side. In fairness, one presumes that the Patent Law's drafters were aware that the PRC's initial Law on Civil Procedure gave courts a residual authority to issue injunctions, impose fines, and require compensation. That general power, however, hardly substitutes for the statutorily set damages that virtually every sophisticated patent system has instituted in order to cope with the fact that victims of infringement will rarely be in a position to know with any precision how much damage they have suffered. Nor have the generic remedies of the provisional or final laws on civil procedure or subsequent pronouncements made by the Patent Office or the Supreme People's Court concerning patent disputes contained the particular injunctive powers, provisions for reimbursing litigation costs, or other special measures that many other jurisdictions have found helpful in establishing effective civil remedies for patent infringement.[102]

Although the 1984 Patent Law was a centerpiece of the PRC's early post–Cultural Revolution efforts to use law to foster economic change, the tensions that marked it had their counterparts in other key undertakings in the intellectual property area. As with patent, the Trademark Law of 1982 was widely heralded by both Chinese and foreign observers as representing a clean break from previous efforts to regulate the area in question. What was less thoroughly understood, or, at least, less thoroughly acknowledged at the time, was the extent to which the 1982 Trademark Law, like the Patent Law, was concerned with more than the establishment of private ownership rights and so tempered such rights even as they were being created and publicized.

To be sure, the 1982 Trademark Law did offer protection "for the exclusive right to use a trademark" but it created such rights in significant measure for the part they were perceived as capable of playing in fostering the "development of the socialist market economy."[103] Through the early years of post–Cultural Revolution law reform, the PRC lacked much of the formal legal framework needed to define and structure emerging market forces.[104] Nor was such a framework perceived as likely soon to be forthcoming, given the enormous challenge posed to legislative drafting work by such politically vexing questions as that of how to deter anticompetitive and other unfair trading practices in an economic system still largely characterized by powerful and relatively unresponsive state-owned enterprises. Trademark was looked to, at least by some in China's leadership, as providing an interim device for bringing order to a fledgling market. So it was that the law directed that trademarks were to be used to "exercise supervision over the quality of goods and . . . stop any practice that deceives consumers."[105] Toward this end, the massive bureaucracy of the SAIC, charged with administering the law, was empowered to cancel marks "where manufacture is rough or poor, or where superior quality is replaced by inferior quality" and to criticize, fine, or refer violators of the law for more serious punishment.[106] And so it was that although the Patent Law was to deny producers of medicines patent protection, the Trademark Law's implementing regulations sought to use trademark as a proxy for legislation on pharmaceuticals by requiring that all such producers "use registered trademarks" whether they wished to or not, and in their trademark applications include "papers . . . from the health department . . . approving [the drug's] production."[107]

As with patent, trademark rights and remedies were more constrained than might initially have seemed to be the case. To begin with, the law denied protection to service marks, collective marks, certification marks, and defensive marks, as well as to trademarks falling into such undefined categories as "being detrimental to socialist morality or customs or having other undesirable influences," "promoting goods in an exaggerated or deceptive manner," or "being ethnically discriminatory."[108] It also diminished the likely value of those marks eligible for registration by requiring that contrary to the practice of many nations, applications be filed on a "per mark, per class" basis, rather than on a multiclass basis—thereby both making it more difficult and expensive for individuals to secure protection in multiple classes and increasing the possibility that persons acting in bad faith might register marks generated by others. The potential for occurrence of the latter problem—particularly with respect to well-known foreign marks—was, in turn, further exacerbated by the law's rigid adherence to a first to file rule and its limited procedures for opposing or seeking the cancellation even of registrations made in bad faith, as well as the narrow definitions of class generated by the vagaries of Chinese distribution channels.[109]

Remedies were also problematic in the 1982 Trademark Law. As was to be the case with patent, the law's emphasis was on the administrative resolution of problems, notwithstanding its provision of a right of access to the people's courts. But as with patent, the law and its implementing regulations failed to articulate in meaningful detail how the competent administrative authority was to proceed, the specific actions it or the courts might take, or how any such administrative actions were to be enforced. And those sanctions that the law provided were of modest severity relative to both Chinese law generally and international practice.[110]

The difficulties inherent in generating patent and trademark laws that might create new forms of property without compromising basic state interests were all the more evident in efforts to develop a copyright law—which took "a road as tortuous as that of Chinese intellectuals," according to Jiang Ping, a noted civil law specialist and head of the Committee on Legal Affairs of the Standing Committee of the NPC in the late 1980's.[111] Commencing on instructions from Deng Xiaoping himself soon after the conclusion of the 1979 U.S.–PRC trade agreement,[112] Chinese officials in effect picked up where they had left off prior to the Cultural Revolution in endeavoring to assimilate artistic output into the state plan. The initial result was a series of regulations and related measures, developed (in many instances for internal circulation only) between 1980 and 1986, that addressed the production of both written and audiovisual materials, covering matters ranging, for example, from the submission of manuscripts to publication to remuneration.[113] Typical of these were the 1984 Trial Regulations Concerning Basic Payment for Book-Writing, which divided the universe of Chinese authors, editors, translators, proofreaders, indexers, and other literary personnel into nine categories and fixed firm boundaries for the payment of each such group, even down to the number of free copies that one was to receive. Thus, for example, indexers were to receive 10 to 20 *yuan* per 1,000 characters, while translators were only to receive from 4 to 14 *yuan* per 1,000 characters. For all their specificity about the relative worth of indexers and translators, however, these pronouncements rarely spoke of illegal copying and even less often of "copyright"—and then typically in the context of listing categories of potentially subversive materials (especially in the audiovisual area) that ought not to be disseminated, rather than with reference to the protection of private rights.[114]

The "tortuous road" took yet another turn with the promulgation of the General Principles of the Civil Law in 1986.[115] Article 94 of the General Principles provides the PRC's first major public recognition of copyright, albeit in the most general of ways. "Citizens and legal persons," it indicates, "shall enjoy rights of authorship (copyright) and shall be entitled to sign their names as authors, issue and publish their works and obtain remuneration in accordance with the law."[116] The operative terms, however, are not defined and no more is said in the General Principles about copyright. As a consequence, the authorities had little more than Communist party policy and their own sense of fairness on which to rely in endeavoring to resolve the 500 court cases and 400 administrative actions touching on authorship that arose during the four and a half years between the promulgation of the General Principles and the effective date of the Copyright Law. In the words of two Chinese commentators, the "lack of relevant laws . . . made things difficult for the courts and it took years for some cases to be closed."[117]

The debates surrounding both the inclusion of Article 94 in the General Principles and the subsequent development of the Copyright Law raised many of the same issues that marked debates over the Patent Law.[118] Notable among these were the appropriateness of establishing new private property interests in what was still said to be a socialist society, China's capacity to meet royalty payments denominated in hard currency, and the extent to which at least formal protections for intellectual property rights were needed to spur the further transfer of advanced technology. In copyright, as with patent, these concerns were not amenable to genuine resolution.

These tensions were reflected in the drafting process. Termed "the most complicated" in the PRC's history by NPC Vice President Wang Hanbin,[119] it produced more than 20 drafts of a copyright law, many of which differed substantially as power shifted among individuals falling roughly into three major groups. Proponents of a law approximating international standards—drawn chiefly from among officials concerned about the disappointingly low quality of much of the technology that China had received from abroad through the 1980's, domestic software producers, and assorted other entrepreneurs and individuals hopeful of using this law as a device for fostering a more general openness—insisted that a China aspiring to be competitive internationally had no alternative, however painful it might be in the short term. Opponents—who ranged from politically orthodox central government officials concerned about creating new rights, particularly prior to the completion of a Publications Law intended to reinforce control over print media, to important personnel in educational circles and other spheres of society heavily reliant on the unauthorized use of foreign copyrighted materials—took a decidedly more skeptical stance. And yet a third group contended that China should commit herself to copyright more in name than substance, with the objective of buying time gradually to adapt to the inevitability of adherence to international standards.[120]

As with patent and trademark, and reflecting the divisions evident during its drafting, the law on copyright that the NPC finally promulgated on September 7, 1990, provided an appreciably more curtailed grant of rights than suggested by its rhetoric and much of the initial commentary, both at home and abroad.[121] For example, although Article 16 specified that works "created by citizens in carrying out assignments given to them by legal persons or non-legal person units"[122] generally belong to the author, closer inspection highlights an array of reasons for viewing this seemingly expansive statement of rights in a more markedly narrow light. This is evident, from an economic viewpoint, beginning with Article 16 itself, which indicates that an author's work unit—in a nation in which most authors had been and still were "cultural workers"— shall have "the priority to exercise their copyrights within their businesses." Nor, under this law, was the work unit the only entity free to use an author's creation. The law's open-ended fair use provisions, *inter alia*, give "state organs," which at the time pervaded much of Chinese political, economic, and social life, the right to make unauthorized use of copyrighted materials "to execute official duties," with only the vaguest of protective caveats about not prejudicing "without reason" the rights of owners.[123] And, perhaps most important economically, the continuation, with but modest alteration, of the so-called *gaofei* system meant that even those authors able to enjoy their economic rights were essentially limited to receiving no more than the rather modest and uniform levels of compensation set by the state, irrespective of the individual merit of their work.[124]

If the Copyright Law is restrictive in its grant of economic rights, it is no less so with regard to the spectrum of political views it tolerates. Unwittingly echoing historic efforts to use copyright as a means of limiting the spread of heterodox ideas, the law provides that "works prohibited by law to be published and disseminated" are not entitled to copyright protection, while also specifying that "copyright holders shall not violate the Constitution and the law, or infringe upon the public interest, while exercising their copyrights."[125] Although the limits of this provision are intentionally not spelled out, the debate surrounding the drafting of both the Copyright Law and the Publications Law indicates that the provision is intended to "take account of ideological considerations"[126] and ban items inconsistent with the Four Cardinal Principles, as well as those that "split the unity of minority nationalities, advocate theft, pornography, violence, and arson, or other criminal activities, and . . . are against Constitution."[127] Nor were these idle words, given the power that the State Administration on Press and Publications (SAPP) was capable of exercising in this area—both directly through its work as state censor and its control over access to *shuhao* (the "book number" that must be secured before publication is permitted) and indirectly as the organ from which the State Copyright Administration (SCA) had emerged and on which it remained dependent.[128]

Mirroring a bifurcation evident in the Patent Law, the Copyright Law endeavors to satisfy the demands of the international marketplace by offering foreigners the prospect of terms more favorable than those available to Chinese. Unlike their Chinese counterparts, foreign authors are free to earn whatever royalty they can negotiate—or, as the law puts it more indirectly, "where a contract contains additional agreements, payment for the use of works may also be made according to the contract."[129] And efforts were made early on to assure foreigners that the restrictions of Article 4 regarding publications would not apply as rigidly to "acceptable works from abroad." [130]

As with patent, however, the position accorded foreign nationals was less favorable than it might have seemed. This was explicitly borne out, for instance, in Article 2 of the law, which specified that whereas the works of Chinese citizens were protected "whether published or not," those of foreigners had first "to be published" in the PRC absent a treaty creating more extensive rights. [131] It was further suggested by the vesting of responsibility for administering the law in the SCA. Not only was the SCA new, understaffed, and weak relative to other governmental agencies, [132] but it drew many of its early personnel from and continued closely to be linked with the SAPP. Given that the SAPP's principal contribution to international copyright, apart from exercising its censorship powers, had for decades consisted of overseeing the mass production by Chinese publishers of unauthorized copies of foreign copyrighted materials, one may perhaps be excused from wondering whether such apparently evenhanded provisions of the law as those on fair use might, in fact, have a disproportionate impact on foreign parties. And other advantages seemingly granted foreigners by the law—such as the freedom to take whatever royalty one might negotiate—were in turn diminished by the limits that China's foreign exchange regime imposed on the capacity of entities that did not earn their own foreign currency—such as schools, libraries and the like—to secure such funds, whether to purchase original copies of materials, pay royalties for copies made, or for any other end. [133]

The Copyright Law's provisions on remedy are consistent with those of the patent and trademark laws. Although the law explicitly provides parties with the right to proceed directly to the people's courts, its emphasis is on administrative solutions. Thus, for example, administrative remedial measures, such as fines and apologies, are set forth in greater detail than their judicial counterpart, although even they are skeletal by international standards. [134]

The PRC's Regulations for the Protection of Computer Software, published three days after the Copyright Law, and the subsequent Measures for the Registration of Copyright in Computer Software tell a similar story. [135] Once again, a seemingly broad statement of rights is subject to a variety of qualifications. At the basic definitional level, the regulations fail to indicate whether software is to be viewed as a literary work, leave uncertain what is meant by first publication, and do not cover programs embedded in semiconductor chips. More substantively, the regulations' expansive provisions regarding the national interest limit the scope of the rights granted. Thus, Article 31 specifies that similarities between newly developed and existing software will "not constitute infringement of . . . copyright . . . [i]f the similarity is necessary for the execution of national policies, laws, regulations, and rules . . . or for the implementation of national technical standards" but neither defines "national policies" or "national technical standards" nor requires compensation for software developers affected. Software developed by state enterprises that is of "great significance to national interests and public interests," the regulations further stipulate, shall potentially be subject to appropriation, but again without providing criteria for helping to identify such interests. Article 28 bars Chinese from licensing software to foreigners without prior state approval, much as the 1985 technology import regulations required parties to seek prior approval of agreements to import technology.[136] And software published prior to the issuance of the software regulations on June 4, 1991—a disproportionate share of which belonged to foreigners—is effectively presumed to have been in the public domain.[137]

As with the other forms of intellectual property discussed herein, upon close examination, it is evident that the software regulations' remedies further curtail the very rights they are intended to buttress. Thus, as a "prerequisite" to seeking either administrative or judicial enforcement of their rights, software developers are required to provide key proprietary data to the Ministry of Electronics Industry in a registration process that is far more exacting than that of many nations, particularly in view of the regulations' liberal invocation of the national interest.[138] The regulations' liberality with respect to national interest is not, however, matched in its provisions on infringement. These, in effect, exonerate persons accused of infringement if they did "not know or have no reasonable basis for knowing that the software is infringing"—which leaves software copyright holders with the burden of having to seek out the "suppliers" of infringing items in order to secure the rather ill-defined forms of redress available under the regulations.[139]

By and large, both Chinese officialdom and foreign observers were quick to proclaim this initial generation of post–Cultural Revolution intellectual property laws successful. As Ren Jianxin, President of the Supreme People's Court and long one of China's most visible spokespersons on intellectual property issues, put it in extolling the effectiveness of China's new laws before an international audience soon after their promulgation, "the Chinese legal and intellectual property system can give full protection to patent right . . . and exclusive right to use a trademark and copyright which have been legally obtained in China."[140] A closer consideration of how these new rules have played themselves out in society, however, tells a rather more complex tale—as some Chinese observers have begun lately to acknowledge.[141] Nor ought the difficulties involved in giving effect to China's new intellectual property laws to be wholly surprising, when one considers the inhospitability of both traditional political culture and ideological orthodoxy during much of the PRC's history to the privatization and commodification of knowledge, the unresolved tensions evident in the laws themselves, and the serious shortage of well-trained, independent jurists, legal professionals, and civil servants to whom one might turn to vindicate rights and resolve uncertainties surrounding them.[142]

Perhaps the most compelling data Chinese officials have been able to offer in support of the proposition that the PRC's first generation of intellectual property laws achieved their stated purpose are statistics concerning the number of patent and trademark applications filed. Official sources have exhibited great pride in the fact that during the eight years prior to the revision of the 1984 Patent Law, over 284,000 applications were filed, including over 40,000 from foreign parties representing some 65 jurisdictions,[143] and that during the decade between the 1983 Trademark Law's promulgation and its most recent major revision, some 366,000 applications for trademark registration were accepted, including more than 53,000 from foreign parties representing some 68 jurisdictions.[144] The general trend toward increased applications, especially from abroad, has been duly cited as providing validation of the PRC's new intellectual property system. In the words of Zheng Songyu, general manager of the China Patent Agency (H.K) Ltd., which is the Chinese state patent agency in Hong Kong, this has had a "highly salubrious effect in mobilizing the enthusiasm of the broad masses of the people engaging in inventive/creative activities, promoting the popularization and application of inventions/creations, introducing advanced technology from abroad, improving China's investment environment and actively carrying out economic-technical cooperation and exchange between China and other countries." [145]

Closer scrutiny of these figures, especially in patent, at least raises questions as to what one means by success, even with respect to this particular aspect of intellectual property law. Patent applications did, indeed, increase over much of the eight-year life of the PRC's initial patent law, but it is also true that some two-thirds of those filed by Chinese were for utility models and design patents, whereas over 80 percent of those submitted by foreigners were for invention patents. [146] By their very nature, utility models and design patents concern less advanced technology and provide less extensive rights than invention patents, as they carry far shorter terms, do not require extensive substantive pre-grant examination, and permit applicants to amend claims during invalidation proceedings (thereby complicating enforcement). Additionally, over two-thirds of all Chinese applications between 1984 and 1992 were for nonservice inventions, which typically involve lower-level technology, being made by individual entrepreneurs or workers in state or collective enterprises acting outside the scope of their employment. Nor do more recent statistics suggest any significant shift, as illustrated by the figures for 1993, which indicate that over 80 percent of the applications filed by and over 95 percent of the rights granted to Chinese were for utility models or design patents, with more than two-thirds falling into the nonservice category, while over 75 percent of applications filed and rights granted with respect to foreigners were for invention patents. [147]

Arguably, one could construe these statistics as evidence that the 1984 law succeeded in creating a patent system that is inspired in its market segmentation, offering foreigners sufficiently attractive rights to entice them to part with technology of international quality, while, in effect, requiring locals to yield up their innovations in return for lesser benefits. This, of course, is not an argument that Chinese officials, vociferous though they have been about the myriad successes of this law, have made or are likely to make. But even if they were to do so, defining success so narrowly runs the risk of ignoring other key objectives of China's new intellectual property system—such as fostering the growth of important indigenous technologies and the exchange of data between Chinese scientists. With rare exceptions, Chinese enterprises have done little to generate their own technology worthy of advanced intellectual property rights. Thus, for example, in 1992, even though Chinese filed eleven times more applications, foreigners obtained two-thirds of all invention patents granted.[148] And these statistics do not disaggregate Sino-foreign joint ventures—many of which have been active in patenting—but instead treat them as domestic enterprises.[149]

The phenomenon of foreign multinationals securing a disproportionate share of patents granted is hardly unique to China, but rather typical of developing nations that have yet to generate extensive indigenous technology with a high commercial value.[150] The fact is, however, that China is neither typical of developing nations nor wishes to think of itself in such terms, save for when it is convenient to do so for purposes of building alliances or gathering votes in international organizations. It should not be forgotten that the PRC produced its own nuclear weapons in the 1960's and soon after the end of the Cultural Revolution embarked on one of the world's most ambitious efforts to foster scientific and technological development, as evidenced in small part, for example, by the allocation in 1991 of 6.6 billion yuan (U.S.$1.2 billion) to support the work of 130,000 new research scientists.[151]

To some extent, the relative indifference of Chinese enterprises to patent rights, through the 1980's and even beyond, cannot be understood without reference to the continued prominence of state-owned entities, especially in the heavy industrial and capital-intensive sectors, notwithstanding many accounts over the years of their demise.[152] One study indicates that from 1985 through June 1992, the 12,000 largest state-owned enterprises on average had filed less than a single patent application of any type annually, bearing out *Renmin ribao*'s assertion that "large enterprises do not think much of the invention patent, or support it with manpower, materials and capital."[153] But the record of nonstate enterprises, many of which are small, thinly capitalized, and in the service sector, has not been significantly better. Nor have Guangdong or other of China's most economically open areas revealed an appreciably different pattern. In short, if the Patent Law was intended to stimulate serious Chinese inventiveness, success is as yet elusive.

The confusion of the quantitative with the qualitative is also evident in the vision of the future articulated by the leaders of the Chinese patent system. Although expressing satisfaction that China already ranked among the "first 15 countries in the world in terms of patent applications received," late in 1991, Director General Gao Lulin of the Patent Office declared that China needed to do still more if it was to become a "patent powerhouse" by the turn of the century. This worthy goal, Gao indicated, in an unwitting epitome of a contradiction at the heart of the PRC's intellectual property policies, could be attained because the Patent Office had developed a plan that called for it to grant 400,000 patent rights over the next decade, thereby allowing China to "edge into the list of the top 10 countries in terms of the number of patents granted.[154]

The issuance of rights is, of course, not the same as their vindication. If statistics as to patent applications filed are amenable to different readings, how much more so the necessarily more fragmentary numbers available with respect to infringement. To take but one example, albeit an especially important one, it is not altogether clear whether the existence of a surfeit of infringement actions should be read as indicating that the laws of the jurisdiction in question are effective (in the sense of being vigilantly enforced) or ineffective (in the sense of so often being broken). Indeed, in the Chinese case, the SAIC has pointed with pride to the many thousand infringement cases it hears annually as proof that the Trademark Law is working, while the Patent Office has stressed, with no less pride, that the "fact" that few infringement cases involving the interests of foreigners have come to its attention shows that the Patent Law has taken hold as intended.[155]

Whatever one chooses to make of such statistics, there are a good many anecdotal data gleaned from a variety of sources—Chinese and foreign, open and secret—to suggest that infringement has been and remains a massive problem, even with the stepping up of enforcement efforts. From the launching of China's "open policy" of the late 1970's onward, Chinese enterprises have turned out a broad array of infringing items. These include fake IBM computer components, Levi's jeans, Johnny Walker scotch (Black Label, no less), Heinz and Nestle's baby food, Mars confectioneries (such as the infamous "W&W" candies, said to "dissolve" in one's mouth), Coca-Cola soft drinks, Bass footwear, Rolex watches, and a host of other consumer items. In most instances, these are pale imitations that appear intended for a domestic market eager, after years of limited access to the outside world, to acquire foreign goods but not overly familiar with them. In at least a few cases, however, these infringing items are virtually indistinguishable from the originals in question and have already turned up in export markets from Taiwan and Southeast Asia to North America and Europe.[156]

It is, however, not only with respect to trademark, which by its very nature is a particularly visible form of intellectual property, that in 1991, China was deemed the "single largest pirate worldwide," according to Joseph Massey, whose responsibilities as Assistant United States Trade Representative (USTR) also included protecting American rights in a number of other leading contenders for the aforementioned title, or that his successors have reiterated such sentiments.[157] Throughout the 1980's and well into the 1990's, China's publishers liberally reproduced foreign materials without authorization. So it is, for example, that China's elite can turn each day to *Cankao xiaoxi* and an array of other internal-circulation-only newspapers and magazines filled with unauthorized translations of foreign news reports deemed too sensitive to share with China's populace.[158] But the latter are by no means deprived of foreign copyrighted information. Students can find shelf after shelf in libraries and research centers filled with unauthorized copies of foreign works, as well as computer centers in which they can fulfill university-wide requirements to become computer literate without ever seeing an authorized piece of software.[159] Consumers more generally have been able to avail themselves of whole floors of state-owned bookstores that are closed to foreigners so as to specialize in pirated editions of foreign works, each marked "for internal circulation only," meaning that foreigners are barred by law from reading them and from taking them out of the country. Nor are such titles restricted to those that would seem to bear on the modernization process, which one might expect given the contention of some Chinese officials during the 1980's that, as a developing nation, China could not afford to pay royalties for important works on science, medicine, technology, and other fields pertinent to growth. Instead, interspersed with the inevitable and often outdated (but still copyrighted) editions of *Gray's Anatomy*, American law casebooks, and, in a reprise of history, *Webster's Dictionary*, one finds works as central to the building of a socialist commodity economy as Nathaniel

Hawthorne's *The Scarlet Letter* and Isaac Bashevis Singer's *The Magician of Lublin*.[160]

Indeed, not even the sacred visage of Mickey Mouse has been spared, in spite of extensive pressure brought to bear by the Disney Company resulting, *inter alia*, in much publicized agreements with Chinese authorities. Proving that it is, indeed, a small, small world, unauthorized reproductions of the immensely popular Mi Laoshu (Mickey Mouse, or, literally, Old Mouse Mi) and friends abounded during the 1980's—and still are liberally spread through the land— in plastic masks sold in parks, on doorbells adorning hotel rooms, in comic books offered by street vendors, and on a range of other items.[161] As the essayist Bill Holm has so aptly put it:

On any day down any street in Xi'an, a parade of cartoon mice, ducks, hound dogs and rabbits walks past you. In the thermos shop, you can buy decorated plastic cylinders painted in gaudy colors with Mickey, Minnie, Donald and Goofy. The precious "only" toddlers wear dancing cartoon mice T-shirts. The red-kerchiefed Young Pioneers carry school notebooks decorated not with pictures of Marx but with the perpetually smiling Mickey. In the candy store, small fists that will build the Four Modernizations reach over the counter clutching aluminum *fens* [pennies] in sweaty fingers to order Shanghai *tang guo*, hard fruit candy that comes in plastic sacks stamped with Minnie Mouse holding hands with the famous Shanghai white rabbit. "Trixon" and "Mow the Helmsman" didn't open China to the West; Walt Disney did.[162]

Overseas victims of infringement are not alone, although they seem neither to have taken consolation from that fact nor, more important, to have recognized the potential alliances that it suggests. Chinese pharmaceutical manufacturers have found their marks infringed—at times with fatal consequences for consumers.[163] Although having fewer public safety implications, the "Cadillacs of Chinese bicycles"—the Feige (Flying Pigeon), Fenghuang (Phoenix), and Yongjiu (Everlasting) bicycles—which themselves bear more than a faint resemblance to classic Raleigh bikes of the 1950's— have been the subject of rampant unlawful copying for years. And much the same has been true of the "best-known" Chinese liquor, Maotai, Hongtashan cigarettes, an array of items bearing the famed Hou Wang (Monkey King) brand name, and hundreds of other products in a society that still has far fewer marks than our own.[164] Indeed, one news account reported that "one-fourth of the 1,400 orders involving trade-mark labels which local printers accepted" lacked proof of authority to use the marks in question.[165]

Nor do China's printers appear to be much more careful with respect to copyright. China has of late had a number of highly publicized copyright cases, such as the successful case brought by Deng Xiaoping's daughter against an infringer of her biography of her father and those leading to the awarding of royalties to the descendants of the famed revolutionary writer Lu Xun and of Li Jiefu (for the unauthorized use of his recently revived, highly popular composition "Wishing Chairman Mao Unlimited Long Life").[166] Nonetheless, infringement is rampant and administrative and formal legal redress seem even more difficult to secure in this than in other areas of intellectual property law. Indeed, according to one study of publishing in post-Mao China, "most books available on the market . . . were pirated in one form or another" throughout the 1980's and into the 1990's.[167]

The plight of Professor Zheng Chengsi illustrates the problem with particular poignancy. Although the "sole academic member participating in the Copyright Law drafting from beginning to end" and the only individual in China to be honored by being named a "National Expert on Intellectual Property" by the State Council,[168] over the years Professor Zheng had not escaped the ravages of infringers, some of whom were so brazen as to appropriate for themselves without attribution sizable excerpts from his many works on intellectual property. These events, however, hardly prepared him for the actions during the late autumn of 1992 of the China Procuratorial Publishing House, which operates under the aegis of the Supreme People's Procuracy, the arm of the Chinese government charged with prosecuting crimes (including those concerning intelletual property). Seeking to capitalize on the attention that the January 1992 Memorandum of Understanding with the United States focused on copyright, the Procuratorial Publishing House published and distributed a so-called *Complete Book of Intellectual Property.* The book was, indeed, complete, incorporating without permission or even acknowledgement portions of no fewer than five different works by Zheng on copyright and other areas of intellectual property. After overcoming disbelief, Zheng persuaded Beijing copyright officials to fine infringers, but his efforts to secure the royalties he believes are his have been unavailing, as the courts, not surprisingly, have been loathe to give a full hearing to an action directed against their procuratorial colleagues.[169]

Although more difficult to discern, patent infringement has also been a problem. Chinese patent officials report fewer than 2,000 administrative actions and 500 lawsuits during the period between the 1984 Patent Law's promulgation and its revision in 1992.[170] Anecdotal data, such as the tale of one patent holder who some six months after receiving his patent found it being infringed by no fewer than 45 factories in a single county in Henan, suggests that these figures may well understate the case.[171] And even in those instances where the problem has been uncovered and brought to the attention of the relevant authorities, its resolution at times has been directed toward goals other than protection of property interests, as suggested, for example, by a 1989 Jiangsu suit in which the local court exonerated the alleged infringers on the grounds that by improving the quality of the patented item they had made a valuable contribution to society.[172]

To be sure, even in earlier days when they were more reluctant publicly to acknowledge intellectual property problems, Chinese officials were by no means wholly oblivious to their existence and, indeed, at times sought to turn such difficulties to advantage—as evidenced, for example, by their handling during the mid and late 1980's of cases involving Vitasoy and the Stone Group (Sitong jituan gongsi). The former, concerning the trademark for a soybean milk (*doujiang*) drink popular in Chinese communities throughout the world, in many ways typified the situation of prominent multinationals capable of shaping foreign perceptions of the Chinese business environment, particularly as the PRC first opened its doors to investors from abroad. Long before entering the Chinese market, the proprietors of the trademark Vitasoy had obtained registration throughout the world, thereby establishing by the standards of the Paris Convention that it was a "well-known" mark, which status, in turn, should have eased the way for registration in the PRC, given Beijing's accession to the Convention. Nonetheless, Chinese trademark examiners not once, but twice, flatly rejected Vitasoy as a registrable mark, contending that it was "generic," given that its English name was derived from the words "vitamin" and "soy" and its Chinese name from the characters "vitamin" and "milk." Only when Vitasoy and its counsel pressed their case did Chinese trademark officials do an about-face, ordering registration of the mark in question to "keep a friend of China satisfied" and suggesting for foreign audiences that this happy result demonstrated China's willingness to use "every means possible to eliminate opposition and obtain approval for its registration, thus winning the trust of the general public," most of whom knew nothing about it and cared less.[173]

The case of the Stone Group was also presented to—and initially received by—the outside world as providing important evidence of China's firm commitment to the protection of intellectual property, but it, too, involved a more complex set of events, which similarly conveyed a more mixed moral regarding efforts to build a new Chinese legality.[174] The dispute that launched the case, at least ostensibly, revolved around the question of whether computer engineers from the state-run China Research Institute for Printing Science and Technology (CRIPST) in moving to Stone had taken with them proprietary data in violation both of the General Principles of the Civil Law's provisions on intellectual property and their employment agreement. Soon, however, the dispute became a focal point for a larger test of wills between, on the one hand, Stone, which was at the time China's largest private enterprise, and its politically ambitious principal owner, Wan Runnan (who through the company founded the "first privately-funded think tank in China specifically concerned with politics, the economy and law"),[175] and, on the other, the SPPA, to which the CRIPST reported, and additional governmental entities with a decidedly conservative bent. Before the initial dispute over CRIPST could be resolved, however, the Beijing Spring of 1989 intervened and Wan, who was accused of having helped instigate those events, fled to Paris. Ironically, *Renmin ribao* chose soon thereafter to affirm the link between intellectual property and politics by running an extraordinary notice declaring that as a bad and dangerous element, Wan no longer enjoyed the right to use the Stone name or any associated trademarks.[176]

In the years since Vitasoy, Stone, and other celebrated, if questionable, self-proclaimed affirmations of the vitality of Chinese intellectual property law, PRC officials have begun to make somewhat more concerted attempts to enforce such laws. Thus, in the months leading up to the January 1992 Memorandum of Understanding, Chinese state agencies stepped up enforcement measures, even as the government denied the existence of significant problems.[177] Similar, if no more successful, measures were undertaken in the immediate aftermath of the Memorandum. Special tribunals dedicated to intellectual property issues have subsequently been established in a handful of China's most important commercial centers.[178] What semi-official Chinese sources have described as "nationwide crusades," which seem at least to echo campaigns (*yundong*) of earlier days, have been commenced with the goal of securing a higher level of compliance, leading Vice Premier Li Lanqing recently to say with reference to persons involved in the manufacture and distribution of "fake and inferior goods, . . . no one should be lenient towards these evil doers and evil deeds."[179] And in a futile effort to deter Washington from pursuing possible trade sanctions, in the summer of 1994, the Standing Committee of the NPC adopted legislation that would impose substantial criminal penalties for copyright infringement and the State Council issued a White Paper extolling progress over the past decade on intellectual property.[180]

Notwithstanding such undertakings, which, *inter alia,* have led to the imposition of the death penalty on at least four individuals, life sentences for no fewer than five others, and the imprisonment of some 500 more for trademark violations, major problems persist. Trademark infringement is so widespread, the *China Daily* reported in September 1993, that "stronger measures" need be taken to address the surfeit of "illegal practices [that] have seriously disturbed the normal economic order, infringed consumers' rights, harmed people's health and life and annulled the image of China-made goods on the world market."[181] Copyright problems, according to some observers, have only gotten worse. *Time* has recently dubbed China "home to the world's largest gang of CD [compact disc] pirates," some of whom the *Wall Street Journal* suggests are affiliated with the very governmental authorities who should be policing them. Experts estimate that 95 percent of the software in use consists of unauthorized copies and "in book-publishing at least, there has been a significant increase in violations of copyright," according to one Chinese publishing executive—all of which is consistent with USTR Mickey Kantor's June 1994 assertion that enforcement is "virtually non-existent."[182] And there are increasing accounts of powerful industries infringing patents belonging to entities from distant jurisdictions, knowing that their local courts—which are heavily dependent financially on local tax revenues collected from such industries—are unlikely to rule against the home team in suits brought by entities from other provinces.[183] In sum, at least at this juncture, the attempt to build an intellectual property law with "Chinese characteristics" capable of serving a new socialist market economy at best remains a long march with many steps yet to be traversed.

Energetic though they have been, the Chinese government's attempts to promote more vigorous adherence to its intellectual property laws have been overtaken by a simultaneous and far more strenuous effort to reassert a strong degree of direct state control over the flow of ideas. Commencing in the autumn of 1993, Beijing has launched what one experienced observer has termed an "onslaught against dissent and journalists . . . [in] an attempt to continue its control on all information."[184] This effort has taken a variety of forms. Journalists, including Hong Kong reporters, and others alleged to have shared classified information (such as an advance text of a public address to be delivered by President Jiang Zemin) have been arrested and, in some instances, received sentences as steep as life imprisonment.[185] The resale of *shuhao* has been prohibited in an attempt to reassert direct central control over which books may be published. The installation and use of satellite dishes, other than by state-approved entities, to receive foreign-originated programming has been barred because, in the words of Vice Minister of Radio, Film and Television Wang Feng, it is "beneficial to the cultivation of patriotism among our citizens, safeguarding the superior tradition of the Chinese race, promoting socialist civilisation, and maintaining social stability."[186] The "Communist Party . . . has taken" what *New York Times* correspondent Patrick Tyler calls "an end-of-empire approach to [film] censorship."[187] And the government is limiting imports of foreign CDs to 120 titles a year, which may be one reason, along with the chance to earn considerable export revenues, that Chinese factories are now churning out tens of millions of unauthorized copies of popular foreign CDs from Michael Jackson to Madonna and beyond.[188] To be sure, as the example of CDs illustrates, these measures designed to control information have not necessarily proven themselves much more effective than those concerning intellectual property, but they nonetheless represent an unwitting reaffirmation by the state of the priorities of its imperial and Nationalist predecessors with respect to the dissemination of ideas.

The tensions evident with respect to the PRC's first generation of post–Cultural Revolution intellectual property laws in many respects typify those that mark the broader effort during this same period at law reform. As with patent, trademark, and copyright, the more general effort at establishing a formal legal system has held considerable appeal for China's leaders. It has constituted an unparalleled vehicle for legitimation both at home and abroad, distinguishing the post–Cultural Revolution leadership from its predecessors (even as some of the latter reemerged amongst the former), while easing the anxieties of foreigners about parting with the technology and capital needed to fuel China's modernization. No less important, it has represented an instrument perceived as uniquely suited to serving the leadership's seemingly contradictory objectives of moving away from the rigidities of a planned economy (through, for example, the gradual substitution of contract for administrative fiat) without surrendering central political authority and jeopardizing stability. Indeed, some may have been drawn to the idea of building up a new legal order in the belief that it might provide a way of reversing an excessive devolution of power to provincial and local officialdom, and as such might be an instrument for national consolidation.

That elements of China's leadership have seen benefits to be derived from further development of a formal legal system does not necessarily mean, however, that these same individuals, let alone their colleagues, either fully appreciate or are entirely willing to accept the associated costs. The introduction of new rights for both citizens and foreigners in what is still said to be a socialist state has posed disquieting questions about the nature and direction of Chinese society at home and in relation to the international economy— at a time of wrenching transition in many parts of the world. And at a more personal level, imbued as they are with a traditional political culture that calls for the retention of a high degree of discretion by those exercising authority, a modern ideological orthodoxy that dismisses the ideal of the autonomy of law, and no small degree of hubris and self-interest, many in leadership circles have been hesitant, at best, to subordinate themselves and their decisions to rules and institutions beyond their control.

As was the case in intellectual property, this tension has expressed itself in doctrine from the Constitution on down that has all too often endeavored to set out new rights while tightly circumscribing their ambit and providing minimal means for their vindication, by either ordinary citizens or foreign nationals. To be sure, it would be misleading to assess Chinese law reform either presuming the existence of absolute rights in other societies or ignoring the highly instrumental nature of legality in all jurisdictions. The laws of every nation—and, perhaps, particularly those that are at an early stage in the development of their systems of formal legality or engaged in recasting fundamental dimensions of social order—exhibit strains between individual and collective concerns, between the rights of citizens and the prerogatives of their leaders, and between instrumentality and autonomy. But whereas many societies seek to mediate such strains by recasting the law itself with greater definition and fixity, by reposing the power to provide such definition with a professionalized judiciary and civil service, or by facilitating the vindication by citizens of their stated rights,[189] through the 1980's and into the 1990's, the PRC's leadership has, at best, displayed profound ambivalence, if not an outright lack of enthusiasm, for such measures.

Ironically, the Chinese leadership's attempt to have it "both ways" —in the sense of proclaiming rights without being constrained by comprehensively providing for their realization—has resulted in having it neither way, at least through the first decade and a half of the post–Cultural Revolution law reform. Although it would be unfair not to acknowledge the gains made since the 1970's in generating and making efforts to give effect to a growing body of legislation, the continued unwillingness of those in positions of real power to cede major authority to the law in a meaningful and consistent fashion has undercut the very stability, predictability, neutrality, and autonomy that comprise the essence of legality, distinguish it from politics, and, ultimately, constitute its particular virtue. This has diminished sharply many of the benefits that the leadership had anticipated reaping in establishing its post–Cultural Revolution legal order. At the same time, it is also beginning to engender expectations and provide a focus for persons with shared interests that, if not met, may well impair, rather than burnish, the party's legitimacy. For, as will be discussed in chapter 5 with reference to Taiwan and in chapter 6 with regard to Sino-American interaction, the nurturing of effective and sustainable law reform—whether in the area of intellectual property or more generally—cannot be divorced from larger issues of political reform.

Five

As Pirates Become Proprietors: Changing Attitudes Toward Intellectual Property on Taiwan

> We still have to twist the arms of our engineers to file
> a patent . . . we have lots of incentive programs for
> them and those incentive programs, of course, include
> money. The amount of money is about five times as
> much as what IBM paid us years ago and we still can't
> get them to file . . . that's one area where we are trying
> very hard to change.
> Alvin Tong, executive vice president, Acer, Inc.

With the defeat of the Nationalist government on the Chinese mainland at the hands of the Communists, the protection of intellectual
property was hardly high on the Guomindang's list of priorities
when it relocated to Taiwan in the autumn of 1949.[1] On the contrary, during its first years on Taiwan, the Guomindang was far
more concerned with closely regulating the dissemination of ideas
in order to keep any materials deemed subversive from the populace.[2] As was the case in so many areas, the resolution of other, less
immediate concerns regarding intellectual property could await return to the mainland, which many in the leadership hoped would be
fairly rapid.

Although it became increasingly apparent through the 1950's that
a return to the mainland was not imminent, the ROC government's
focus with respect to intellectual property remained on questions

of censorship. Indeed, in order to subsidize the cost of its elaborate censorship apparatus, the government early on set its copyright registration fees for books at 25 times the cover price.[3] The unsurprising result was that throughout the entire first decade of Nationalist rule on Taiwan, fewer than 600 books were registered, of which fewer than 30 were foreign,[4] in spite of the fact that "by mid-1959, the number of Western titles that had been reprinted there numbered more than two thousand."[5]

At first, foreign publishers seemed little concerned about the pirating of their property on Taiwan. At least for American publishers and authors, this may have been attributable both to lack of interest in foreign markets during the early postwar years (evidenced in the practice, then common throughout the U.S. publishing industry, of selling international rights on a wholesale basis to British firms)[6] and to particular ignorance about the problems and possibilities posed by the Taiwan market. To be sure, neither the original American nor the less expensive "Far Eastern" editions of their works licensed in Japan and elsewhere in East Asia sold in large numbers in Taiwan, but closer attention to Taiwan would have revealed that the market there for foreign books—many of which local printers pirated from one another, as well as from abroad—was growing rapidly among both Chinese nationals and American garrison troops.[7] Nor was help forthcoming from the U.S. government, which, eager to buttress the Nationalist regime, did little to promote the interests of the U.S. publishing industry.

By the late 1950's, however, several factors combined to rouse American publishers. The unauthorized reprinting of some of the latest and most expensive foreign works, including current editions of the *Encyclopædia Britannica*, *Webster's Dictionary*, and *Gray's Anatomy*, and their export both to the West and to potential markets elsewhere in the world, drew the attention of foreign publishers.[8] For example, the publishers of the *Encyclopædia Britannica* were greatly annoyed at the extensive pirating of their work. They saw the Chinese government's delay in registering its copyright— which ROC authorities said was necessary to censor "incorrect information contained therein concerning the Republic of China . . . , Outer Mongolia . . . , opium-smoking . . . [and Mao Zedong]"[9]— as a deliberate effort to assist local pirates. These culprits, they believed, reaped enormous profits, which they "immediately sank . . .

into the unauthorized reprinting of literally hundreds of additional Western titles."[10]

So bestirred, Western publishers urged their governments to take diplomatic action against Taiwan. American publishers, for example, argued that the Mutual Security Program that served as a defense lifeline for Taiwan ought to be reexamined. They also questioned Taiwan's eligibility for the Informational Media Guarantee Program, which provided nations whose currency was not freely convertible with the dollars needed to purchase American books and films. Only through such measures, they contended, could the ROC be persuaded to revise its intellectual property laws, join the Universal Copyright Convention, and generally take whatever measures were necessary to live up to its obligations under the provisions of the 1946 Friendship, Commerce and Navigation Treaty meant to protect U.S. intellectual property.

The ROC government sought to counter this pressure by arguing that unauthorized reprinting grew out of its students' need for the latest foreign information, especially in the sciences, which they could not afford to purchase.[11] Dependent as it was on U.S. financial, military, and diplomatic support, the ROC was, however, unable wholly to resist American entreaties. In 1959, in an effort to ameliorate American pressure while keeping alive the domestic reprint industry, the Nationalists reluctantly amended the ROC's fledgling rules concerning copyright.[12] These amendments reduced the fees to be paid on registration and provided foreigners with the same period of copyright protection to which Chinese were entitled. A year later, the government followed this up with a proclamation declaring that persons exporting unauthorized copies of books and records would be subject to prosecution for smuggling. And in 1964, the Legislative Yuan passed additional revisions to the Copyright Law directed toward ending the piracy of foreign works.[13]

Notwithstanding these measures, the situation failed to improve appreciably. Nor did much-publicized additional governmental initiatives in the areas of enforcement and mass education,[14] taken during the remainder of the 1960's or through the 1970's largely in response to intensifying U.S. pressure, prove any more effective. This was chiefly because of the immense difficulty that foreign and domestic parties alike had in proving infringement under existing procedures and in securing meaningful sanctions in the handful of actions actually tried.[15] As a consequence, few among the more than 1,400 publishers and reprinters in business on Taiwan in the mid 1970's thought it worth the expense and effort to obtain copyright registration, even though unregistered works enjoyed no legal protection from unauthorized reproduction.[16] Indicative of their lack of confidence in the law was the fact that in 1975, a typical year, fewer than 1,000 copyrights were registered, almost all by a mere 35 publishers.[17] Much the same point is borne out by the fact that during that year, a mere dozen infringement cases were filed in the Taipei District Court, one of the island republic's more active, of which eight were withdrawn before judgment and only one resulted in a full sentence.[18] Not surprisingly, unauthorized reproductions of books, records, tapes, and, by the 1970's, computer software found their way to buyers throughout the world, including the United States, Europe, Africa, the Middle East, and even the PRC.[19]

Counterfeiters of trademarked and patented foreign products were no less active during the 1960's and 1970's.[20] Knowledgeable observers suggest that government officials may originally have encouraged such piracy for reasons both of import substitution and export promotion.[21] Revisions of trademark and patent laws during those decades did little to constrain such piracy, since these statutes continued to provide scant recourse for foreign holders, lacked effective methods for assessing damages, assigned penalties that could be redeemed by modest payments, and, in any event, were not rigorously enforced.[22] By the 1970's, the ROC was furnishing a burgeoning world market with a host of counterfeited products, including pharmaceuticals, "pens, watches, clothing, car parts, computers, chemical processes," "dolls, toys . . . cameras . . . batteries, puzzles," and airplane and helicopter parts, among other items.[23] As a consequence, in 1982, *Newsweek* labeled Taiwan the counterfeiting capital of the world, and the *New York Times* soon thereafter described it as being "to counterfeiting what Miami is to drug trafficking."[24] More official condemnation came from the U.S. International Trade Commission, which in 1984 identified Taiwan as the source of as much as 60 percent of the $6 to $8 billion worth of counterfeited goods believed to be produced worldwide annually in a sampling of only five major industries.[25]

With the pace, scope, and quality of counterfeiting expanding[26] and with a growing awareness of the impact of such activity on the rapidly increasing U.S. trade deficit,[27] the American government began in the early 1980's to apply more concerted pressure on Taiwan. In particular, efforts were made to play on Taiwan's overwhelming dependence on American markets. At first these efforts were focused on the Generalized System of Preferences (GSP), a program intended to aid developing nations by eliminating tariffs on specified items.[28] The Trade and Tariff Act of 1984 conditioned continued receipt of GSP treatment on "the extent to which [any given] country is providing adequate and effective means under its laws for foreign nationals to secure, to exercise, and to enforce exclusive rights in intellectual property, including patents, trademarks, and copyrights."[29] This step was hardly inconsiderable, given that Taiwan had long been among the greatest beneficiaries of the program, reaping more than $3 billion in tariff benefits annually.[30] Nonetheless, in 1988, the U.S. government chose to relinquish this tool. In an effort to stem the trade imbalance, it removed Taiwan and the other three Little Dragons of East Asia from GSP eligibility.[31] This loss of leverage was eased somewhat, however, by the amendment soon thereafter of Section 301 of the 1974 Trade Act, which, as will be discussed below, authorized the president to take extensive retaliatory action against nations failing to respect American intellectual property adequately.[32]

Such pressure, together with the increased efforts of Apple Computer, International Business Machines Corporation, and other leading U.S.–based multinationals to protect their property, and extensive publicity by international news media, helped produce changes in the intellectual property laws of the ROC, as well as widely trumpeted educational and enforcement campaigns.[33] Thus, in 1981, the ROC promulgated regulations requiring would-be exporters of trademarked goods to supply customs authorities with documentation establishing their right to use the marks in question.[34] Two years later, Taiwan's Trademark Law itself was amended to protect unregistered "well-known foreign trademarks," authorize confiscation by police of infringing goods, and raise criminal penalties for the infringement of registered trademarks to a level—a maximum of five years' imprisonment—at which monetary redemption was no longer possible.[35] And in 1985, the law was still further revised to permit foreign enterprises, even if not registered, to initiate cases, while also reducing the claimant's burden of proof on the issue of damages.[36]

During the 1980's the ROC's copyright and patent laws also were the subject of amendments concerning coverage, standing, and infringement. As revised in 1985, the Copyright Law provided that for Chinese nationals, copyright—which was redefined to include computer programs,[37] films, sound tracks, lectures, musical and artistic performances, dance, sculpture, and scientific and engineering drawings, as well as more conventional media previously covered—attached "upon . . . completion" of the work, rather than registration.[38] Subsequently, the Taipei District Court followed the Executive Yuan's urging and extended this right to American works.[39] Although registration continued to be required for the works of most other foreign nationals, this burden was somewhat eased by the fact that the 1985 revisions provided that an unrecognized foreign entity would have standing "to file a [civil] complaint or a private prosecution against" infringers, if its own nation accorded such rights to Chinese nationals.[40] Additional enforcement measures, mirroring those of the Trademark Law, clarified the circumstances under which works believed to be pirated might be seized, mandated minimum civil damages of 500 times the retail price of the infringed work, and increased the maximum sentence of imprisonment to five years so as to eliminate the possibility of monetary redemption.[41] Comparable measures respecting standing and enforcement lay at the heart both of the revisions made in 1986 to the Patent Law and of proposals then made for an unfair competition law.[42]

Although providing substantial clarification in many respects, the intellectual property law reforms of the mid 1980's neither resolved all questions addressed nor addressed all important questions. Typical of this first shortcoming was the much-heralded 1983 amendment to the Trademark Law providing protection for unregistered "world-famous" trademarks.[43] Neither the law, concurrent implementing regulations, nor other official pronouncements contained a definition of the operative term. Not surprisingly, even with these amendments, throughout the 1980's only a handful of foreign holders availed themselves of this protection, despite ongoing difficulties with infringement, evidenced by the continuing sale in Taiwan of would-be Eveready batteries, Champion spark plugs, Rolex watches, Chanel perfumes, Super K basketballs, Dunlop sporting goods, and a veritable orchard of imitation Apple computers, including the Pineapple, the Golden (Delicious), the Orange, and even the Lemon.[44] Moreover, the intellectual property law reforms of the mid 1980's failed meaningfully to speak to such key matters as retro-activity, the interface between these laws and Taiwan's treaty commitments, and the ability of those whose intellectual property had been infringed to prove damages.[45] Nor was progress made on such vexing issues as duration, translation rights, compulsory licensing, and *ex parte* seizures of counterfeited items.

The ROC's intellectual property law reforms of the mid 1980's were promulgated with great fanfare. Much publicity was directed toward efforts to enhance the work of relevant governmental offices, including the Ministry of Economic Affairs, the Board of Foreign Trade, the police and prosecutors, of the courts, and of private organizations such as the National Anti-Counterfeiting Committee.[46] This was complemented by the focusing of attention on prosecutions in which severe penalties were dispensed, by a spate of friendly articles in journals at home and abroad, by mass educational campaigns by government and private groups, and by increased news about discussions between Taiwan and the United States aimed at producing a copyright agreement.[47]

Although prosecutions for infringement increased substantially and some of the more visible forms of piracy diminished appreciably, the problems prompting these reform measures continued into the late 1980's.[48] Counterfeiting of computer hardware and software, electronic goods, video and audio cassettes, watches, textiles, and a range of other products continued, in some instances being taken over from small-time back-alley pirates by more serious criminal elements. "Piracy is rampant in Taiwan. It is carried out openly and in defiance of the law," noted a local observer at a 1987 forum sponsored by the American Institute in Taiwan (AIT) and the National Anti-Counterfeiting Committee.[49] Others suggested that "despite protestations of innocence, the Taiwan government is . . . aware of what is going on [by way of counterfeiting] . . . Taiwanese counterfeiters use the Trademark Office as a positive aid in their stealing—searching to discover the potential of a trademark and then adapting a product to fit it."[50] Much the same sentiment was expressed by those alarmed at the government's seeming willingness to tolerate continued pirating of the *Encyclopædia Britannica*, supposedly in retaliation for its American publishers having prepared a special bilingual edition for sale in the PRC.[51]

Believing the problem to be worsening, in the late 1980's, the

U.S. government adopted a more aggressive stance.[52] Foreign infringement was, as recounted above, nothing new, but during the
Reagan administration, American companies succeeded in linking
intellectual property protection and international trade by way both
of diagnosing what ailed their nation's economy and of prescribing
a remedy for those ails.[53] The burgeoning trade deficit, which was
especially large with the nations of East Asia, would have been far
smaller, they contended, had those very nations purchased, rather
than pirated, American intellectual property. Only by condition-
ing the access of exports from these nations to the U.S. market
on greater protection, the argument continued, would such abusive
practices cease.

"Special 301" was the vehicle through which the linkage was to
be effected. A part of the Omnibus Trade and Competitiveness Act
of 1988, Special 301 is a variant of Section 301 of the 1974 Trade Act
that requires the USTR both to notify the Congress regularly of
"priority foreign countries" failing adequately to protect American
intellectual property and to take all measures needed to address these
deficiencies within statutorily mandated deadlines.[54] To enhance the
effectiveness of Special 301 as a negotiating tool, soon after the law's
passage, the USTR additionally commenced the compilation of both
a "priority watch list" and a "watch list" for nations that did not
yet warrant designation as "priority foreign countries" but might if
their standard of protection did not improve.[55]

In May 1989, the USTR placed the ROC on its priority watch
list—thereby sparking an intense diplomatic struggle that has yet
fully to be resolved.[56] Knowing that a failure to reach agreement
would result in the ROC being named a priority foreign country,
which, in turn, could lead to retaliatory measures limiting access to
the U.S. market, the AIT and the Coordination Council for North
American Affairs (CCNAA) engaged in what one knowledgeable
observer has termed "the most difficult . . . trade talks" yet between
the United States and the ROC.[57] The result, initialed in July 1989,
was a comprehensive pact in which the ROC's negotiators agreed
to undertake changes intended to address long-standing American
concerns. Proposals to amend the ROC's Copyright Law covering
matters such as first sale, public performance, translation rights and
the duration of copyright would be forwarded to the Legislative
Yuan, while steps would be taken administratively to improve the

enforcement of those laws already on the books. Pleased with these promises, in November 1989, the USTR moved Taiwan from the priority watch list to the less threatening regular watch list.[58]

If American interests were at first pleased with the 1989 agreements, the same could not be said for many in the ROC. Newspaper and other commentators denounced American pressure, arguing, in the words of the *Jingji ribao* (Economics Daily), that the "government should not rush out to legislate laws that benefit others and harm our own."[59] Chinese academic observers echoed that sentiment, contending that U.S. negotiating techniques and subsequent pressure on Taipei to "request its judges to mete out more severe sentences in infringement cases" and provide Washington with monthly statistics of enforcement performance" infringed ROC sovereignty. Indeed, some went so far as to denounce ROC lawyers who had represented American intellectual property holders in Taiwan as "traitors" (*hanjian*). And even members of the ROC negotiating team, including one of its leaders, Executive Secretary Louis Wang (Wang Chuanlu) of the Ministry of Interior's Copyright Committee, expressed their concern, threatening to resign in order to draw further attention to what they described as American excesses.[60]

This anger helps explain why the agreements wrung so painfully from the ROC had little real effect. If modest progress was made with respect to traditional forms of infringement, such as the sale of $10 "Rolex" watches on street corners and unauthorized reprints of American texts, there was more than a countervailing increase in more sophisticated and costly types of infringement, particularly with regard to software and audio materials.[61] Nor did an amendment to the Copyright Law designed to halt the unauthorized commercial screening of American and other films staunch the flow of business at Taipei's notorious MTV (movie television) parlors. And the government's much-vaunted mechanisms to prevent the exportation of infringing goods proved of scant value, as the "elaborate trademark screening program for exports" established in 1985 failed to result in even a single exporter losing its export license during its first six years of operation.[62]

These and other instances of the ROC's perceived unwillingness to move rapidly enough to give effect both to the letter and spirit of the 1989 agreement did not escape notice. As early as 1990, Eric Smith, general counsel for the International Intellectual Property Alliance (IIPA), observed that "enforcement in the copyright area has fallen off since Taiwan pledged to improve its law," raising questions, as he put it, about the seriousness of Taipei's commitment.[63] In 1991, "Taiwan accounted for approximately 70 percent of Customs seizures of infringing computer and electronic products imported into the United States."[64] And a year later, counsel for a major American software producer declared that Taiwan remained the world's biggest source of counterfeit software. Nor were these views limited to foreign observers. So it was that the former general manager of the Microsoft Corporation's Taiwan operations could declare in 1992 that "90 per cent of the pirated software we [Microsoft] uncover in the world market originates in Taiwan."[65] Similar sentiments were expressed by Simon Huang, executive vice president of the ROC's largest domestic producer of software, who also indicated in 1992 that "at present for every one copy of legal software in the domestic market, there are three pirated copies in use. . . . People don't expect to pay for software."[66]

Spurred by the complaints of the IIPA and a growing number of associations and individual companies, early in 1992, the USTR again turned its attention to the ROC. Bitter negotiations, described "as the most contentious . . . in years" ensued,[67] but for months yielded no results, notwithstanding far from subtle intimations by the USTR that continued ROC resistance might complicate American support for Taipei's accession to the GATT.[68] Exasperated, on April 29, 1992, the USTR finally designated Taiwan a "priority foreign country" pursuant to Special 301, terming it "a center for copyright piracy and trademark counterfeiting of U.S. products."[69] In compliance with Special 301, a formal investigation was launched, requiring the USTR within a six-month period either to resolve the problem or recommend the imposition of sanctions.

The USTR's decision to deploy what some have termed the "nuclear weapon of trade remedies" (i.e., better brandished than detonated) did not escape Taipei's attention. Within a week, President Lee Teng-hui expressed his concern and called on the Executive, Legislative, and Judicial *yuan* to take the steps needed to defuse this weapon.[70] Heeding President Lee's injunction, on May 22, the Legislative Yuan approved amendments to the Copyright Law that had been under consideration for some two years. From June 12, 1992, unauthorized translations of foreign-copyrighted works were outlawed, the copyright term was extended to life plus 50 years, penalties for infringement were substantially stiffened (to include, *inter alia*, destruction of infringing materials) and a number of other changes designed to accommodate foreign intellectual property holders were made.[71]

Although the 1992 amendments represented what one Taiwanese specialist has described as the "largest scale amendment [of Chinese] copyright law [since] . . . 1928,"[72] the USTR believed that their passage alone did not fully comply with the changes in copyright law called for in 1989 AIT–CCNAA agreement—particularly with respect to matters such as parallel imports, public performance, fair use and retroactive protection.[73] Nor, of course, did these amendments speak to other areas of intellectual property law troubling to the United States or to the issue of enforcement in general.

Accordingly, on June 5, 1992, the AIT and CCNAA reached an "understanding" designed to address these matters.[74] "The authorities represented by the CCNAA" pledged to use their "best efforts" to secure ratification of the 1989 bilateral agreement as soon as possible and, in any event, no later than January 31, 1993. In addition, the ROC agreed to submit to the Legislative Yuan amendments to the ROC's patent and trademark laws and to draft cable television, trade secret, and semiconductor protection laws designed to bring the ROC into compliance with the standards articulated in the so-called Dunkel draft of the Uruguay Round of the GATT trade negotiations.[75] And to improve the quality of enforcement, the June 5 understanding called on the ROC to issue "directions to the public prosecutors to . . . consider the adverse impact of counterfeiting activities on the [nation's] economy and international image . . . [and therefore] to request a stiff penalty" and also to step up export monitoring, crack down on unlawful operators of MTV studios and cable stations, and to compile detailed statistics that would facilitate periodic review of the ROC's intellectual property regime.[76]

Far from resolving a nettlesome controversy, the June 5 understanding seems to have exacerbated it, principally because of the ways in which the negotiated settlement evoked tensions regarding both the allocation of power in Taiwan's increasingly democratic political life and the island state's international posture, especially vis-à-vis the United States.[77] Critics of the Guomindang in particular and of the ROC's long-standing subordination of the Legislative

Yuan more generally were quick to attack the Executive Yuan for usurping the legislature's responsibilities by committing it to pass particular measures into law within a set period of time.[78] Moreover, they and others indicated, the June 5 understanding constituted a "national humiliation," in that Taipei was allowing the United States not only to dictate to its elected representatives, but also to demand an even higher standard of protection than required by the Berne Convention.[79] This was especially irksome in view of the unwillingness of the United States to support Taiwan's participation in Berne or any other multilateral intellectual property agreement. Small wonder, then, that legislators belonging to the opposition Democratic Progressive Party "demanded that details of the . . . negotiation process be released and called for the punishment of ROC negotiators,"[80] while others abandoned use of the traditional Chinese term for traitor (*hanjian*, or, literally, one who betrays the Han) in favor of the phrase *taijian* (literally, one who betrays Taiwan) to denounce ardent supporters of the understanding.[81]

As legislatures worldwide are wont to when dealing with difficult matters, the Legislative Yuan delayed taking action until the eleventh hour before ratifying the 1989 agreement days ahead of the January 31, 1993 deadline.[82] In finally ratifying it, however, the legislature added no fewer than eight reservations to the 22-article pact. Although those reservations concerning parallel importation, public performance, and retroactivity, in particular, cut back on provisions of the agreement that the United States had emphasized, members of the Legislative Yuan believed them to be contrary either to the ROC's Constitution or law, or to exceed international norms.

The American reaction was unambiguous. Trade associations and individual companies alike plied the USTR and the Congress with data suggesting that piracy was increasing on Taiwan. The IIPA, for example, contended that copyright counterfeiting alone in 1992 was double that of 1991 and joined with a host of other entities in identifying the Taiwan situation as a first priority, leading one veteran ROC observer to suggest that in spite of years of trade negotiations, "Taiwan remains the jurisdiction where the broadest segment of U.S. industry continues to face its most pernicious counterfeiting and IP protection problems."[83] Even discounting for industry hyperbole, it was evident that American business was unwilling to accept the compromise put forward by the Legislative Yuan.

For its part, the USTR indicated that the reservations were unacceptable, save for a modest exception to the ban on parallel importation. If the ROC persisted, cautioned the USTR, there would be no alternative but to once again designate Taiwan a priority foreign country. In that situation, the U.S. government would be free to retaliate against its exports immediately without even the six-month investigation period required for first-time offenders. Retaliation, it was suggested, could well entail both the imposition of a large punitive tariff or sharp quantitative restrictions on ROC exports and a diminution of U.S. support for Taiwan's GATT application.[84]

The USTR's threats triggered a sharp decline in the Taipei stock exchange and led President Lee personally to take active part in trying both to convince legislators of the need for action and to encourage greater vigilance on the enforcement side.[85] Finally, on April 26, 1993, the Legislative Yuan ratified the 1989 agreement in a manner satisfactory to the American side, but not without adding measures designed to deter the Executive Yuan from again unilaterally binding the legislature. In return, when releasing its annual listing of nations misusing American intellectual property on April 30, the USTR chose not to designate Taiwan as a priority foreign country but instead to place it on the priority watch list. There the ROC remained, notwithstanding Taipei's subsequent passage of legislation intended to deter infringement by cable television operators and the launching of a so-called Comprehensive Action Plan for the Protection of Intellectual Property Rights that, *inter alia,* calls for the establishment of special intellectual property court chambers and of a new agency with a mandate to improve coordination between the governmental entities dealing with intellectual property matters, the police, and the courts.[86] And there, according to USTR Mickey Kantor, Taiwan is likely to remain until the Legislative Yuan undertakes significant additional measures regarding copyright, patent, and trademark.[87]

That American pressure has been the immediate catalyst for an unprecedented revision of intellectual property law in the ROC is undeniable. But for the specter both of a diminished access to its largest export market and of alienating its most important ally, the ROC would not have amended its copyright and other intellectual property laws in the way or at the pace it has since 1989. Nonetheless, foreign pressure alone provides neither a full explanation of the legal reforms that have already occurred nor, more important, a basis for inculcating the appreciation for intellectual property rights necessary if these laws are to take hold in a sustained fashion and thereby attain their stated goals. After all, were foreign pressure as certain an answer as its proponents believe, why was the ROC able to resist it for decades during which the island state was highly dependent on U.S. economic and military support, only to yield to it at a time when Taiwan has the world's largest per capita foreign currency reserves and has carved out its own position in the international community?[88]

An answer to this question lies in extraordinary economic, political, technological and diplomatic changes that have occurred in Taiwan over the past decade and their implications for the society and its culture. Taiwan's explosive economic expansion, increasing awareness of the need for indigenous technology, ever-more-pluralistic political and intellectual life, growing commitment to formal legal processes, and international aspirations have made evident the need for intellectual property law and nurtured domestic constituencies with good reasons for supporting it.

On the economic front,[89] it is evident that the type of low-wage, low-technology exports that fueled Taiwan's phenomenal growth of prior decades no longer will suffice to nurture the quality of life to which its people have become accustomed. As both government and industry have discerned, the ROC needs to generate its own world-class technology if, in the years ahead, it is to compete with other advanced economies. Greater protection for intellectual property, in the words of the former Minister of Economic Affairs Vincent Siew, "is crucial to Taiwan's own industrial upgrading, [as] inadequate efforts . . . would dampen research and development."[90] So it is that groups as varied as entrepreneurs involved in the famed Xinzhu science park, engineers behind the ROC's burgeoning software business, publishers confronted with mainland piracy and many in the indigenous film and entertainment industries, among others, have of late raised voices in support of stronger protection.[91]

Nor are such concerns limited only to those at the cutting edge—as evidenced by the budding concern of local businesses for trademark protection. At one time, so much of the ROC's industrial output was marketed under foreign brand names that one foreign wag suggested that Taiwan was not "an exporting nation . . . but simply a collection of international subcontractors serving the American market."[92] But now locally developed trademarks such as Kenex, Acer, and Ta-t'ung have developed such a high reputation for quality that they have become the victims of infringement both at home and abroad.[93] It ought, therefore, not to be particularly surprising that a range of actors, including the august Chinese National Federation of Industries, representing many of the ROC's largest businesses, have taken to lobbying for more serious trademark protection.[94]

These innovators and entrepreneurs would not have been able to give voice to such concerns, however, had it not been for the ROC's ongoing political transformation. Over the course of the past decade, the ROC has in many respects transformed itself from a highly centralized single-party state to a vibrant multiparty democracy. To be sure, the Guomindang's efforts to retain a high degree of control over electronic media and otherwise keep its upper hand in the political process, as well as the corruption that cuts across party lines, continue to impede this evolution.[95] Nonetheless, the changes under way are clearly without precedent in Chinese (or, for that matter, much of world) history and are seemingly irreversible.

If Taiwan's growing democratization has complicated the conclusion of a copyright agreement with the United States by virtue of introducing multiple voices into the negotiating process, it has also helped diminish Chinese civilization's long-standing link between censorship and copyright, while additionally facilitating circumstances conducive to expanding sharply the numbers and range of persons interested in having their voices heard. Prior to the late 1980's, through both direct and indirect means, such as the "three limitations" (*san xian*), the Guomindang had, in the mode of its predecessors, essentially retained a high degree of control over print media.[96] But by 1988, the substance, if not the form, of such control fell away dramatically, giving rise to as varied and independent an array of publications as has ever existed in a Chinese society. Operating in and reinforcing a setting of increasing pluralism, these media have created unparalleled opportunities for the expression of views other than those of the state and party.[97] And this, in turn, has added appreciably to the core of persons interested for political, as well as economic, reasons in the public use of their words, and so in the concerns addressed through copyright.

The political liberalization of the past decade has also, at least indirectly, enhanced the viability of the ROC's courts as a venue for the resolution of problems concerning intellectual property, as well as civil disputes more generally. For many years, the judicial system on Taiwan suffered problems comparable to those that afflicted ROC courts on the mainland prior to 1949 and that beset PRC courts to this day.[98] Burdened with an excessive number of persons of less than optimal competence, integrity, and independence and saddled with substantive and procedural laws that all too often bore little relation to local conditions, the court system was seen more as an obstacle than a means of remedying infringement and associated difficulties.

In recent years, however, the ROC's judicial system has begun to change. Spurred by a democratizing society increasingly able to express its concern that justice be done and by the breakdown, thanks to urbanization, industrialization, and internationalization, of traditional fora for the resolution of disputes, the courts have been broadening their mandate beyond the maintenance of order. With this has come a continuing effort to upgrade the status, quality, and independence of the judiciary, the public and private bars, and other personnel associated with the administration of justice.[99] And although questions remain, the political, societal, and economic factors that have been so central in the courts' improvement—and with it, the willingness of intellectual property holders to use them—seem certain to persist.

The prospect for Taiwan of playing a new and bolder role on the world stage provides yet another rationale for supporting intellectual property laws. With the end of the Cold War in Europe and the changing character of communist rule on the Chinese mainland, the ROC now finds itself with both the opportunity and a good deal of domestically generated pressure to assume a more vigorous stance internationally.[100] This may mean not only joining key economic entities such as GATT[101] but also efforts to secure further international legitimation through such measures as membership in the United Nations or the judicious use by Taipei of its newfound wealth to foster worthy developmental or educational endeavors abroad. But whatever may be entailed, it is clear that Taiwan's lingering image as a haven for counterfeiting that fails to live up to international norms despite great prosperity impedes the drive toward greater international involvement and respectability.[102]

That economic growth, political liberalization, diplomatic ambition, and other indigenous concerns, as well as external pressure, are fostering a greater regard for intellectual property law in the ROC by no means ensures that Taiwan will soon cease to be perceived as the land of $10 Rolex watches and knocked-off software. But, over time, it does suggest that Alvin Tong will have more important concerns about which to think than "twist[ing] the arms of [his] . . . engineers to file a patent."

Six

No Mickey Mouse Matter: U.S. Policy on Intellectual Property in Chinese Society

> As far as intellectual property is concerned, the practice
> of the United States asking large numbers of Chinese
> students to stay in the United States is itself a big plun-
> der of intellectual property.
>
> Wang Ke, "Essence of Escalation of
> Sino–U.S. Trade Frictions" (January 5, 1992)

The occupation of Tiananmen Square in late May 1989 by thousands of Chinese students, workers, and other citizens stirred the imagination of millions throughout the world, but evoked far less response from the U.S. government than did the possibility of successfully concluding discussions then under way with the PRC concerning intellectual property protection.[1] The Bush administration's professed concern about interfering in China's internal affairs, which supposedly constrained it from pushing with vigor, either publicly or privately, for a peaceful resolution of the occupation of the square, simply did not carry over to intellectual property. Instead, even as tensions mounted between hunger strikers in the square and elders of the Chinese Communist party, the U.S. government repeatedly threatened the PRC with massive and unprecedented trade sanctions if China did not promise to devise legal protection for computer software to America's liking.[2] And so it was that as the Chinese government spent May 19 putting the finishing touches to the declaration of martial law that was to signal a tragic end to the Beijing

Spring of 1989, American negotiators were busy putting their own finishing touches to a memorandum regarding computer software protection.[3]

The decisions that led the U.S. government to pay insufficient heed to the epochal events culminating on June 4, 1989, and instead to devote a goodly portion of its available diplomatic leverage to securing promises about software, were neither inadvertent nor passing tactical errors. On the contrary, they exemplify the high priority that intellectual property protection has assumed in American foreign policy with respect to the Chinese world and beyond since the mid 1980's, and the concomitant conviction that the key to securing such protection is the passage of new legislation, through pressure if need be. As discussed in chapter 5, the Bush and Clinton administrations have made intellectual property a centerpiece of America's quasi-official relations with Taipei. Nor has Taipei been singled out in this respect. Even after the tragic ending of the occupation of Tiananmen Square and the resultant expansion of concern in the United States about human rights in the PRC, intellectual property issues have remained at or very close to the forefront of the U.S. negotiating agenda with Beijing.

The degree to which intellectual property protection became a defining issue in relations with the PRC is graphically illustrated by an extraordinary series of events that occurred late in the Bush administration, leading up to the conclusion of the bilateral Memorandum of Understanding on Intellectual Property of January 17, 1992. In November 1991, then Secretary of State James Baker made the first visit to China by an American cabinet officer since the crushing of the Beijing Spring movement of 1989. Picking up on increasingly direct messages delivered by lower-level officials throughout the preceding two years, Baker informed the Chinese that the misuse of American intellectual property stood with the sales of weapons of mass destruction to international outlaws such as Iran and abuses of fundamental human rights as one of three issues impeding better bilateral relations.[4] On December 16, the U.S. government moved to separate out and highlight intellectual property, as USTR Carla Hills delivered an ultimatum demanding that Beijing agree within a month's time to rewrite its intellectual property laws to the satisfaction of Washington or face the imposition of hundreds of millions of dollars of punitive tariffs.[5]

Within days, Beijing responded in kind to the Hills ultimatum, indicating that it might impose comparable tariffs on American exports to China. This, in turn, led the Bush administration, which throughout its tenure had steadfastly resisted congressional efforts to limit MFN preferential tariff rates for China on human rights or any other grounds, to threaten to end MFN, discourage further American investment in China, and impede the PRC's GATT application.[6] Faced with the most substantial threats made against it by the United States in over two decades, hours before Ambassador Hills's deadline, Beijing capitulated and signed the desired agreement.[7] But the deal was not without its benefits for Beijing, as to compensate for the bitterness of the negotiations, President Bush agreed to receive Premier Li Peng, a principal architect of the suppression of 1989, a mere fortnight later, thereby "implicitly complet[ing] Peking's [post-Tiananmen] diplomatic rehabilitation."[8]

During its first year and a half in office, the Clinton administration does not appear to have steered a substantially different course from that of George Bush. Indeed, it has exhibited an even greater singularity of purpose regarding intellectual property in relations with Taipei than its predecessor, demanding, as outlined in chapter 5, that further law reform be undertaken to American specifications on Washington's timetable. Little attention seems to have been devoted to the possibility that such demands may have placed ROC negotiators in a difficult position constitutionally and in a more vexing one politically in terms of the intricate internal underpinnings of the ROC's unprecedented moves toward greater democratization and a more active role on the world stage. In its dealings with Beijing, the Clinton administration initially suggested that it was placing a greater emphasis on human rights and strategic concerns than its predecessors, but as the seeming costs to American exporters of stressing such concerns have become more apparent, it has, in the words of *New York Times* diplomatic correspondent Thomas Friedman, "put human rights issues on the back burner," with the result that "one of the main sources of friction between Washington and Beijing will be over trade issues and particularly copyright violations" as evidenced in USTR Kantor's June 30, 1994 decision to designate the PRC a "priority foreign country" under the so-called Special 301 provision of the 1988 Trade Act.[9]

That, in spite of their other differences, Republican and Democratic administrations should have made intellectual property issues so central a feature of Sino-American relations is not surprising when one considers the manner in which affected American industries have brought such concerns to the foreground politically, commencing in the mid 1980's. Although counterfeiting had long been a problem, it was at that time that key domestic industries succeeded in fostering a politically potent perception that their losses were linked to the nation's larger trade difficulties.[10] Calculating losses on the presumption that current infringers would buy at list price rather than cease using their products, they contended that infringement accounted for much of the burgeoning U.S. trade deficit—especially in East Asia—and, moreover, that it threatened those very service and high-technology industries on which a rosier future was supposed to be based. For politicians, the possibility of shifting attention away from America's seemingly intractable domestic economic problems and onto foreigners—and particularly distant foreigners who neither purchased our goods in abundance nor showed compunction about misappropriating the fruits of our technological prowess—was too tempting to resist. And the fact that a sizable number of the key industries raising these concerns were located in such electorally important areas as Southern and Northern California, Texas, and New York, and were involved in mass communications, only made such temptations more appealing.

To be sure, the unprecedented pressure brought to bear by the Bush administration did lead to the signing of a so-called Memorandum of Understanding, in which China pledged to strengthen its principal intellectual property laws. As regards patent, the PRC agreed to revise its Patent Law to extend the term of invention patents to 20 years; to cover pharmaceutical, chemical, and alimentary products; to enhance process patent protection; and to ease compulsory licensing requirements. With respect to copyright, China agreed to accede to the Berne Convention prior to the end of 1992, and to the Geneva Phonograms Convention no later than June 1, 1993; to treat software as a literary work deserving of protection even in the absence of formal registration; and to provide at least some modest limits on open-ended provisions that had the effect of treating materials already published as in the public domain. And additional promises were made to use "best efforts" to promulgate trade secrets legislation prior to January 1, 1994, and to develop more "effective procedures" in the trademark area.[11]

The PRC has, indeed, carried through on the formal commitments made in the January 1992 Memorandum of Understanding—certain of which it had already begun contemplating making. The Patent Law has been revised to incorporate measures discussed in the Memorandum. Beijing has not only acceded to the Berne, Geneva, and Universal Copyright conventions, but has also issued regulations reaffirming Article 142 of the General Principles of the Civil Law, which provides that treaty obligations are to prevail in the event that they conflict with municipal law.[12] A new Anti–Unfair Competition Law provides China's first direct protection for trade secrets.[13] And the Trademark Law has been amended to cover service marks, simplify opposition and cancellation procedures, heighten penalties for infringement, and take a number of more modest steps to improve this area of the law.

Clearly, China's agreement in January 1992 to supplement its intellectual property laws, and the steps taken thereafter to amend doctrine, offered advantages to both sides. At an immediate level, one of the most serious, if little publicized, disputes between the two nations in decades was, at least in the short term, defused. More substantively, both countries have benefited from China's elaboration of its formal legal regime in an area of growing importance and increasing complexity, just as efforts to bring the law closer to broadly followed international standards facilitate a policy of integration into the world economy.[14] And at a more general level, the further articulation of rights, albeit in a highly formalistic fashion, can be said to have laid another stepping-stone on the long path toward a society more shaped by legality, or at least to have established an ever more finely calibrated standard against which to measure the Communist party's ability to live up to its promises.[15]

Whatever advantages these steps may be seen as having provided, it is critical that one not equate the promulgation of new law on intellectual property with a meaningful transformation of Chinese life, notwithstanding the tendency of both the PRC and U.S. governments, each in its own way, to impart the impression that this is the case.[16] For although it is as yet too early to reach a definitive judgment as to the full effect of what might be termed a second generation of post–Cultural Revolution intellectual property laws, there is also no indication that these new laws are meaningfully altering prior practice in this area, even taking into account much-publicized government propaganda efforts associated with their promulgation. On the contrary, one might well contend that the very tensions that marked the PRC's first generation of intellectual property laws, as well as the post–Cultural Revolution law reform effort more generally—and, in each instance, limited the realization of stated objectives—remain essentially unaltered in the new generation of intellectual property laws and, for that matter, the ongoing project of law reform.[17]

As discussed in chapter 4, the PRC's early post–Cultural Revolution law reform efforts in general were characterized by the creation of rights without adequate provision for their realization. More recent measures do help to clarify many ambiguities and fill in gaps, and as such have, some would contend, begun the process of establishing meaningful municipal standards, departure from which will entail sanctions. Nonetheless, even granting this point, these measures neither address the problem of an insufficiency of remedial measures in contemporary Chinese doctrine nor speak to the more difficult questions involved in fostering institutions and values that might make possible a fuller realization of those rights provided. Thus, even after the revisions of the 1990's, PRC intellectual property law on its face either still fails sufficiently to address the issue of remedies, as in the cases of patent and copyright, or remains heavily dependent on administrative remedies redolent of the days of the controlled economy, as in the case of trademark. But even if remedies that parties could invoke and shape were stated more fully, the institutional vehicles through which these might be realized— be they administrative or judicial—remain insufficiently independent and professional. And, perhaps most vitally, before even those remedial measures and institutions that do exist can be fully utilized and others advanced, there remains a need further to foster what might be called a rights consciousness—that is, a belief that individuals are endowed with rights that they are entitled to assert even with respect to those in positions of authority.

While it would be disingenuous to suggest that a foreign government unable to preserve the integrity of Mickey Mouse somehow can and should play an important role in seeking to transform another people's attitudes toward rights, it is a contention of this study that a policy consisting in large measure of the use of extensive pressure to secure formal modifications of doctrine is deeply flawed in both its methodology and its objectives, and ultimately self-deluding as to the process and implications of legal change. The ready and frequent use by one nation of massive threats to secure changes in the municipal laws of another sovereign state may extract short-term concessions designed chiefly to ease such pressure, and may even help set in place standards against which a nation's citizens may be able to assess their government's willingness to adhere to its own rules. It is, however, incapable of generating the type of domestic rationale and conditions needed to produce enduring change and, moreover, runs a serious risk of discrediting the very message it, at least ostensibly, is intended to impart of the need for a greater respect for rights and the legal processes through which they are to be protected.

Arguably, this danger is accentuated with regard to the PRC, where more than a century's history of foreign states' using their greater power to extract concessions in the name of legality and supposedly higher ideals has combined with the current growing abuse by powerful Chinese of legal process for private gain to produce a widespread skepticism about appeals to the law.[18] The further fact that one prominent end toward which such pressure has been brought to bear and resisted in Sino-American relations during both the 1900's and 1990's has been the promulgation of Western-style intellectual property law is surely ironic and reflective of the unduly static and monodimensional vision that both the U.S. and PRC governments have of what legal change means. For without a concomitant nurturing of the institutions, personnel, interests, and values capable of sustaining a liberal, rights-based legality— which has hardly been a prime concern of either American or Chinese negotiators at either the beginning or the end of the twentieth century—freestanding foreign-derived rules on rarified private property rights, held in significant measure by foreign parties, are, ultimately, of limited utility. Stated differently, in its choice of means and ends, the United States has, in effect, devoted considerable diplomatic capital to securing concessions that fail meaningfully to speak to the chief impediments to the development in China of respect for legality and, through it, of a greater commitment to the protection of intellectual property rights.

To take issue with the means utilized and ends sought by the United States in its dealings with the Chinese world over intellectual property is not to suggest that foreign parties should desist from seeking to assert their interests or otherwise make their presence felt in the PRC or ROC. Clearly, in an increasingly interdependent world, where ideas, items, and individuals move across borders in profusion, whether governments wish them to or not, that is no longer an option. Rather, it is to stress the need to weigh with great care the rationale, character, and implications of such intervention prior to undertaking it; to emphasize the capacity of means to define, if not distort, ends; and to underscore the importance of remembering that the sovereign affairs of a state should ultimately be shaped principally by those whose polity it is.

If the purpose of U.S. policy toward the PRC concerning intellectual property is to secure meaningful protection for American property interests, it is necessary, therefore, first to understand why such protection is no more readily available for Chinese—as it is inconceivable that a system designed largely to protect the former, but not the latter could be sustained in modern China, given the bitter legacy of more than a century of foreign privilege. Although it is impossible to prove a negative, and perhaps as difficult to isolate interwoven variables in the laboratory of life, this study suggests that we need to move beyond the written rule itself to a consideration of the broader social and intellectual circumstances, and, in particular, the political culture within which law arises and within which it must operate. Obviously, political culture is an inexact notion, the contents of which have hardly remained constant over four millennia of Chinese history, interact with economic and other variables, and in any event are not wholly unique to China. Nonetheless, recognizing the limitations of this concept, it is a central contention of this book that the most important factor in explaining the late appearance and relative insignificance of the idea of intellectual property in the Chinese world lies in what, for lack of a better term, we might describe as its political culture, and especially in the central importance to the state, for purposes of legitimation and power, of controlling the flow of ideas. A system of state determination of which ideas may or may not be disseminated is fundamentally incompatible with one of strong intellectual property rights in which individuals have the authority to determine how expressions of their ideas may be used and ready access to private legal remedies to vindicate such rights.[19]

Political culture is not impervious to change, as the experience of the ROC on Taiwan, to cite but one example, shows. There, an extraordinary, if still evolving, political liberalization has spawned an unprecedented degree of pluralistic expression and openness of association that, in conjunction with the economic, diplomatic, and other factors discussed in chapter 5, offers the prospect of a more realistic foundation than has heretofore existed in the Chinese world for sustained support for intellectual property protection for both nationals and foreigners.[20] Undoubtedly, such change is a far more uncertain and complex proposition on the Chinese mainland, given its relative size, poverty, level of educational attainment, and the extent to which until recent years it has been isolated from alternative currents of political thought. Nonetheless, as suggested in chapter 4, even in the PRC, its beginnings are evident, although the state's ambivalence about the very rights it has been busy creating, and its concomitant hesitance to cede to individuals a greater capacity for enforcing them, raises questions as to the potential of such steps genuinely to transform fundamental tenets of Chinese political culture.

To the extent that political culture, broadly defined, has been a prime impediment to the growth of modern intellectual property law in the Chinese world, Americans interested in the protection of such rights would do well to concern themselves more directly with it, for without further political liberalization and a greater concomitant commitment to the institutions, personnel, and values needed to undergird a rights–based legality, detailed refinements in intellectual property doctrine itself will be of limited value. The challenges so posed are daunting, for by its very nature, political culture comprises enduring values and practices central to a nation's identity, which foreigners, perforce, should not too readily assume they have either the moral authority or capacity meaningfully to influence. Nonetheless, it is here that attention should be focused, for a state that encounters serious difficulties in protecting its citizens' basic civil and political rights is unlikely to be able to protect their property rights, which in turn means that it will be even less likely to protect the highly sophisticated property interests of foreigners.

The question of what constitutes fundamental civil and political rights also, of course, poses daunting challenges of definition, particularly if one subscribes to the idea that political culture and the differing historical experiences of which it in part consists are of consequence.[21] It is not my intention here either to define the contours of such rights, beyond referring to the broad standards set forth in the major international conventions—certain of which neither the PRC nor the United States have ratified—or to attempt a precise delineation of the relationship between economic and social rights on the one hand and civil and political rights on the other. Nor am I seeking to endorse the alluring, but overly simplistic, equation that many Americans would make between concern over issues of human rights and a belief that China's shortcomings therewith warranted a cessation of MFN—for as I have suggested elsewhere, the MFN issue in many respects fell victim to domestic American political considerations that obscured the search for convincing answers to the truly difficult question of what best advances the cause of international human rights in China (or other nations, for that matter.)[22] Rather, my point is to underscore my contention that the United States would, in the end, have been far more pragmatic in advancing its intellectual property interests during May 1989 had it not expended considerable political capital on computer software protection, but instead used what leverage it had to more vigorously seek a resolution of the occupation of Tiananmen Square compatible with respect for fundamental human rights, even while recognizing the limits of its ability definitively to shape such events.

Daunting though they may be, the foregoing are not the only challenges confronting those who would hope to foster a greater respect for intellectual property and other legal rights in China. As the PRC's efforts at law reform proceed, there is a growing need for vigilance as to who is seeking to use the law and toward what end. Obviously, such concern is necessary in any society, but both history and the novelty and fragility of many of PRC's new formal legal institutions underscore its importance in the current Chinese context. Already, law is being enlisted in a highly instrumental fashion as a weapon in intensifying struggles within and between units of government and party, center and region, and various other entities and individuals.[23] If rights are to be protected, legal reform will need not only to facilitate the assertion by various entities and individuals of their particular interests, but also to provide a generalized and visible means through which competition between them can be fairly resolved.

Close scrutiny will also be necessary to discern and think through the implications of how ministries and individuals once at the heart of the planned economy and administrative state are now, under the rubric of reform, pouring forth a torrent of new and often highly parochial rules in order to recast themselves as agents of change, lay claim to resources, and ensure themselves an ongoing role in tomorrow's China. Advocates of the growth of respect for intellectual property rights will need, for example, to assess carefully such seemingly unalloyedly positive undertakings as the SAIC's recent 6,000-strong cadre campaign against trademark infringement. Are the benefits of reducing such counterfeiting worth the risk of providing an agency that in pre-reform days tightly oversaw virtually all facets of local commercial activity with a ready excuse to exercise sweeping administrative authority over retail enterprises not controlled by the state? Undoubtedly, many such entities are engaged in activities contravening intellectual property laws, and, indeed, with further economic liberalization, and the resulting emphasis on profitability, they are prime candidates for carrying out further infringement. Nonetheless, these entities are among the most ardent advocates of the very economic reform that has facilitated much of whatever growth of intellectual property law has already occurred and that is in general bringing China closer to the world economy.

Americans and other foreigners concerned about intellectual property rights may also have to face variants of this conundrum with respect both to access for Chinese goods in their home markets and competition from PRC entities more generally. Earnings from exports to major foreign markets and investment induced thereby have been important factors in enabling Chinese exporters, particularly in southeastern China, to enjoy autonomy—principally economic, but in a modest, but growing, degree political—from central state and party authorities (if not always their local counterparts). If reform is to continue and if, in the future, Chinese enterprises are to accumulate sufficient capital from sources other than the state to conduct the research needed to develop commercially valuable intellectual property of their own, increased exports are a certainty. The United States, to take but one example, already limits imports of textiles, shoes, and other labor-intensive items in which the PRC enjoys a comparative advantage, and, concerned about its burgeoning trade deficit with Beijing, Washington is making serious noises about imposing further such restrictions.[24] Although providing more open markets will not necessarily directly produce a rapid growth of intellectual property law in the PRC, constricting access to the markets of major industrialized countries almost certainly will retard it. Americans concerned about their intellectual property in the PRC would do well to recognize that the conditions likely to be conducive to the further growth of respect for intellectual property in China are those that may also dictate permitting PRC exports to compete more, rather than less, freely in the American marketplace.

Embedded in the problems of increased infringement and further market access is a challenge—namely, that the circumstances likely to lead to greater protection for intellectual property in the PRC are also likely to enhance China's overall capacity to compete with the United States economically. If it is true that serious protection for foreign intellectual property in the PRC must await the further development of Chinese-generated intellectual property of commercial importance, it follows that a PRC willing to accord American holders of intellectual property more of the rights they now seek will likely have many more enterprises that are technologically sophisticated and increasingly commercially competitive internationally. In short, the conditions that breed protection for intellectual property are also those that breed competition with regard to intellectual property.

Acknowledgement of the problems engendered by current efforts to graft limbs grown in one setting onto trunks that have matured in another will not of itself provide remedies to the many and vexing problems of transplantation discussed in this book. It may, however, reduce friction resulting from misunderstanding, while bringing into starker relief the difficult, but inescapable, questions that confront the PRC as it seeks to generate a legal system capable of serving nation building. For only if we have some understanding of why in Chinese civilization it has been an elegant offense to steal a book will China and its foreign friends know how in the future to discern and protect one another's legitimate interests.

Reference Matter

Notes

One. Introduction

The aphorism in the epigraph to this chapter appears in Lu Xun's short story "Kong Yiji." See *Selected Stories of Lu Hsün*, trans. Yang Hsien-yi and Gladys Yang (New York: Oriole Editions, n.d.), 39–45.

1. The history of these innovations is described in Ch'ien, *Paper and Printing*.

2. The PRC's formal undertaking to revise its intellectual property laws is contained in a Memorandum of Understanding signed with the government of the United States on January 17, 1992. The efforts of the PRC to revise its copyright, patent, and trademark laws are discussed in detail in chapter 4, while the negotiations leading to the Memorandum are considered in chapter 6. The ROC's intellectual property laws form the subject of chapter 5. The pressure brought to bear by the U.S. government on the PRC is treated in Alford, "Perspective on China." That applied to the ROC is considered in Baum, "Taiwan on a Tightrope." See also Alford, "Intellectual Property."

3. Treatises providing an introduction to the current state of doctrine in these fields in the United States include Nimmer, *Nimmer on Copyright*; Peter Rosenberg, *Patent Law Fundamentals*; and McCarthy, *Trademarks and Unfair Competition*. Legal protection is also available in the United States for other forms of intellectual property, including semiconductor mask works, trade secrets, and know-how.

4. The early history of copyright in the West is treated in Patterson, *Copyright in Historical Perspective*; Rose, *Authors and Owners*; and Woodmansee, "Genius and the Copyright."

5. The early history of patent in the West is discussed in Kaufer, *Economics of the Patent System*.

6. See, e.g., Zou, "Baohu banquan . . . ?" and Zheng and Pendleton, *Copyright Law in China*, 9–17.

7. See, e.g., Adelstein and Peretz, "Competition of Technologies and Markets for Ideas," 209.

8. See "Memorandum of Understanding . . . on the Protection of Intellectual Property"; Alford, "Perspective on China"; Lachica, "China Settles Dispute."

9. This is not to contend that intellectual property law in the West has been or is unidimensional. A strong argument can be made that a central objective of copyright in contemporary American society is to facilitate a marketplace of ideas (even as one recognizes how private ownership in some respects curtails the flow of the information). See Boyle, "Theory of Law and Information."

10. Students of comparative intellectual property law would be quick to note that fundamental dimensions of U.S. intellectual property law, such as our patent law's reliance on the principle of being the first to invent rather than the first to file, suggest that the experience of the United States hardly provides a "normal" pattern of growth relative to other Western nations. In fact, U.S. insistence on retaining the first to invent rule has effectively derailed a decade-long international effort at harmonizing patent laws. Teresa Riordan, "Patents: The Patent Office Takes a Stand on International Patent Policy, But It Is Confusing to Many," *New York Times*, Feb. 7, 1994, D2.

11. Despite increasing convergence in recent years—or, at least, increasing claims of convergence, given the decision of the United States in 1989, finally, to ratify the International Union for the Protection of Literary and Artistic Property (the Berne Convention)—Continental and Anglo-American notions of copyright sprang from different roots. Although there are considerable differences between French and German copyright law, both can be traced to ideas of natural law current in the aftermath of the French Revolution. See Stewart, *International Copyright*. The roots of Anglo-American copyright, on the other hand, appear to have been more terrestrially based in economic considerations. See Kaplan, *Unhurried View of Copyright*. For an overview of the ways in which modern technology is challenging many assumptions in this area of law both here and in other industrialized democracies, see U.S. Office of Technology Assessment, *Intellectual Property Rights*.

12. Tough questions regarding the extent to which intellectual property law achieves its stated aims anywhere are raised in Priest, "What Economists Can Tell Lawyers"; Breyer, "Uneasy Case for Copyright"; Fisher, "Reconstructing the Fair Use Doctrine"; and Merges, "Commercial Success and Patent Standards." Also worth considering are empirical efforts by economists, including Mansfield, "Patents and Innovation"; Levin et al., "Appropriating the Returns from Industrial R & D"; and Levin, "Appropriability, R & D Spending and Technological Performance." The question of

effectiveness is no more easily resolved with respect to developing nations. A number of commentators (some in the employ of developed world enterprises that stand to profit through increased protection for intellectual property globally) contend that the benefits for developing nations of embracing greater formal legality far outweigh the costs. See, e.g., Francis Brown and Carole Brown, eds., *Intellectual Property Rights*; Sherwood, *Intellectual Property*; Gadbaw and Richards, *Intellectual Property Rights*; and Rapp and Rozek, "Benefits and Costs." Certain of these writers deploy extensive statistics in making their cases, although in some instances, such data rest on questionable assumptions (as, e.g., when Rapp and Rozek essentially conflate legislative enactment and enforcement) and offer little insight as to whether intellectual property law spawned prosperity or prosperity spawned intellectual property law. Other commentators are somewhat more skeptical about the impact of intellectual property protection on the economic and political situation of developing nations. See, e.g., Goonatilake, *Aborted Discovery*; Oddi, "International Patent System"; Adikibi, "Multinational Corporation and Monopoly of Patents"; and Kirim, "Reconsidering Patents."

13. The U.S. International Trade Commission, a semi-independent federal agency whose responsibilities include preparing reports on the international economic activity of the United States, estimates that foreign infringement of American intellectual property costs this country more than 133,000 jobs and from U.S.$23.8 to U.S.$61 billion in lost profits annually, and that the PRC and ROC account for a sizable portion of that infringement; see U.S. International Trade Commission, *Effect of Foreign Product Counterfeiting* and *Foreign Protection of Intellectual Property Rights*. See also Eduardo Lachica, "U.S. Steps Up Efforts to Form Pact on Patents," *Wall Street Journal*, Feb. 29, 1988, 46. These figures should not be taken at face value, as they are based on data supplied by domestic industries seeking government assistance against infringers and typically calculate losses by multiplying estimated instances of infringement by full list prices. Even assuming the accuracy of estimates of the numbers of infringers, there is no reason to presume that each infringer would prefer to pay a list price rather than cease using the item in question, were these the only two alternatives available. It seems far more likely, to take but a single example, that law students in the PRC, who typically live on less than U.S.$35 a month, would cease using pirated American texts rather than pay full price for such books, which typically list for more than U.S.$35 each. Nonetheless, there is little doubt that infringement of U.S. intellectual property not only exacts a great cost in terms of lost revenues and jobs but also has a deleterious impact on unwitting consumers here and abroad of a range of substandard products, from improperly constituted polio vaccine to fake automobile parts to defective contraceptive devices. See Rakoff and Wolff, "Commercial Counter-

feiting." The various forms of infringing activity and the damage they cause are discussed in General Accounting Office, *International Trade*.

14. Intellectual property rights have largely been territorial in scope. That is, they essentially provide protection only with respect to infringement occurring within the territory of the nation granting the right in question. Commencing with the International Union for the Protection of Industrial Property of 1883 (the Paris Convention), which deals with patent and trademark, and the Berne Convention, which addresses copyright, efforts have been made to enable nationals of one nation to secure counterpart rights within the territory of other nations.

The development of a Benelux patent, work toward a European patent, and attempts to promote a "world" patent suggest the possibility of further extending intellectual property rights beyond their current territorial status. Nonetheless, given the difficulties that have marked such efforts to harmonize the law, as well as the problems that would ensue from subsequent divergent national interpretations, meaningful harmonization of intellectual property law remains only a distant possibility. In its absence, the United States and other nations frustrated with the problem of infringement were able in the recently concluded Uruguay Round of the General Agreement on Tariffs and Trade (GATT) to link access to their markets for foreign goods to respect for their intellectual property rights. The international treaty structure for intellectual property protection and proposals to strengthen it are described in General Accounting Office, *International Trade*. Efforts at addressing such issues through the GATT are considered in Alford, "Intellectual Property."

15. The United States was notorious through much of the nineteenth century for its lack of respect for authors' rights. In one of the more celebrated examples, Charles Dickens's work was sold in the United States in numerous pirated editions. *A Christmas Carol*, for instance, was offered for as little as six cents in the United States (as opposed to the equivalent of $2.50 in Great Britain) and altered in different parts of the United States to suit local tastes. For more on the early history of U.S. copyright law, see Aubert Clark, *Movement for International Copyright*.

Although it took the United States over a century to recognize foreign copyrights, even that step was limited by the introduction in 1891 of the so-called "manufacturing clause." In an effort to boost the American publishing industry, the manufacturing clause specifically limited protection to those foreign copyrighted works actually produced within the United States, and these requirements remained in effect until 1986. Chinese officials and scholars have been quick to point to this history in seeking to justify China's record of protection for foreign copyrighted material. For more on developing countries's concern about the expenditure of limited foreign exchange holdings for royalty payments in order to obtain access to needed foreign intellectual property, see Shen Yuanyuan, "To Copy or Copyright."

16. See, e.g., Rakoff and Wolff, "Commercial Counterfeiting."

17. The complexity and impracticality of fair use doctrine is nicely illustrated in UCLA Policy No. 1160—Reproduction of Copyrighted Materials for Teaching and Research (Nov. 25, 1986), which devotes some fifteen largely impenetrable pages to endeavoring to explain to faculty the limits of the fair use doctrine. An overview of fair use is provided in Nimmer, *Nimmer on Copyright*. The fair use doctrine is insightfully discussed in Fisher, "Reconstructing the Fair Use Doctrine," and Weinreb, "Fair's Fair."

18. The Eurocentric quality of Marx's thinking is demonstrated in Karl Marx, "Revolution in China and Europe," *New York Daily Tribune*, June 14, 1853, reprinted in Alford, "Role of Law in Chinese Society."

19. See Vogel, *Four Little Dragons*. See also Alford, "When Is China Paraguay?"

20. For more on this problem, see Alford, "On the Limits of 'Grand Theory.' "

21. Thus, for example, in the otherwise stimulating debate regarding patent between Edmund Kitch and his critics, certain basic questions—such as why the United States limits patent protection to seventeen years (or any specified period) irrespective of the value of the invention involved—are essentially taken for granted and so not probed. The article that initiated this debate was Kitch, "Nature and Function of the Patent System." The debate is continued, inter alia, in Smith and McFetridge, "Patents, Prospects and Economic Surplus" and Kitch, "Patents, Prospects and Economic Surplus: A Reply."

Similar concerns might be voiced with respect to important scholarship concerning copyright. For example, Richard Epstein's recent foray into copyright uses the celebrated case of *International News Service v. Associated Press*, 248 U.S. 215 (1918), as a vehicle for contending that we ought to pay greater heed to "custom and industry practice" and less to the "positive law" of judges and legislators in considering such property rights. Ironically, however, notwithstanding the increased role he advocates for custom relative to law, Epstein's central discussion of custom in the news-gathering business at the time of World War I is drawn from fewer than a half-dozen judicial opinions and from fragmentary anecdotal data from two sources about journalistic behavior in the period since World War II. Epstein seems unconcerned with how journalists in the early twentieth century (or, for that matter, anyone other than judges, whose "techniques of rational analysis" he questions elsewhere in the same article) conceived of "custom and industry practice" in news-gathering. Nor does he evidence any appreciation at a more general or theoretical level of the difficulties inherent in ascertaining what constitutes custom, particularly some seven or more decades after the fact. See Richard Epstein, "*International News Service v. Associated Press.*"

Scholars with a very different political orientation than Kitch and Epstein have recently turned their attention to copyright law. Among the most important pieces are Martha Woodmansee, "Genius and the Copyright"; Jaszi, "Towards a Theory of Copyright"; and Boyle, "Theory of Law and Information." Although they take a fresh, imaginative, and stimulating view of copyright, these scholars seem torn between their desire on the one hand to take apart what they term the societal constructs of authorship and copyright and on the other to preserve the economic, moral, and psychological prerogatives that such constructs provide. For example, at a conference organized by Woodmansee and Jaszi in 1991 entitled "Intellectual Property and the Construction of Authorship," participants paused in the midst of three days of strenuous attacks on the idea of authorship and the notion of copyright to pepper the Registrar of Copyrights of the United States with a stream of questions concerned, in large measure, with how they might secure fuller protection for their work under current copyright law.

22. Arguments for and against treating intellectual property differently from other forms of property are set forth in Gordon, "Inquiry into the Merits of Copyright."

23. See Yankelovich et al., "Public Perceptions of the Intellectual Property Rights Issue"; Shattuck, "Public Attitudes and the Enforceability of Law." It should be noted that the leading software producers trade association, the Business Software Alliance, believes software piracy is far worse throughout Asia than in the United States.

24. Both the PRC and the ROC are pressing to secure GATT Contracting Party status. The array of issues involved are discussed in Feinerman, "Taiwan and the GATT."

25. See, e.g., Alford, " 'Seek Truth from Facts.' " On the disruptions of the Great Proletarian Cultural Revolution, which is described in the PRC as having lasted from 1966 to 1976, see Thurston, *Enemies of the People.*

26. The role of the PRC government in the unauthorized production and distribution of foreign intellectual property, as well as its censorship activities, are discussed in chapter 4.

27. The role of internal circulation (*neibu*) laws and legal materials in the PRC is thoughtfully discussed in Jones, "Some Questions." See also Nicholas Kristof, "What's the Law in China? It's No Secret (Finally)," *New York Times*, Nov. 20, 1988, pt. 1, 21. In response to a U.S. threat to impose substantial trade sanctions, the PRC agreed in principle, on October 10,

1992, to eliminate *neibu* laws concerning foreign trade by issuing "regulations . . . that state only laws and regulations published and readily available to foreign governments and travelers are enforceable [after October 10, 1993]," according to the principal U.S. negotiator involved (Massey, "301: The Successful Conclusion," 9). Even taking account of exceptions found elsewhere in the October 10, 1992, "Memorandum of Understanding . . . on Market Access" (such as that permitting the exclusion of undefined "information contrary to the public interest," it strains credulity to believe that this will transform fundamental long-standing Chinese practices any more effectively than the U.S. undertaking—as part of the so-called Structural Impediments Initiative with Japan—to reform our elementary and secondary education will, indeed, result in a drastic improvement in the overall quality of our public schools. Motivated largely by the presidential election, the U.S. drive in 1992 to secure the PRC's agreement to open its markets to foreign goods or face massive retaliatory tariffs, all the while paying scant attention either to how such promises were to be met or to the implications of using U.S. leverage for such purposes, exemplifies the type of problem in trade policy discussed in chapter 6 of this book with reference to intellectual property. Succinctly stated, flexing one's muscles is no substitute for thinking through how respect for particular types of legality grows.

28. See, e.g., Ren Wei, "World-Wide Symposium."
29. See U.S. Congress, House, *Unfair Foreign Trade Practices*.

Two. Don't Stop Thinking About . . . Yesterday

1. See, e.g., Zou, "Baohu banquan . . . ?"; Zheng and Pendleton, *Copyright Law in China*; and Chan, "Control of Publishing."
2. The point is perhaps most explicitly made in Adelstein and Peretz, "Competition of Technologies and Markets," whose views may be seen as a specific application of the broader contention of economic historians such as Douglass North and Robert Paul Thomas that innovation spurs the need for well-defined private property rights, which in turn provide the incentive needed to foster further innovation (see, e.g., North and Thomas, *Rise of the Western World*). See also Libecap, "Property Rights"; Rapp and Rozek, "Benefits and Costs"; and Mansfield, "Intellectual Property."
3. Zheng and Pendleton, *Copyright Law in China*, 11.
4. Bodde and Morris, *Law In Imperial China*, 3.
5. Imperial law codes are discussed in ibid. See also Chiu Hanping, ed., *Lidai xingfa zhi*, which reproduces the section on law of the official dynastic histories from the Han to the Ming. Portions of the Qing code have been translated by George Staunton into English and by Guy Boulais into

French. William Jones of Washington University has recently completed a modern translation. A useful guide to the *Da Qing lü li* is Xue Yunsheng, *Duli cunyi.*

6. Needham, *Science and Civilization,* 2: 524. Philip Huang and Kathryn Bernhardt of UCLA have launched a major and impressive research project delving into the question of whether there was a "civil law" in late imperial and early Republican China.

7. Needham, *Science and Civilization,* 2: 524–30.

8. Chang Wejen, "Chuantong guannian."

9. This extraordinary emphasis on the imperial codes' penalties seems attributable to a number of factors, among them the Confucian ideological antipathy toward formal legality, which discouraged scholars from considering the "civil" side of such law; widespread popular perceptions of the legal system; and early reports by foreign observers as to the quality of Chinese justice relative to that of their home jurisdictions. For more on why Western scholars have misunderstood Chinese law, see Alford, "Law, Law, What Law?"

10. The so-called Ten Abominations are listed in Article 2 of the General Principles section of the Qing code.

11. The classic work on clan rules is Liu Wang Hui-chen, *Traditional Chinese Clan Rules.*

12. Guild charters are discussed in detail in Rowe, *Hankow.*

13. Mann, *Local Merchants.*

14. Hsiao, *Rural China;* Watt, *District Magistrate.*

15. Susan Mann's *Local Merchants* suggests that this was the case with respect to tax farming and related fiscal issues.

16. The Four Books are the *Lünyu* (*The Analects of Confucius*), *Mengzi* (*The Mencius*), *Daxue* (*The Great Learning*), and *Zhongyong* (*The Doctrine of the Mean*).

17. Ray Huang, *1587,* 149.

18. On the role of hierarchy, see Alford, "Inscrutable Occidental."

19. The Chinese vision of world order also mirrored family structure, with the Chinese at the apex exercising fiducial responsibilities toward less civilized peoples.

20. Waley, trans., *Analects of Confucius,* bk. 2, ch. 21.

21. See Rowe, *Hankow,* 292–99; Mann, *Local Merchants,* passim.

22. Rowe, *Hankow,* 292–99; Liu Wang Hui-chen, *Traditional Chinese Clan Rules,* 143.

23. See Liu Wang Hui-chen, *Traditional Chinese Clan Rules.*

24. The work being done by Philip Huang and Kathryn Bernhardt on civil law suggests that legal issues were far more numerous than previously assumed.

25. Zhang Xujiu, *Shangbiaofa jiaocheng.*
26. Bodde, *China's First Unifier.*
27. Chang and Alford, "Major Issues in Chinese Legal History."
28. Historians locate the invention of woodblock printing between 590 and 650 and the development of movable type by Bi Sheng at around the year 1000. Zheng Chengsi and Michael Pendleton assert that whereas in the West "the adoption of woodblock printing was not sufficient to dramatically speed up the publication of books . . . in China the situation was different," owing to the use of Chinese characters rather than a phonetic alphabet (*Copyright Law in China*, 11–12). The history of printing in China is discussed in Ch'ien, *Paper and Printing*; Carter, *Invention of Printing*; Pelliot, *Debuts de l'imprimerie*; Poon, "Books and Printing"; and Twitchett, *Printing and Publishing.*
29. Chan, "Control of Publishing," 2. See also Qi Shaofu, "Zhongguo gudai de chuban," 31; Ch'ien, *Paper and Printing.* Wallace Johnson has published a translation of the General Principles section of the Tang code and completed translations of other major portions of the code. See Johnson, *T'ang Code.*
30. Printed versions of state laws were rarely disseminated widely in preimperial and imperial China. Although the populace's limited literacy was obviously a factor, the notion that law ought not to be widely distributed may have been attributable more to a sense that the populace had no need for the law, as those persons who had properly cultivated their virtue would know how to behave without resort to legal rules, while those of lesser character would simply study the written law in order to find ways around its strictures. Interestingly, the PRC government continues to restrict access by both Chinese nationals and foreigners to laws to which they are potentially subject. See chapter 1.
31. Chan, "Control of Publishing"; Twitchett, *Printing and Publishing.*
32. The Imperial College, which housed China's "first officially-run publishing house," is discussed in Zheng and Pendleton, *Copyright Law*, 12.
33. Ye Dehui, *Shulin qinghua*, 145.
34. Ibid.; Zheng Chengsi, "Printing and Publishing in China"; Thomas Lee, *Government Education*, 42. The most comprehensive study of Song printing is Poon, "Books and Printing."
35. Chan, "Control of Publishing"; Ye Dehui, *Shulin qinghua*; Lu Guang and Pan Xianmou, *Zhongguo xinwen falü gailun*, 4. Concern about using the names of those in power has been a regular theme in Chinese history. Celebrated instances include those concerning the Hongwu Emperor during the mid fourteenth century, the Qianlong Emperor during the late eighteenth century, and Mao Zedong during the Cultural Revolution (1966–76).
36. Ye Dehui, *Shulin qinghua*, 143–45. The penalties in the Song dynasty's

publication laws are discussed in detail in Niida, *Chūgoku hōseishi kenkyū*, 4: 445–91.

37. The original colophon is reproduced in Poon, "Printer's Colophon," 39. Ye Dehui discusses local efforts to bar unauthorized reproduction in *Shulin qinghua*, 37–41 and 143–45. See also Twitchett, *Printing and Publishing*, 65.

38. Even the late Qing study *Shulin qinghua*, which deals more extensively with Song prohibitions on printing than any other, consists of little more than isolated anecdotes.

39. See Yuan, "Zhongguo gudai banquan shi kaolüe."

40. Ye Dehui, *Shulin qinghua*; see also Ku, "Study of the Literary Persecution," 254. For a thorough treatment of mid-Qing efforts to control publication, see Goodrich, *Literary Inquisition*.

41. Hucker, *Ming Dynasty*, 70; Wu Kuang-ch'ing, "Ming Printers and Printing," 230.

42. Goodrich, *Literary Inquisition*.

43. Wu Kuang-ch'ing, "Ming Printers and Printing," 229.

44. Chan, "Control of Publishing," 23–24.

45. Mann, *Local Merchants*; Santangelo, "Imperial Factories of Suzhou."

46. See, e.g., the *Da Qing lü li*, Art. 429. The sumptuary laws are described in detail in Ch'ü, *Law and Society*.

47. Hamilton and Lai, "Jinshi zhongguo shangbiao."

48. Edwards, "Imperial China's Border Control Law," 57–58.

49. The original mark is reproduced at Zhang Xujiu, *Shangbiaofa jiaocheng*, 18.

50. Examples are discussed in Hamilton and Lai, "Jinshi zhongguo shangbiao." See also Rowe, *Hankow*.

51. Hamilton and Lai, "Jinshi zhongguo shangbiao," 4–15.

52. Ibid.

53. Zheng Chengsi, *Chinese Intellectual Property*, 21; Hamilton and Lai, "Jinshi zhongguo shangbiao," 4–15.

54. See Hamilton and Lai, "Jinshi zhongguo shangbiao."

55. The best source for evidence of these efforts is Ye Dehui, *Shulin qinghua*. For more on the history of real property in China, see vol. 4 of Niida, *Chūgoku hōseishi kenkyū*. James Feinerman of the Georgetown University Law Center is now working on the mortgage-like transaction known as the *dian*.

56. With respect to England, see Patterson, *Copyright in Historical Perspective*, 36–41. See also Eisenstein, *Printing Press*. With regard to France, see Darnton, *Literary Underground*. Others would link copyright far more to the rise of the Romantic construct of "authorship." See Woodmansee, "Genius and the Copyright," 425.

57. Machlup, "Patents," 461.

58. Klemm, *History of Western Technology*, 171–73.

59. See Patterson, *Copyright in Historical Perspective*; Machlup, "Patents," 462; Nathan Rosenberg and L. E. Birdzell, Jr., *How the West Grew Rich*; North and Thomas, *Rise of the Western World*.

60. Alford, "Inscrutable Occidental"; Alford, "On the Limits of 'Grand Theory,'" 975.

61. See, e.g., Temple, *Genius of China*, 9–12; Ross, *Oracle Bones*; Needham, *Science and Civilization*.

62. See, e.g., Zou, "Baohu banquan," or any of the writings of Zheng Chengsi.

63. Martha Woodmansee and those who have adopted her thesis that copyright is an outgrowth of the Romantic conception of the author as an inspired genius whose creativity should be seen as individual rather than societal, are noteworthy exceptions. See Woodmansee, "Genius and the Copyright."

64. See, e.g., Adelstein and Peretz, "Competition of Technologies and Markets for Ideas."

65. Needham, *Science and Civilization*; Elvin, *Pattern of the Chinese Past*.

66. Adelstein and Peretz, "Competition of Technologies and Markets for Ideas." Similar views are voiced by Zheng Chengsi and Michael Pendleton, who assert that the "fact that the concept of copyright was formed after such a leap [to movable type] shows that the development of law always follows the development of technology" (*Copyright Law in China*, 14).

67. Ch'ien, *Paper and Printing*.

68. Berman, *Words Like Colored Glass*, 105.

69. Richard Smith, *China's Cultural Heritage*, 201.

70. Eastman, *Family, Field and Ancestors*.

71. In using the term political culture, it is not my intention to invoke the work of Lucian Pye. As I endeavor to demonstrate below, I seek to bring both a broader and a more nuanced content to this admittedly elastic concept.

72. For a compelling discussion of the importance of the idea of the past in Chinese civilization, see Owen, *Remembrances*.

73. The importance of these relationships is discussed in Alford, "Inscrutable Occidental."

74. Hsiao, *History of Chinese Political Thought*, 1: 90–94.

75. Tu, *Centrality and Commonality*.

76. Alford, "Inscrutable Occidental."

77. Confucius, *Analects*, bk. 2, ch. 3 (Waley translation modified by this author).

78. See Hall and Ames, *Thinking Through Confucius*.

79. Alford, "Inscrutable Occidental."

80. Waley, trans., *Analects of Confucius*, bk. 13, ch. 3. The idea of a "rectification of names" has had enduring currency in China, as evidenced, for example, by the use of that term by the leadership of the Chinese Communist party to describe efforts in the early 1980's to encourage the retirement of certain cadres resistant to Deng Xiaoping's policies.

81. Keightley, "Religious Commitment," 220.

82. Chan, *Legitimation in Imperial China*.

83. In the words of the *Shu jing* (Book of Documents), one of the great classics of the Chinese tradition, the last Shang (1700–1122 B.C.) ruler had "no clear understanding of the respect due the people; he maintained and spread far and wide resentment and did not change. Therefore, Heaven sent down destruction on Yin . . . [and replaced it with the next dynasty, the Chou]. . . . It was due to [such] excesses. Heaven is not tyrannical" ("Announcement About Drunkenness," trans. Karlgren, 1).

84. The invalidating power of the past, was evidenced, for example, by the controversial late Qing scholar and reformer Kang Youwei (1858–1927), who believed that the state orthodoxy of his day was impairing China's modernization. In his book *Xinxue weijing kao* (A Study of the Forged Classics of the Xin Period), Kang sought to expose as inauthentic certain of the key Confucian classics relied on heavily by conservatives surrounding the Guangxu Emperor. In turn, he argued that an accurate reading of authentic Confucian texts provided unmistakable support from the Master himself (who Kang claimed had written, rather than edited, the texts in question) for a host of reforms. These included a curtailing of imperial power, the introduction of elections, and the abolition of the family in favor of voluntary cohabitation arrangements that could be altered annually. Kang's efforts to appropriate and recast the past earned him widespread denunciation and an imperial ban (later briefly lifted) on much of his writing. Among his critics was the conservative scholar Ye Dehui, whose book on Song publication practices is relied on elsewhere in this study. "K'ang Yuwei's face," wrote Ye, "is Confucian . . . but his heart is barbarian." Quoted in Hsü, *Rise of Modern China*, 456.

85. See Kuhn, "Taiping Rebellion," 264.

86. See Teng Ssu-yü, "Chinese Influence on the Western Examination System," 267, which traces the impact of the Chinese method for selecting imperial officials on the British civil service system.

87. Centuries before the Sui—during the third century B.C.—would-be Confucian advisors were already being attacked for their emphasis on knowledge of the past. "They [the Confucianists], neither study affairs pertaining to the law and government nor observe the realities of vice and wickedness but all exalt the reputed glories of remote antiquity and the achievements of Ancient Kings." Han Fei Tzu, "On the Dominant Systems

of Learning," quoted in De Bary et al., trans., *Sources of Chinese Tradition*, 1: 142.

88. Thomas Lee, *Government Education*.

89. Bodde and Morris, *Law in Imperial China*.

90. Ibid., 63. In reaching this estimate, Bodde and Morris rely on the *Duli cunyi*, in which Xue Yunsheng lays out in meticulous detail the origins and subsequent history of revision for the various provisions of the Qing code.

91. The use of substatutes is discussed in ibid., 63–68. Evocation of the past was, of course, not the only way in which the Chinese state used its legal system to evidence its majesty. Centuries before Foucault wrote *Discipline and Punish*, the Chinese state displayed a keen appreciation of the fact that symbolic infliction of punishment might have an even greater impact than its actual counterpart. At least from the Han dynasty (206 B.C.–A.D. 220) onward (and some would suggest long before the formation of imperial China in 221 B.C.), the death penalty was divided so that execution of all but the most egregious offenders was to be delayed until "after the autumn assizes." Although this procedure may have had its genesis in the effort to align human and natural affairs by deferring executions until the time of greatest death in the natural world, the Chinese soon took to using it simultaneously to display the state's awesome power and its great benevolence. Individuals were often sentenced to death "after the assizes" (*jianhou*), which typically entailed waiting two years, only to be spared by a state wishing to appear magnanimous once the requisite time had elapsed.

A comparable appreciation of the value of symbolic punishment is also evident in the Qing code directive that officials only inflict a fraction of the blows with a bamboo cane (either heavy or light) to which criminals might be sentenced. Again, it was presumed that those so sentenced would both understand the severity of the punishment due them and appreciate the state's decision to accord them leniency.

As these examples and much of this chapter illustrates, many of the ideological and psychological devices that Jürgen Habermas suggests (in *Legitimation Crisis*) result from the efforts of modern states to legitimate themselves appear to have had clear antecedents in imperial China.

92. One such compilation was the *Xing'an huilan*, comprising cases recorded by the Board of Punishments, compiled on an unofficial basis by officials of the board for the benefit of magistrates.

93. Much has been made of what Ch'ü T'ung-tsü three decades ago termed the "Confucianization" of the law, by which he meant the absorption during the Han dynasty of Confucian values into the law. This process led, for example, to the law's mandating far harsher penalties when juniors struck their seniors than vice versa. Work remains to be done, however,

on what might be termed the "legalization" of the Confucians—by which I mean the impact that use of the law had on the thinking of Confucian-oriented scholar-officials, for whom formal legality was said to be an inferior social norm. It is hard to imagine that such officials could have used the law as extensively and adroitly as many in fact did without its ways of looking at the world influencing them, consciously or otherwise. For a brief further discussion of this, see Alford, "Law, Law, What Law?" Extremely interesting work on related concerns is being done by Karen Turner (focusing on notions of legality in early China) and by Mary Buck and Adam Alfert (each of whom is exploring the interaction between formal legality and Confucian ideals in magisterial decision making).

94. Pulleyblank, "Chinese Historical Criticism," 135.

95. Watson, *Ssu-ma Ch'ien*; Pulleyblank, "Historiographical Tradition," 143, 152–53.

96. Bodde, *China's First Unifier*. In a fascinating example of the vitality of the past for contemporary discourse, articles published about the Qin dynasty in the PRC in the wake of the June 1989 suppression of the pro-democracy movement attempt to play down the number of persons executed 2,200 years ago and suggest that they were unworthy individuals. See, e.g., Wang Ningjun, "Tale of Qin Scholars Being Buried Alive Is Challenged," *China Daily*, Aug. 1, 1989, 5.

97. Goodrich, *Literacy Inquisition*.

98. Sima Qian, *Shi ji*, quoted in De Bary et al., trans., *Sources of Chinese Tradition*.

99. Goodrich, *Literary Inquisition*.

100. Metzger, "Foreword," xiv. This same mentality may be evident in a principal PRC translation of U.S. Supreme Court cases, which essentially excludes all dissenting opinions on the grounds that they represent incorrect views and so do not warrant study.

101. Attempts to stretch that collective memory included not only the denunciation of texts as unauthentic (as Kang Youwei did) but also the "discovery" of what were said to be long-lost versions of classics. Indeed, by the late Qing, there were so many key texts being "rediscovered" that Liang Qichao (who commenced his public career as an ally of Kang's) later deplored what he saw as efforts retroactively to add passages to ancient texts and then claim their discovery. Liang Qichao, *Yinbingshe heji*.

102. The evaluation of magistrates was based, in part, on the extent to which they maintained "harmony" within their districts, giving them a strong incentive to discourage litigation and other actions that would be seen as disharmonious by their superiors. See Bodde and Morris, *Law in Imperial China*.

103. Waley, trans., *Analects of Confucius*, bk. 7, ch. 1.

104. Schwartz, *World of Thought in Ancient China*.
105. Owen, *Remembrances*, 18.
106. As Zhu Xi (1130–1200), the progenitor of Neo-Confucianism, observed "at that time [i.e., when Confucius lived], the work of creation was fairly complete; the Master [i.e., Confucius] therefore made a Great Synthesis [*dacheng*] of the various Sages and struck a Mean. Although this was 'transmission,' his merit was twice that of 'making.' One must understand this also" (quoted in Murck, *Artists and Traditions*, xii). See also Ju-hsi Chou, "Through the Disciples' Eyes," 11–22.
107. Owen, *Remembrances*, 22.
108. Ibid., 14–15. See also Alford, "Inscrutable Occidental."
109. Owen, *Remembrances*, 15.
110. Eliot, *Notes Toward a Definition of Culture*, 118.
111. Levenson, *Confucian China*, xvii.
112. Lynn, "Alternative Routes to Self-Realization," 322.
113. Quoted in ibid., 317.
114. Quoted in Chaves, "Panoply of Images," 357.
115. Ibid., 343.
116. Pulleyblank, "Historiographic Tradition," 150.
117. Cahill, *Compelling Image*, 57.
118. Mote, "The Arts and the 'Theorizing Mode' of Chinese Civilization," 7.
119. Bush, *Chinese Literati on Painting*, 50–66.
120. Quoted in Levenson, *Confucian China*, 1: 21.
121. Murck, *Artists and Traditions*.
122. Bush, *Chinese Literati on Painting*.
123. Cahill, "Orthodox Movement," 180.
124. Quoted in Cahill, *Compelling Image*, 57.
125. See Ho, *Eight Dynasties of Chinese Painting*.
126. Quoted in Cahill, *Compelling Image*, 155.
127. Murck, *Artists and Traditions*, xi.
128. Wen Fong, "Problem of Forgeries," 100.
129. Ibid., 100.
130. Ibid.
131. Wen Fong, "Problem of Forgeries," 100. These suggestions, of course, indicate that some were concerned about unauthorized copying.
132. Quoted in Lin Shuen-fu, "Chiang K'uei's Treatises," 307.

Three. Learning the Law at Gunpoint

1. See Richard Smith, *China's Cultural Heritage*.
2. Hao and Wang, "Changing Chinese Views," 156–72.

3. Edwards, "Ch'ing Legal Jurisdiction," 222.
4. Edwards, "Canton System."
5. Edwards, "Ch'ing Legal Jurisdiction," 223.
6. The *hong* are described in Fairbank, *Trade and Diplomacy*.
7. In so doing, the Chinese sought to have the "barbarians" structure their activities along Chinese lines. As was the case with guilds and a range of other groups, the Chinese expected group leaders to be responsible for the behavior of members.
8. Fairbank and Teng, eds., *China's Response to the West*, 19–21.
9. Quoted in Edwards, "Canton System," 245.
10. The *Lady Hughes*, a British merchant ship, had the misfortune of firing a salute that resulted in the death of a Chinese seaman. At first the British captain refused to surrender a gunner to the Chinese side, arguing that it was difficult to ascertain who was responsible for the errant volley, and that, in any event, British courts would see that justice was done. Relenting under pressure, the British were shocked when the Chinese executed the sailor by strangulation. The Chinese believed that this demonstrated leniency, inasmuch as it enabled the sailor to die with his body intact, in keeping with Confucian mores to the effect that one should leave this world without damaging the body one's parents had given one. The British, who would have preferred a quicker—and to their minds more humane—means of execution, instead took this as a sign of Chinese barbarism, and they refused thereafter to allow their subjects to be tried by Chinese courts. The record of the *Lady Hughes* case has been translated by Dr. Fu-mei Chen and others affiliated with the Harvard East Asian Legal Studies program. It is reprinted in Alford, "Role of Law in Chinese Society."
11. Chang Hsin-pao, *Commissioner Lin*, 1–15.
12. Spence, "Opium Smoking," 143–73.
13. Hao Yen-p'ing, *Commercial Revolution*, 121.
14. Chang Hsin-pao, *Commissioner Lin*, 95, 39–46.
15. Cohen and Chiu, *People's China and International Law*, 14.
16. The letter to Queen Victoria is translated in Fairbank and Teng, eds., *China's Response to the West*, 24–27.
17. By virtue of enjoying most-favored-nation status with Qing China, a foreign Treaty Power was entitled to whatever privileges China granted to any other foreign power. Key treaties establishing these privileges are reprinted in Mayers, ed., *Treaties*.
18. Article 12 of the Treaty of Peace, Amity and Commerce Between the United States of America and the Chinese Empire signed at Wangxia on July 3, 1844, reprinted in Mayers, ed., *Treaties*, 76.
19. See Fishel, *End of Extraterritoriality*; Kotenev, *Shanghai and Its Mixed Court*; Hsia Ching-lin, *Status of Shanghai*.

20. Although so-called *songgun* (litigation tricksters) and others provided informed advice to persons involved in Chinese legal processes (see Alford, "Of Arsenic and Old Laws," 1180), it is generally agreed that prior to Wu Tingfang's appearance in the Shanghai Mixed Court in 1877, "legal representation of the Chinese parties had been deemed unnecessary" (Ch'en, *China and the West*, 231). Indeed, even as late as 1926, there were fewer than 250 Chinese lawyers available to Shanghai's population of over three million.

21. Lobingier, "American Courts in China," 24.

22. Relevant U.S. laws are described in "Jurisprudence and Jurisdiction," 503–5, 508–11.

23. "Those who have to administer [these] . . . laws are destitute of all legal requirements," J. W. Davis, the American commissioner to China at midcentury, reported to the U.S. Senate (Senate Executive Document 72, 31st Cong., lst sess. [Sept. 1850], 8–19, reprinted in Fishel, *End of Extraterritoriality*, 13).

24. Act Creating the United States Court for China and Limiting Jurisdiction of Consular Courts in China, 34 U.S. Stats at L., ch. 74 (1906).

25. Although the Exclusion Act of 1882 was aimed at Chinese "laborers," the imprecise definitions contained in the legislation served as a deterrent to Chinese thinking of coming to the United States for a range of different purposes. See Hunt, *Making of a Special Relationship*, 85–96.

26. Chinese images of Western justice are addressed in Cohen and Chiu, *People's China and International Law*, 10.

27. The most noteworthy exception seems to have been the abortive proposal of Hong Ren'gan, one of the leaders of the Taiping revolutionary movement of the mid nineteenth century, that a patent system be adopted. See Zheng Chengsi, *Chinese Intellectual Property*, 51–52.

28. Gardella, "Boom Years of the Fukien Tea Trade," 69–70.

29. See, e.g., Morse, *International Relations*, 3: 378.

30. Hao, *Commercial Revolution*, 263. See also Allen and Donnithorne, *Western Enterprise*.

31. Jernigan, *China in Law*, 270.

32. Hao, *Commercial Revolution*, 265.

33. Machlup, "Patents." The conventions are discussed in Machlup and Penrose, "Patent Controversy," 1; Ricketson, *Berne Convention*.

34. Morse, *International Relations*, 3: 377–78.

35. It remains difficult to render Western trademarks in Chinese, particularly in view of differences in oral renderings that speakers of different dialects give the same characters. Thus, at times, a trademark that may sound felicitous in one dialect may contain a hidden (and not necessarily pleasant) meaning in another.

36. Crow, *400 Million Customers*, 15–31.

37. See, e.g., Gutzlaff, *Sketch of Chinese History*, 34–53; Doolittle, *Social Life*, 335–41; MacGowan, *Sidelights on Chinese Life*, 272–96.

38. Jones, *The Great Qing Code*.

39. Guojia dang'anju Ming-Qing dang'an guan, comp., *Wuxu bianfa dang'an shiliao*, 453–54.

40. Yuan, "Zhongguo jindai banquan de yanbian shiqi," 46–47.

41. Cochran, *Big Business in China*; Hamilton and Lai, "Jinshi zhongguo shangbiao."

42. Morse, *International Relations*, 3: passim.

43. Heuser, "Chinese Trademark Law of 1904," 187–88.

44. Morse, *International Relations*, 3: 157–87.

45. Quoted in Heuser, "Chinese Trademark Law of 1904," 183.

46. Morse, *International Relations*, 3: 191. Although the *likin* theoretically applied only to Chinese goods, the requirement that foreign goods be covered by a "transit pass" equal to half the duty charged Chinese and the uneven quality of administration in general led the treaty powers to see this tax as impeding their trade in China.

47. The problems engendered by the absence of a uniform national currency are described in King, *Money and Monetary Policy in China*, 113.

48. Morse, *International Relations*, 3: 360–80.

49. The 1903 treaty between the United States and China, reprinted in MacMurray, ed., *Treaties and Agreements*, Arts. 12 and 15.

50. See Feuerwerker, *China's Early Industrialization*.

51. This was also the case in contemporaneous discussions between the Chinese and other foreign powers, such as Germany, that did not culminate in comprehensive commercial agreements.

52. The Mackay Treaty, reprinted in Allman, *Protection of Trademarks*, Art. 7.

53. "Lun shangbiao zhuce buying yanqi," 143.

54. The 1903 treaty between the United States and China, reprinted in MacMurray, ed., *Treaties and Agreements*, Art. 9. That the concern with reciprocity may have been symbolic is suggested by the fact that at the time in question, owing to the Exclusion Act of 1882 and other legislation directed against Chinese immigrants, there were scarcely 100,000 Chinese in the United States, few of whom presumably had the time to worry about the niceties of securing trademark protection.

55. The Mackay Treaty, reprinted in Allman, *Protection of Trademarks*, Art. 7.

56. Clark, *Analytic Summaries*.

57. The 1903 treaty between the United States and China, reprinted in MacMurray, ed., *Treaties and Agreements*, Art. 9.

58. Ibid., Art. 10.

59. Ibid., Art. 11. The most commonly used Chinese words for copyright, *banquan* and *zhuzuoquan*, appear not to have been used in official public documents in China prior to this time. To be sure, individual Chinese authors—including, most notably Yan Fu, the famous translator of Locke, Hobbes, Montesquieu, and other key figures in Western philosphy—had made brief mention of copyright shortly before. Xie and Guo, "Sounds of History's Footsteps," 20.

60. The 1903 treaty between the United States and China, reprinted in MacMurray, ed., *Treaties and Agreements*, Art. 11.

61. Heuser, "Chinese Trademark Law of 1904," 192.

62. Joseph K. H. Cheng, "Chinese Law in Transition," 111.

63. "Gaiding shangbiao tiaoli" (1909), Art. 2.

64. Joseph K. H. Cheng, "Chinese Law in Transition," 96.

65. Heuser, "Chinese Trademark Law of 1904," 200–201.

66. Trademark regulations, reprinted in *Foreign Relations of the United States*, Aug. 15, 1904, item no. 1681, Art. 1.

67. Ibid., Art. 27.

68. Ibid., Art. 8.

69. Ibid., Art. 2.

70. Order to the Ministry of Commerce, reprinted in *Dongfang zazhi*, Guangxu 30th year, 2d month, 25th day (1905).

71. Conger, "Letter to Secretary of State John Hay, Oct. 13, 1904."

72. Heuser, "Chinese Trademark Law of 1904," 203.

73. "Inclosure to Letter of U.S. Minister Conger to Secretary of State Hay, Dec. 8, 1904."

74. *North China Herald*, Sept. 16, 1904.

75. Ministry of Commerce memorial quoted in Heuser, "Chinese Trademark Law of 1904," 204–5.

76. Coolidge, "Letter to Secretary of State John Hay, Jan. 7, 1905."

77. Allman, *Protection of Trademarks*, 1–13.

78. Ibid.; Willoughby, *Foreign Rights*, 902–18.

79. Wang Jiafu and Xia Shuhua suggest no more than 360 patents were issued (*Zhuanlifa jianlun*, 66–68), while Zheng Chengsi puts the number at 692 (*Chinese Intellectual Property*, 51). This was at a time when U.S. patent authorities "faced a continuously increasing flood of applications," yielding far more patents annually than China granted over this entire period (Noble, *America by Design*, 102).

80. These laws may be found in Ke, *Zhongguo baoxue shi*, 334–79.

81. Allman, *Protection of Trademarks*, 178–79.

82. Ibid., 107. The practice of using "stamps . . . as corroboration of ownership" dates from this period (Zheng Chengsi, *Chinese Intellectual Property*, 87).

83. Allman, *Protection of Trademarks*, 107.

84. Fishel, *End of Extraterritoriality*, 26–50.

85. See, e.g., the correspondence of U.S. minister to China W. W. Rockhill with the German minister, A. V. Mumm, Aug. 22, 1905, reprinted in *Foreign Relations of the United States* (1906), 232.

86. See the notes between the United States and Belgium, Denmark, France, Germany, Great Britain, Italy, Japan, the Netherlands, Russia, and Sweden, reprinted in MacMurray, ed., *Treaties and Agreements*, 1: 542, 641, 538, 544, 502, 546, 735, 540, and 2: 1002.

87. Willoughby, *Foreign Rights*, 902–18.

88. May and Fairbank, eds., *America's China Trade*, 151–203.

89. The *baihua* movement is discussed in Fairbank, *Great Chinese Revolution*, 189–91.

90. *Foreign Relations of the United States* (1907), pt. 1, 262.

91. Allman, *Trademark Protection*, 96.

92. Zhang Jinglu, *Zhongguo xiandai chuban shiliao*, 334; Dregé, *Commercial Press*, 58.

93. Zhang Jinglu, *Zhongguo xiandai chuban shiliao*, 335.

94. Willoughby, *Foreign Rights*, 905. Believing efforts to obtain redress through the Chinese futile, by the 1920's the British authorities did not even bother to contact Chinese officials.

95. "Trade-marks in China," *North China Daily News*, Aug. 20, 1907.

96. Willoughby, *Foreign Rights*, 912–18.

97. Zhang Jinglu, *Zhongguo xiandai chuban shiliao*, passim.

98. Link, *Mandarin Ducks*, 150.

99. Ibid., 51.

100. Ibid., 53.

101. Quoted in Heuser, "Chinese Trademark Law of 1904," 50.

102. Conger, "Letter to Secretary of State John Hay, Oct. 13, 1904."

103. Shen Jiaben (1840–1913) was a paramount figure in late Qing law reform. Following a distinguished career on the Board of Punishments, in the course of which he served as its vice president and conducted groundbreaking research on Chinese legal history, Shen was named imperial commissioner for law reform in 1902 (along with Wu Tingfang). In that capacity, Shen proposed sweeping changes in such fundamental notions as the differentiation of punishments according to the relative rank of the perpetrator and victim. Although few of the proposals generated under his direction were enacted, he is rightly considered a major figure in Chinese legal history.

104. Wu Tingfang (1842–1922), who was born in Singapore and educated in the West, became Hong Kong's first Chinese barrister in 1877. After successfully practicing in Hong Kong, he joined the staff of Viceroy Li Hongzhang in 1882, through which he was able during the next decade and

a half to play an important role in a range of commercial, legal, diplomatic, and other activities. He was made China's ambassador to the United States in 1896 and later was selected as an imperial commissioner for law reform along with Shen Jiaben.

105. Meijer, *Introduction of Modern Criminal Law in China*; Joseph K. H. Cheng, "Chinese Law in Transition."

106. *Dongfang zazhi*, Guangxu 32d year, 3d month, 25th day (1907).

107. Ibid., Guangxu 31st year, 2d month (1906).

108. Jiangnan Bureau of Commerce, report, in ibid., Guangxu 30th year, 9th month, 25th day (1905).

109. Ibid., "Reasons for Drafting the Trial Provisions of Trademark Registration."

110. The 1903 treaty between the United States and China, reprinted in MacMurray, ed., *Treaties and Agreements*, Art. 9.

111. Letter of Prince Qing to Minister Rockhill of June 1, 1907, reprinted in *Foreign Relations of the United States* (1907), item no. 284.

112. Link, *Mandarin Ducks*, 161–70.

113. Bai, *Outline History*, 491.

114. McKee, *Chinese Exclusion*.

115. Chow, *May Fourth Movement*, 117–70.

116. Arnold, *China*, 343–47.

117. In Shen's words, "Being surrounded by the powers and compelled by the situations of international interaction, it is extremely difficult for China to stick to the old way" (quoted in Cheng, "Chinese Law in Transition," 209).

118. Bai, *Outline History*, 447–48, 480–83; Meijer, *Introduction of Modern Criminal Law in China*.

119. Berman, *Words Like Colored Glass*, 100–121.

120. Joseph K. H. Cheng, "Chinese Law in Transition," 196–258.

121. Ibid., 196–258.

122. Madeline Zelin's recent work suggests that at least in the salt industry in Sichuan during this period, some chambers of commerce acted with dispatch and skill to resolve disputes among Chinese merchants. Zelin, "Merchant Dispute Mediation."

123. Fairbank, *Great Chinese Revolution*, 156.

124. Levenson, *Confucian China*, 1–21. As had the Qing, Yuan Shikai instituted restrictive press laws during his brief interlude as China's ruler.

125. Thus, the Chinese resisted foreign pressure in 1913 and 1920 to join the Berne Convention, contending that adherence would only hurt China's economy and educational system. See Zheng Chengsi, *Chinese Intellectual Property*, 88.

126. Meijer, *Introduction of Modern Criminal Law in China*.

127. Quoted in Allman, *Protection of Trademarks*, 179.

128. Eastman, *Abortive Revolution*.

129. Sheridan, *China in Disintegration*.

130. Tang, *America's Failure in China*, 48–49.

131. Sun's vision is described in his *San Min Chu I* (The Three People's Principles). The Guomintang's early years in government are the subject of Eastman, *Abortive Revolution*.

132. Ch'en, *China and the West*, 231 and 728–29; Alford and Shen, " 'Law Is My Idol.' "

133. A translation of the Copyright Law and its detailed regulations was published in 4 *China Law Review* 4, no. 2 (1929).

134. Ibid. This law was amended in 1944, in response to American objections, to place Chinese and foreigners on an equal footing.

135. Ibid., Art. 22.

136. The full Publication Law is reprinted in Ke, *Zhongguo baoxue shi*, 334.

137. Ting, *Government Control*, 126–59.

138. Reprinted in Ke, *Zhongguo baoxue shi*, Art. 19.

139. Ibid., Art. 15.

140. Ibid. See also Ting, *Government Control*.

141. The 1930 Trademark Law, Art. 2.

142. These are discussed in National Foreign Trade Council, Subcommittee on Intellectual Property "Protection of Industrial and Intellectual Property in China," 6.

143. The 1949 Patent Law, Arts. 4 and 14.

144. Hall, "Pirating of American Books," 1914.

145. Kaser, *Book Pirating*, 19.

146. Shen Ren'gan and Zhong Yingke, *Banquanfa*, 101.

147. He Defen, *Zhuzuoquanfa lunwen ji*.

148. Beale and Pelham, *Trade and Economic Conditions*, 48–49.

149. National Foreign Trade Council, Subcommittee on Intellectual Property "Protection of Industrial and Intellectual Property in China," 6.

150. Quoted in Eastman, *Abortive Revolution*, 11.

151. The paucity of legally trained individuals is discussed in Qian, *Government and Politics*, 249.

152. Ch'en, *China and the West*, 328.

153. Ibid., 254.

154. Qian, *Government and Politics*. Kathryn Bernhardt in her research on divorce in early Republican China suggests that formal legal processes may not have been as daunting as is posited here. See Bernhardt, "Women and the Law."

155. Fairbank, *Great Chinese Revolution*, 223. The Control Yuan was one

of the five branches of government envisioned by Sun Yatsen. It was intended, broadly speaking, like the imperial-era censorate, to oversee officialdom so as to deter both misfeasance and malfeasance.

156. Quoted in Edwards, Henkin, and Nathan, eds. *Human Rights in Contemporary China*, 90.

Four. Squaring Circles

1. See, e.g., Mao, "On the Tactics of Fighting," 153–78.
2. See, e.g., Zhu Xisen, *Shangbiao yu shangbiao fa*, 20–31.
3. "Zhongguo renmin zhengzhi xieshang huiyi de gongtong gangling."
4. Wang Jiafu and Xia Shuhua, *Zhuanlifa*, 68–69.
5. Soviet intellectual property law of the relevant period is discussed in Levitsky, *Copyright, Defamation, and Privacy*; Swanson, *Scientific Discoveries*; Hazard, *Communists and Their Laws*.
6. Marx, *Early Writings*, 157.
7. Alford, "Inscrutable Occidental," 975.
8. "Baozhang famingquan." The PRC has routinely published important laws and regulations initially in "provisional" (*zanxing*) or "trial" (*shixing*) form. This device enables the PRC to issue rules of considerable generality, to test out particular formulations, and, in Marxist terms, to adapt law and, for that matter, other elements of the superstructure to the changing economic base. As will be discussed below, the flexibility that marks this and other features of the legal system are not attained without a considerable cost.
9. Shen Yuanyuan, *Faming yu faxian quan*, 4; Hsia Tao-tai, "China's New Patent Law," 19.
10. Kay, "Patent Law," 343–44.
11. The PRC's initial Constitution, promulgated in 1954, explicitly recognized private property. 1954 Xianfa, Arts. 5, 8–12, 14.
12. Cheng Kaiyuan, "Yibu juyou zhongguo tese," 42.
13. "Zhengwuyuan guanyu jiangli youguan shengchang de faming, jishu gaijin ji helihua jianyi de jueding." Discussed in Wang Jiafu and Xia Shuhua, *Zhuanlifa*, 70–72.
14. Persons holding Guomindang trademarks were given six months to turn in their old trademark certificates and apply for registration under the PRC's rules. Interestingly, prior to assuming power, the Chinese Communists had issued trademarks in areas under their control. See Liu Li, "On the Legal System of China Governing Trademarks."
15. Sidel, "Copyright, Trademark and Patent," 270.
16. Shen Ren'gan and Zhong Yingke, *Banquanfa*, 260–61.
17. Ibid.

18. Ibid.

19. "Guanyu guoying chuban bianji jigou ji gongzuo zhidu de guiding." For more on contract in a PRC setting, see Lucie Cheng and Arthur Rosett, "Contract with a Chinese Face"; Potter, *Economic Contract Law*. Other contemporaneous legal measures included the "Guanli shukan chubanye yinshuaye faxingye zanxing tiaoli" and "Guanyu jiuzheng renyi fanyintushu xianxiang de guiding." Shen Ren'gan and Zhong Yingke, *Banquanfa*, 106–8.

20. Shen Ren'gan and Zhong Yingke, *Banquanfa*, 262.

21. Ibid. These early efforts are also discussed in Xie Xiang and Guo Jiakuan, "Sounds of History's Footsteps," 20.

22. Zheng Chengsi, "Future Chinese Copyright System," 144–45.

23. Richman, *Industrial Society*, 384.

24. Sidel, "Copyright, Trademark and Patent," 271.

25. Tang Zongshun, "Protection of Intellectual Property," 4.

26. "Guanyu guoying chuban bianji jigou ji gongzuo zhidu de guiding." Addressed in Zheng Chengsi, "Future Chinese Copyright System," 148.

27. Alford and Birenbaum, "Ventures in the China Trade," 101–2.

28. The "Anti-Rightist Movement" (1957) was designed to root out intellectuals and others who had been too critical of the Communist party during the preceding "Hundred Flowers Movement." The "Great Leap Forward" (1958–60) sought to accelerate the pace of socialist economic development, leading, *inter alia,* to the transfer of urban intellectuals and others at least temporarily to the countryside. See further MacFarquhar, *Origins,* passim; Goldman, *Literary Dissent in Communist China*, 240.

29. Baum and Teiwes, *Ssu-ch'ing*.

30. Both the 1954 Constitution, which was then operative, and the 1982 Constitution describe the State Council as the executive organ of the highest state authority—"the highest administrative organ of state."

31. "Faming jiangli tiaoli"; "Jishu gaijin jiangli tiaoli."

32. "Faming jiangli tiaoli," Art. 23.

33. Quoted in Hsia Tao-tai, "China's New Patent Law," 20.

34. Richman, *Industrial Society*, 319.

35. *Guangming ribao* (Enlightenment Daily) is the leading official paper for intellectuals and is devoted in large measure to matters of science, education, and culture.

36. Quoted in Gale, "Concept of Intellectual Property," 350.

37. "Shangbiao guanli tiaoli."

38. Ibid., Art. 1.

39. "1963 Shangbiao guiding," Art. 2.

40. Goldman, *Literary Dissent*, 241.

41. Shen Ren'gan and Zhong Yingke, *Banquanfa*, 47.

42. The Cultural Revolution (1966–76) tore apart Chinese political, eco-

nomic, and social life. The official history of it is recounted in "On Questions of Party History: Resolution on Certain Questions in the History of Our Party Since the Founding of the People's Republic of China" (issued June 27, 1981, at the Sixth Plenary Session of the 11th Central Committee of the Chinese Communist Party). Chinese text in *Renmin ribao*, July 1, 1981. English translation in *Beijing Review* 24, no. 27 (July 6, 1981): 10, 20–26. For more detached accounts, see MacFarquhar, *Origins*; Thurston, *Enemies of the People*.

43. Leys, *Chinese Shadows*, 132.

44. In fact, these consisted of five Beijing operas, two ballet-dramas, and one symphonic work.

45. See, e.g., *Fan Peng, Luo hei xian*, a Cantonese Red Guard broadsheet.

46. Lubman, "Emerging Functions," 235.

47. Wang Jiafu and Xia Shuhua, *Zhuanlifa*.

48. Quoted in Gale, "Concept of Intellectual Property," 351.

49. Zheng Chengsi, "Trade Marks in China," 278.

50. Sidel, "Copyright, Trademark and Patent."

51. Leys, *Chinese Shadows*, 132, 135–36.

52. Author's interviews, conducted in Beijing, Chongqing, Shanghai, Guangzhou, and Hong Kong, June–Dec. 1986 and June–Aug. 1987, and in Los Angeles, Apr.–June 1986, Jan.–June 1987, and Sept. 1987–Mar. 1988.

53. Quoted in Zheng Chengsi, "Future Chinese Copyright System," 152. While in China in the 1970's, I visited "art factories" in which artists collaborated on paintings.

54. Zhou Enlai (1899–1976) served as premier of the PRC from its foundation in 1949 until his death in 1976 and was also foreign minister from 1949 until 1958. Deng Xiaoping (b. 1904) has been the principal leader of the PRC since 1977, although he has long since resigned from formal positions. Hua Guofeng (b. 1920), who was designated by Mao Zedong as his successor, was simultaneously premier of the PRC, chairman of the Communist party's Central Committee, chairman of the party's Military Affairs Committee, and editor of Mao's works in the years immediately following Mao's death. He proved unable to sustain leadership in his own name, however, and by 1980 had relinquished the aforementioned posts. For more on the Four Modernizations generally, see Richard Baum, *China's Four Modernizations*. China's post-Mao transformations are portrayed in Harding, *China's Second Revolution*.

55. Kay, "Patent Law," 351.

56. In the PRC, "intellectuals" include those who have graduated from high school, as well as those who have received higher education.

57. The situation of intellectuals in post–Cultural Revolution China is artfully portrayed in Link, *Evening Chats*, passim.

58. For a thoughtful discussion of these efforts at reconstruction, see Lubman, "Emerging Functions."

59. Kay, "Patent Law," 351.

60. These are translated in *Foreign Broadcast Information Service* CHI-80-0005 (Jan. 7, 1980), L-5.

61. The CCPIT was one of the few Chinese organizations to remain relatively unchanged in format during the Cultural Revolution years.

62. Zheng Chengsi, "Trade Marks in China."

63. Thus, e.g., the PRC's first comprehensive criminal code, promulgated in 1979, provides criminal penalties for persons fraudulently passing off goods.

64. "Guanyu zhixing xinwen chuban gaofei ji butie banfa de tongzhi." This notice is discussed briefly by Shen Ren'gan and Zhong Yingke, *Banquanfa*.

65. These regulations are briefly treated in Zhao Xiuwen, *Zhuzuoquan*, 50–51.

66. Section 2435 of the 1974 Trade Act establishes the criteria that must be met before the "President may authorize the entry into force of bilateral commercial agreements providing nondiscriminatory treatment to the products of countries heretofore denied such treatment." In the event that the foreign nation involved is not a party to the major international intellectual property conventions, Section 2435 requires that the agreement "provide rights for United States nationals with respect to patents and trademarks . . . [and] copyrights in such country not less than the rights" specified in such conventions." 19 U.S.C. 2435.

67. Article VI of the U.S.–PRC Trade Agreement of 1979. The United States was willing to accept such broad language from a nation then lacking patent and copyright laws and with relatively little in the way of trademark protection because of its eagerness to "normalize" relations with the PRC and its attempts to generate support in the American business community for its China policy by suggesting a more favorable climate for doing business than existed. In this and a range of comparable steps designed to enlist support for normalization, however, the Carter administration raised undue expectations on the part of the business community, the American public more broadly, and the Chinese themselves as to the suitability of Chinese conditions for international business.

68. The two sides have disagreed as to whether Article VI of the 1979 trade agreement actually committed the PRC to protect American intellectual property or merely to aspire toward such protection. For years, PRC commentators dismissed the notion that Article VI created an obligation to provide any specific protection. Interestingly, with the promulgation of the PRC's Copyright Law in 1990, some Chinese commentators argued that

in fact Article VI constitutes a bilateral copyright agreement for purposes of that law, thereby enabling citizens of one nation to secure rights in the other, regardless of where works are first published. See "Copyright Law Is Put into Effect," *China Daily*, June 1, 1991, 1; Kay, "PRC: Regulations." American negotiating strategy regarding intellectual property rights in China is discussed further both in this chapter and in chapter 6.

69. Wang Jaifu and Xia Shuhua, *Zhuanlifa*, 73–74. The State Science and Technology Commission is dealt with extensively in Saich, *China's Science Policy*; Simon and Goldman, *Science and Technology*.

70. Sidel, "Copyright, Trademark and Patent," 273.

71. "Making the Right Moves," *China Trade Reports* 25 (July 1987): 5–7.

72. See, e.g., Wang Jiafu and Xia Shuhua, *Zhuanlifa*; Cheng Kaiyuan, "Yibu juyou zhongguo tese." Also author's interviews, Beijing, 1986.

73. Kay, "Patent Law," 357. Duan Ruilin, *Zhuanlifa*, 48–50.

74. Duan Ruilin, *Zhuanlifa*, 48–50. The government perceived this as also having the ancillary benefit of enabling it to reduce its direct grants to many research centers. Saich, *China's Science Policy*, 39–42.

75. Zhao Zelu, "Zhuanli quan."

76. Michael Parks, "China Adopts Controversial Patent Law," *Los Angeles Times*, Mar. 13, 1984.

77. Zhang Youyu was a professor of law at Beijing University and the first head of the All-China Bar Association (Quanguo lüshi xiehui). Ren Jianxin is president of the Supreme People's Court and a major figure in the state and party security apparatus. Previously he held prominent positions at CCPIT, with particular responsibility for inducing foreigners to part with their technology.

78. Hsia Tao-tai, "China's New Patent Law," 23.

79. Xia Shuhua, *Zhuanlifa gaiyao*, 13–14.

80. Ibid.; Zhu Wenqing, "Shilun zhuanlifa de renwu," 1238–39. In their effort to legitimate patent law developments, Chinese officials now suggest that late Premier Zhou Enlai was interested in its establishment. See Wang Zhengfa, "Chinese Intellectual Property System," 22–23.

81. Wang Jiafu and Xia Shuhua, *Zhuanlifa*.

82. *Guangming ribao* and *Jingji ribao* (Economics Daily) quoted in Hsia Tao-tai, "China's New Patent Law," 25.

83. Wang Yujie, "Zhongguo tese de shehuizhuyi zhuanlifa," 20.

84. These concerns are addressed in Wang Jiafu, *Shilun zhuanlifa*, 27–32.

85. Author's interviews, Beijing, June 1986 and June–Aug. 1987, and Los Angeles, Feb. 1987. Concerns about foreign exploitation helped spur the passage in 1987 of a law on technology contracts that sought to bar restrictive clauses and called for the central review of sizable agreements.

86. Ibid.

87. Ibid.

88. Wang Jiafu, "Shilun zhuanlifa," 27–32; see also Fang, "Bocai ta guo zhi qiang," 10. Author's interviews, conducted in Beijing, June 1986 and June–Aug. 1987, and in Los Angeles, Feb. 1987.

89. Hsia Tao-tai, "China's New Patent Law," 23.

90. Ibid. Distracted by ongoing skirmishing between proponents and opponents of the proposed legislation, the drafting committee finally secretly left Beijing in order to conclude its work without interruption. With the promulgation of this law, China joined the WIPO, which administers the Paris Union and the Berne Convention. Chwang and Thurston, "Technology Takes Command," 145.

91. See, e.g., Cheng Kaiyuan, "Yibu juyou zhongguo tese"; Haeusser, "Industrial Property," 8.

92. Kay, "Patent Law," 361. A "utility model" is defined as "any new technical solution relating to the shape, the structure, or their combination, of a product . . . [fit] for practical use." "Zhonghua renmin gongheguo zhuanlifa shishi xize."

93. "Zhonghua renmin gongheguo zhuanlifa shishi xize," Rule 10.

94. See Walder, Communist Neo-Traditionalism, passim.

95. PRC officials, including Huang Kunyi, the founding director of the Patent Office, have tacitly admitted as much. See, e.g., Huang Kunyi, "Guanyu zhonghua renmin gongheguo zhuanlifa," 176–82. Patent statistics, which are treated later in this chapter, provide confirmation of this.

96. "Zhonghua renmin gongheguo zhuanlifa shishi xize," Rules 70–75. See also Huang Kunyi, "Guanyu zhonghua renmin gongheguo zhuanlifa," 180–81. The Inventions Regulations live on, having been revised by the State Council in mid 1993. See "Guowuyuan jueding xiugai sange jiangli tiaoli" (The State Council Revises Three Sets of Regulations Concerning Rewards)," Renmin ribao (haiwaiban) (People's Daily [Overseas Edition]), July 15, 1993, 1.

97. "Zhonghua renmin gongheguo zhuanlifa shishi xize," Arts. 51–52.

98. Alford, "When Is China Paraguay?" 124–27. Another example of this bifurcated treatment, although perhaps somewhat less favorable to foreigners, may be found in the distinctive rules governing domestic and foreign technology transfers.

99. See, e.g., Levin et al., "Appropriating the Returns from Industrial R & D."

100. Author's interviews, Beijing, Sept. 1993.

101. "Zhonghua renmin gongheguo zhuanlifa," Art. 63.

102. See, e.g., the "Zhuanli guanli jiguan chuli zhuanli jiufenbanfa" promulgated by the Patent Office in 1989, and the "Zuigao renmin fayuan guanyu kaizhan zhuanli shenpan gongzuo de jige wenti de tongzhi," "Zui-

gao renmin fayuan guanyu shenli zhuanli shenqing quan jiufen anjian ruogan wenti de tongzhi," and "Zuigao renmin fayuan guanyu shenli zhuanli jiufen anjian ruogan wenti de jiehui" promulgated by the Supreme People's Court in 1985, 1987, and 1993 respectively.

103. "Zhonghua renmin gongheguo shangbiaofa," Art. 1.

104. See Alford, "When Is China Paraguay?"

105. "Zhonghua renmin gongheguo shangbiaofa," Art. 6.

106. Ibid., Art. 31.

107. "Zhonghua renmin gongheguo shangbiaofa xize," Art. 4. The decision to regulate the manufacture of pharmaceuticals through trademark (and subsequent additional specialized rules) stood in contrast to the decision made in the 1984 Patent Law not to extend patent protection to such items. The idea that items such as pharmaceuticals are too important to merit patent protection was hardly unique to China. See U.S. Office of Technology Assessment, *Intellectual Property Rights*, 229–30. Unhappy with the exclusion of pharmaceuticals from patent coverage in the PRC, American firms persuaded Washington to make this a high priority in bilateral trade negotiations. In its 1992 Memorandum of Understanding on Intellectual Property with the United States, the PRC committed itself to ending this exclusion—which it soon thereafter did through a revision of its original patent law. The troubled negotiations leading to the Memorandum of Understanding and its implications for the further development of intellectual property law in China are discussed in chapter 6 below.

108. "Zhonghua renmin gongheguo shangbiaofa," Art. 8.

109. Ibid., Art. 18.

110. Remedies are provided for at ibid., Arts. 37–40 and in Art. 127 of the Criminal Law, which provides for up to three years' imprisonment for counterfeiting. By PRC standards, however, this is a relatively modest sanction. At present, there are more than 100 separate offenses under PRC law for which the death sentence may be imposed.

111. Tan Hongkai, "New Copyright Law Is a Welcome Start," *China Daily*, Oct. 12, 1990, 4.

112. Author's interviews, Beijing, Aug. 1990.

113. These included the 1980 "Guanyu shuji gaofei de zanxing guiding," the 1982 "Luyin, luxiang zhipin guanli zanxing guiding," the 1984 "Shuji gaofei shixing guiding," the 1985 "Meixu chubanwu gaofei shixing banfa," and the 1986 "Guanyu zhengdun luyin, luxiang zhipin shichang, zhizhi weizhang fanlu xiaoshou huodong de tongzhi," "Luyin, luxiang chubanwu chuban baohu zanxing tiaoli" and "Luyin, luxiang chuban gongzuo zanxing tiaoli." These are addressed in Zheng and Pendleton, *Copyright Law in China*, 20–35, which also discusses what it means to be a salaried author (54–60).

114. This is particularly evident in the 1986 "Guanyu zhengdun luyin,

luxiang zhipin shichang, zhizhi weizhang fanlu xiaoshou huodong de tong-zhi," issued jointly by the SAIC, Ministry of Commerce, and Ministry of Radio, Film, and Television.

115. "Zhonghua renmin gongheguo minfa tongze." For an insightful critique of the General Principles, see Jones, "Some Questions."

116. On the protection of copyright provided by the General Principles, see, e.g., "Copyright Protected Even Without a Law," *China Daily*, Mar. 7, 1988, 1; Zheng Chengsi, "Jianli qianmian banquanbaohu zhidu yitan" (A Discussion of the Establishment of a Comprehensive System of Copyright Protection), *Guangming ribao*, Nov. 12, 1986, 3; Guo Shoukang, "Common Rules of Civil Law." Ideas of property in the General Principles are treated in Edward Epstein, "Theoretical System of Property Rights," 177.

117. Xie Xiang and Guo Jiakuan, "Sounds of History's Footsteps," 4.

118. "Zhuzuoquanfa." The question of whether to call the law one on author's rights (*zhuzuoquan*) or on copyright (*banquan*) was a contentious one, with the former view prevailing because of the drafters' desire to emphasize their concern with protecting authors. See Shen Ren'gan, "'Copyright' and 'Author's Right,'" 55. Notwithstanding their Chinese language choice, PRC governmental sources continue in English to speak of copyright.

119. Quoted in "Copyright as Industrial Property," *China News Analysis*, no. 1445 (Oct. 15, 1991): 2–9. One important model for PRC drafters, among many, was that of Taiwan. See Wang Guang, "Taiwan yu dalu," 68.

120. Author's interviews, Beijing, July 1990.

121. Schloss, "China's Long-Awaited Copyright Law," 24, 26–27. See also Huang Zhuhai, "Guanyu wo guo zhuzuoquan lifa."

122. Legal persons (*faren*) are defined in the General Principles to include state-owned enterprises, collective enterprises, Sino-foreign joint ventures, organs of government and other institutions, and associations formed between the foregoing.

123. Zheng Chengsi and Michael Pendleton have argued that the "Chinese version [of the law] clearly only refers to copying by departments with judicial or quasi-judicial power and only when involved in procedures dealing with their judicial or quasi-judicial functions" (Zheng and Pendleton, "Response," 259). The relevant portion of Article 22:7 of the law provides no support for their assertion. It refers to *guojia jiguan*, which Zheng and Pendleton translate as "state organs," and *wei zhixing gongwu*, which they translate as "for the purpose of performing its official duties." Liu Gushu, the founding director of the China Patent Agency (H.K.) Ltd., contends that "state organs" means "legislative bodies, the administrative organs, and the judicial organs, etc." and that "official" business is that within the "function of the state" (Liu Gushu, "Questions of World-wide Interest," 21–

23). Although closer to the mark than Zheng and Pendleton, Liu's words exemplify part of the problem described above of substituting personal assurances for clear standards and ready access to neutral dispute resolution which might provide predictability. At no point do the law, the law's implementing regulations, or any other official materials published in conjunction with the law meaningfully limit the broad sweep of its provisions on fair use.

124. Liu Gushu, "Questions of World-wide Interest"; author's interviews, Beijing, Aug. 1990. In recent years, there have been exceptions to this uniform schedule.

125. "Zhonghua renmin gongheguo zhuzuoquan fa," Art 4.

126. Author's interviews, Beijing, Aug. 1990. Efforts were made by more ideologically orthodox officials to delay promulgating the Copyright Law pending completion of the Publications Law.

127. Tan Hongkai, "New Copyright Law is a Welcome Start," *China Daily*, Oct. 12, 1990, 4. The Four Cardinal Principles are a commitment to the socialist road, the leadership of the Chinese Communist party, Marxism-Leninism Mao Zedong Thought, and the people's democratic dictatorship. The implications of the Copyright Law for Chinese intellectuals are thoughtfully explored in Deborah Kaufman, "Intellectual Property."

128. Cary Huang, "CPC Resumes Prepublication Censorship," *Hong Kong Standard*, Sept. 20, 1991, A-8. The State Copyright Administration (SCA) was formed in the mid 1980's to replace the State Publications Bureau (which subsequently became the State Administration for Press and Publications—SAPP) and has sought since to assume responsibilities for copyright-related issues from individual ministries (such as the Ministry of Culture). The SAPP's ideological orthodoxy is suggested by the fact that its initial head, Du Daozheng, was a longtime associate of Deng Liqun, a noted party hard-liner. The state was able to maintain tight control over publication through the mid 1980's in part because it oversaw the supply of both capital and paper to publishing houses and was in charge of *Xinhua* (New China News Agency), which was then the sole lawful distributor of books for the whole country. By the late 1980's, this system began to break down, with the emergence of private publishers and booksellers. Strenuous efforts were made in 1989, after the suppression of the Beijing Spring movement, and are now under way again (as is discussed further later in this chapter) to reassert a high level of state control. For an illuminating overview of the Chinese publishing world through the early 1990's, see Chen Yi, "Publishing in China in the Post-Mao Era."

129. "Zhonghua renmin gongheguo zhuzuoquan fa," Art. 27.

130. Author's interviews, Beijing, Aug. 1990.

131. Zheng Chengsi and Michael Pendleton (*Copyright Law in China,*

112–14) contend that the use in Article 2 of the term *fabiao* (which can be translated as "to publish" or "to divulge") in effect means that Chinese law provides foreigners with wider protection than the copyright laws of the United States and most other nations. Their logic is that this wording opens the possibility that foreigners might seek protection in China by virtue of merely exhibiting a work there, rather than making available a sufficient number of copies to satisfy public demand. Neither the law's implementing regulations, as they acknowledge, nor practice bear out this somewhat strained interpretation.

132. To be sure, the work of the SCA's few dozen permanent employees is modestly supplemented by the efforts of thinly staffed provincial copyright offices. In 1993, the Shanghai copyright office, for example, had a staff of four, who reported not to the SCA but to the Shanghai government—although on cases involving infringement both within and beyond Shanghai, the national and provincial offices did at times work together. Author's interviews, Shanghai, Oct. 1993.

133. Gelatt, "Foreign Exchange Quandary," 28.

134. Article 46 of the law vests both the SCA and the courts with the authority to order the payment of "compensation for damages" resulting from infringement, but reserves to the former the authority to impose civil fines for such activity. In any event, according to one Chinese expert, "Disputes over copyright infringement in general arise mostly among intellectuals, who are often unwilling to go to court, but prefer to have a mediator who can uphold justice . . . the administrative authorities for copyright affairs [the SCA and provincial copyright departments] have become the principal mediators in copyright infringement disputes." Liu Song, "The Role of the Chinese Government in the Protection of Copyright," 65.

135. "Jisuanji ruanjian baohu tiaoli"; Jisuanji ruanjian zhuzuoquan dengji banfa".

136. "Zhonghua renmin gongheguo jishu," Art. 4.

137. The January 1992 U.S.–PRC Memorandum of Understanding on the Protection of Intellectual Property purports to resolve a number of these issues. It is discussed further in chapter 6. The issue of retroactivity has presented difficult questions for the drafters of China's Copyright Law. Article 55 of the Copyright Law indicates that "the rights enjoyed by copyright owners, publishers, performers, producers of sound recordings and video recordings, radio stations, and television stations as provided for in this Law, of which the term of protection specified in this Law has not yet expired on the date of entry into force of this Law, shall be protected in accordance with this Law." Taken literally, this would seem to suggest that China was endeavoring retroactively to accord copyright protection to any work produced by any author who died within 50 years of the effective

date of the Copyright Law. Although the Berne Convention recognizes, at Article 18bis, that a nation joining the Convention may enjoy a measure of retroactive protection for works copyrighted prior to its joining, that would hardly seem to justify the reach of Article 55. That the above reading of Article 55 mirrors the intention of at least one of the law's drafters seems attested to by the somewhat confusing treatment of retroactivity in Zheng and Pendleton, *Copyright Law in China*, 207–9. It is interesting that in the 1992 Memorandum of Understanding, the Chinese government did not fully retreat from its basic position concerning the use of foreign copyrighted materials available in China before the effective date of Chinese protection. Article 3:7 of the Memorandum provides that natural or legal persons who used such items prior to the establishment of U.S.–PRC copyright relations (which took effect, according to the Memorandum, no earlier than March 17, 1992) "may continue to . . . use . . . that copy of the work without liability, provided that such copy is neither reproduced nor used in any manner that unreasonably prejudices the legitimate interests of the copyright owner of that work." Some foreign observers fear that the PRC may invoke this article as justification for continued reproduction and distribution of foreign copyrighted materials, albeit in less than commercial quantities. See Simone, "Copyright-MOU," 14.

138. "Jisuanji ruanjian baohu tiaoli," Arts. 23–24. Foreign concerns about this procedure are voiced in "Software Firms Slow to Export to China," *Chicago Tribune*, Dec. 30, 1991, 7-C. It should be noted that because neither the Berne Convention nor the Universal Copyright Convention requires the registration of software, the PRC, upon acceding to these two treaties, has provided that foreign computer programs need not be registered. As with so much else in this area, there is more here than meets the eye. Foreigners may be free not to register, but if they so choose, they will lack what Article 24 of the software regulations describes as "a prerequisite to instituting . . . an administrative action or a lawsuit concerning any dispute regarding the copyright in such software." Chinese nationals, meanwhile, continue to lack even this Hobson's choice.

139. "Jisuanji ruanjian baohu tiaoli," Art. 32.

140. Ren, "China's Judicial System," 17. In fairness, it should be noted that Chinese officials such as Ren are not the only ones to make overblown claims about the efficacy of the PRC's new intellectual property laws. Witness, e.g., the unstinting praise international civil servants, such as Director General Arpad Bogsch of the WIPO, have for years lavished on Chinese efforts in patent, trademark, and copyright. See, e.g., "When Friends Come from Afar: One-Day Visit to Hong Kong by WIPO Director General Dr. Bogsch and His Party," *China Patents & Trademarks*, no. 1 (1992): 4. Whether prompted by a naiveté as to Chinese circumstances, a

sincere belief that easy praise would best guide the PRC to greater heights, a bureaucratic desire to include as a WIPO member the world's most populous nation (whether or not it was complying with international standards), or susceptibility to the attention that accompanies being an international bureaucrat with something to offer China, Bogsch and company have been all too hasty to equate the PRC's adoption of intellectual property laws with their implementation. See "WIPO Director General Bosch Received by CCP General Secretary Jiang Zemin in Beijing and Granted the Title of Honorary Professor by Peking University," *China Patents & Trademarks*, no. 1 (1992): 118.

141. See, e.g., Liu Chuntian, "The Current Situation."

142. Although professionalism and independence are hardly neutral or self-defining terms, we should not assume that these are wholly foreign constructs thrust on the Chinese and therefore somehow inappropriate for consideration. As noted in chapter 2, the notion of a civil service chosen by criteria aspiring to objectivity has its roots in the Tang dynasty. And as Jerome Cohen has shown, during the first few years of the PRC, the Chinese Communist party itself grappled with providing its judges with some measure of independence—even if only from cadres seeking to abuse legal processes to serve private ends. See Cohen, "Chinese Communist Party and 'Judicial Independence,'" 967.

In fairness, it should be noted that China is now making extraordinary efforts to provide on-the-job training for its judges, fewer than 10 percent of whom as recently as 1985 were recipients of a formal legal education.

143. Jiang Ying, "Looking Back and Looking Ahead"; Gao, "On the Revision of the Current Patent Law"; Yuan Zhou, "Foreign Patent Filings Lag Behind Domestic Increase." *China Daily Business Weekly*, Apr. 12, 1992, 1; "Aiming to be World 'Patent Powerhouse,'" *China Daily Business Weekly*, Oct. 28, 1991, 1.

144. Dong Baolin, "Decade of Mighty Advance," 60.

145. Zheng Songyou, "Sum Up the Past," 6–7.

146. These figures are extracted from the statistics compiled by the Planning Division of the General Management Department of the Chinese Patent Office and published quarterly by *China Patents & Trademarks*. My attention was first drawn to this important body of data by Wang Liwei's useful work in the area of patent law, as exemplified by his article entitled "China's Patent Law," 254.

147. "Data & Statistics," *China Patents & Trademarks*, no. 2 (1994): 85–86.

148. "Data & Statistics," *China Patents & Trademarks*, no. 1 (1993): 109. Domestic applications were up in 1993, but enterprises were still relatively inactive.

149. Indeed, PRC statistics concerning foreign investment in general

warrant careful scrutiny, as they are subject to manipulation to bolster particular arguments. For example, investment on the Chinese mainland by PRC-owned companies chartered in Hong Kong is routinely treated as foreign investment, in part to give the impression of a higher level of confidence in China than statistics on investment by unambiguously foreign capital would warrant and in part so that such entities can enjoy any tax holidays and other advantages available to foreign capital.

150. See Goonatilake, *Aborted Discovery*.

151. See Zhang Lin, "Scientists Complete 11,000 Projects," *China Daily*, Sept. 18, 1991, 1. These efforts are described in "Science and Technology as the Primary Productive Force," *China News Analysis*, no. 1446 (Nov. 1, 1991).

152. For recent observations by the Nobel economics laureate Milton Friedman as to the continuing major role of state-owned enterprises in the Chinese economy, see Agence France Presse, "Friedman Says Beijing Still Controls Economy," *International Herald Tribune*, Oct. 30–31, 1993, 17.

153. "Disproportionately Low Percentage of Invention Patents in Domestic Patents," *Renmin ribao (haiwaiban)*, Aug. 5, 1989, 1, quoted in Wang Liwei, "China's Patent Law." The statistics are from "Gongzuo yanjiu: Guoyou caichan de liushi" (A Practical Study: The Erosion of State Property), *Zhongguo zhuanli bao* (China Patent Newspaper), Aug. 24, 1992, 2.

The low productivity of China's state-owned enterprises relative to collective or privately owned entities is described in Conner, "To Get Rich Is Precarious," 1. In comparing state and other enterprises, one must always, of course, be mindful of important differences in size, social welfare responsibilities, nature of output, access to raw materials, and control over pricing.

154. See "Aiming to be a World 'Patent Powerhouse,' " *China Daily Business Weekly*, Oct. 28, 1991, 1.

155. Gao, "On the Revision of the Current Patent Law"; Author's interviews, Beijing, Aug. 1993.

156. Author's interviews, Washington, D.C., May 1990, Beijing, Aug. 1990 and Aug.–Oct. 1993. See also Crothall, " 'Pirated' Products," 3; "Official on Foreign Trademark Protection," *Xinhua* (New China News Agency), Jan. 23, 1992, in *Foreign Broadcast Information Service* CHI-92-16 (Jan. 24, 1992), 22: "IBM v. Six Shenzhen Companies"; "M&Ms v. W&Ws." In fairness, it should be noted that foreigners—and especially Hong Kong and Taiwan Chinese—have been responsible for instigating some infringing activity, particularly in southern China. See, e.g., Doerner, "Pirates of the High Cs." Chinese officials have complained privately to this author about Hong Kong Chinese using the PRC as a base of operations to produce "for-

eign" items that might then be sold to naive Chinese or taking advantage of the fact that PRC authorities have a poorer track record than their Hong Kong counterparts in deterring the export of counterfeited items. It will be interesting to see how the PRC and Hong Kong interact with respect to intellectual property issues after the former resumes sovereignty over the latter in 1997. For more on intellectual property issues in Hong Kong, see Pendleton, *Law of Intellectual and Industrial Property*.

157. James McGregor, "China Adopts a Harder Line in Trade Talks," *Wall Street Journal*, Dec. 23, 1991, A6; Murphy, "CD Pirates Make China a Home Port as Sales Soar."

158. I have been both flattered and dismayed to discover many of my articles (and even talks) reproduced without permission—including versions edited and translated without authorization and with varying degrees of accuracy. Indeed, shortly before this book went to press, I had the unsettling experience of having a Chinese colleague cite (with praise, fortunately) an article of mine on the need for patent law reform that I am purported to have published in 1992. Early senility may be the explanation, but I have no recollection of ever having written such a piece, although praise is always welcomed, warranted or not.

159. Author's interviews, Beijing, Aug. 1990, and direct observations, 1986–93. Chinese universities may also be playing a less passive role in pirating if Shenzhen University is at all typical. That school's Reflective Materials Institute turns out to have made counterfeit Microsoft holograms so well that "even Microsoft executives could not distinguish them from originals." Blass, "Case for Sherlock Holmes."

160. Mr. Singer reacted to this information with bemusement. "I always thought," he said, "that the Chinese and Jews had a great deal in common—and this proves it" (conversation with the author, Cambridge, Mass., Feb. 1989).

161. Based on the author's direct observations, 1986–93. See also, William Alford, "Perspective on China: Pressuring the Pirate," *Los Angeles Times*, Jan. 12, 1992, D5; Syron, "Year of the Mouse," 5. Mickey Mouse paraphernalia in the author's possession include the unauthorized comic book series "Mi Laoshu, Tang Laoya" (Mickey Mouse, Donald Duck) published in Beijing by the Popular Scientific Press, an array of Disney attire (including Scrooge McDuck and Mickey neckties), and a host of toys and decorative objects.

A "Mickey Mouse" trademark was first registered in China by an overly entrepreneurial Guangdong manufacturer. Subsequently, the Disney Company was able through the China Patent Agency (H.K.) Ltd. to secure registration for Mickey and hundreds of other marks. Although Mickey seems to have enjoyed some protection in idyllic Hangzhou (see "Infringement of the Exclusive Right to Use the Designs of the Registered Trademarks 'Mickey Mouse' and 'Donald Duck' Penalized in Hangzhou," *China Patents & Trademarks*, no. 2 [1990]: 70), nationwide infringement was so rampant throughout the 1980's and into the 1990's that Disney cancelled its popular television program featuring the beloved Mouse in protest. Now back in China, Disney has recently won a judgment in Beijing of more than 600,000 *yuan* (US$70,000) against a Chinese infringer.

162. Holm, *Coming Home Crazy*, 115–16.

163. Wang Yonghong, "Deeper Crackdown Urged"; Wang Zhengfa, "Proliferation of Fake and Inferior Pharmaceuticals," 40.

164. Counterfeiting undertaken during the early years following the 1982 Trademark Law's promulgation is described in Christopher Wren, "China Fighting a Boom in Counterfeit Bicycles," *New York Times*, Oct. 7, 1983, 4; "Shangbiaofa zhi shishi xieze zai Shanghai de zhixing qingkuang" (The Conditions for Carrying Out the Trademark Law and Its Implementing Regulations in Shanghai), *Shanghai fayuan* (Shanghai Legal Garden), Sept. 1986, 5; "Crackdown on Fake Wine Stepped Up," *China Daily*, Apr. 3, 1987, 3. More recent infringement is described in Crothall, " 'Pirated' Products," and Wang Yonghong, "Deeper Crackdown Urged."

165. "Inspections Target Fake Trade Marks," *China Daily*, May 2, 1987, 3. See also "National Crusade Against Fake Goods Successful," *Xinhua* (New China News Agency), in *Foreign Broadcast Information Service* CHI-88-007 (Jan. 12, 1988), 29.

166. Author's interviews, Washington, D.C., June 1994; Liu Chuntian, "Current Situation," 78.

167. Chen Yi, "Publishing in China in the Post-Mao Era"; Freemantle, *The Steal*; Crothall, " 'Pirated' Products."

168. Zheng and Pendleton, *Copyright Law in China*, v–vi.

169. "Fasheng zai zishi baohu lingyu de guaishi: Fanquan fan dao banquan zhuanjia tou shang" (Discovering a Strange Thing in the Area of Intellectual Property Protection: Infringing the Rights of the Leading Specialist on Copyright), *Guangming ribao*, Mar. 22, 1993, 4; Zheng Chengsi, "Wo yu *Zhishicanquan falü quanshu* de banquan jiufen" (My Copyright Dispute with the *Complete Book of Intellectual Property Law*), *Guangming ribao*, Mar. 31, 1993, 5.

170. Gao, "On the Revision of the Current Patent Law."

171. "Patent Violators Fined," *China Daily*, Apr. 30, 1987, 3.

172. See, e.g., the case of *He Peiping v. Research Institute for Economic and Technological Development of Wu County (Jiangsu)*, reported in Wen Yikui and Jiang Tianqiang, "Women zengyang shenli zhuanli jiufen anjian" (How We Adjudicate Patent Disputes), *Fazhi ribao* (Legal System Daily), Dec. 31, 1989, 3.

173. Ren Wei, "Beverage 'Vitasoy'"; Crothall, "'Pirated' Products"; Horsley, "Protecting Intellectual Property"; Tian Ying, "Trademark Controls Are Taking Effect." Author's interviews, Hong Kong, Dec. 1986, June 1987.

174. Author's interviews, Hong Kong, June 1988, Dec. 1989. Seth Faison and Marlowe Hood, "Hi-Tech Dispute Tests Scope of China's Reforms," *South China Morning Post*, June 11, 1988, 1.

175. Howson, "Cao Siyuan," 270.

176. "'Solemn Statement' by Beijing Stone Enterprise Group," *Renmin ribao*, Feb. 10, 1990, 7, in *Foreign Broadcast Information Service* CH-90-031 (Feb. 12, 1990), 11. See also Yao Guang, "Wan Runnan banqi 'Shitou' yao zashui" (Who Did Wan Runnan Want to Smash by Picking Up a Stone), *Renmin ribao*, Aug. 7, 1989.

177. Tian Ying, "Trademark Controls Are Taking Effect," *China Daily Business Weekly*, Jan. 19, 1992, 4. Lu Guangcan, "Second National Conference on Patent Work."

178. In fact, there were predecessor chambers to these new tribunals. See, e.g., Yuan Zhao, "New Court Settles Patent Dispute: China's Legal Eagles Grapple with Intellectual Property Disputes," *China Daily Business Weekly*, Sept. 9, 1991, 1. Whether the new intellectual property chambers, which have been established in Beijing, Shanghai, Fujian, Guangdong, and Hainan, will have the impact suggested by their proponents is unclear. Well over 90 percent of trademark cases are resolved administratively (Wang Zhengfa, "Administrative Resolution," 11), while holders of copyrights and patents—especially from abroad—have been reluctant to utilize the courts generally to vindicate their rights, allegedly because of their doubts about the courts' ability to enforce their judgments. Author's interviews, Beijing, Aug. 1993. The PRC government itself reports that from 1986 through 1993, Chinese courts including the aforementioned new chambers specialized collegial panels and regular judges, heard a total of 3,505 civil cases involving intellectual property. "Zhongguo zhishicanquan baohu zhuangkuang."

179. Wang Yonghong, "Deeper Crackdown Urged." In a cynical moment, one cannot help but wonder whether or not the publicity surrounding such enforcement efforts is in significant part generated for foreign consumption. After all, quasi-official foreign language media in China such as the *China Daily*, which usually are quite reticent about the imposition of severe criminal sanctions, seem only too willing to accord great prominence to executions and other serious punishments handed down under intellectual property laws. For example, the *China Daily* recently carried a front-page story on the execution of a 33-year-old Guizhou man for selling fake Maotai, which the paper termed an "unmistakable warning" to pirates across the nation.

180. "Zhongguo zhishicanquan baohu zhuangkuang."

181. Wang Yonghong, "Deeper Crackdown Urged."

182. Doerner, "Pirates of the High Cs"; Brauchli, "Fake CD's"; Murphy, "CD Pirates Make China a Home Port as Sales Soar"; Geoffrey Crothall, "Copyright Laws Prove Ineffective," *South China Morning Post*, Sept. 6, 1993, B2; Reuters, "China Called Top Pirate of Software," *International Herald Tribune*, Oct. 21, 1993, 16. It is rumored that on his 1992 southern tour undertaken to demonstrate his support for economic reform, Deng Xiaoping visited the Xianke Laser Group, China's most notorious infringer of CD's.

183. Author's interviews, Beijing, Nov. 1993. The Chinese government has been making efforts to publicize its intellectual property laws. For a sample of materials available for factory managers, see Peng Haiqing, *Zhuanli wenjian shiyong zhinan*. Xinhua may have taken this effort to propagandize the new intellectual property laws to an extreme. Take, for example, an article it ran in early 1992 suggesting that dinner guests now seek to "appropriately compliment" their hostesses by saying, "With this skill, you can apply for patent rights." Chen Xianxin, Fu Gang, and Wu Jincai, "Newsletter [on Intellectual Property]," *Xinhua* (New China News Agency), Jan. 23, 1992, in *Foreign Broadcast Information Service* CHI-92-16 (Jan. 24, 1992), 21. For a more serious example of an effort to popularize the law broadly, see *Shangbiao fa tushi*.

184. Robin Munro quoted in Kathy Chen, "Beijing Takes Harder Line on Dissidents and the Press," *Asian Wall Street Journal*, Oct. 25, 1993, 1. See also Jernow, "Amicable Divorce"; Nicholas Kristoff, "Signalling New Hard Line, Chinese Jail a Dissident," *New York Times*, Jul. 12, 1993, A9.

185. "Peking Paper Chase: China Orders Life in Jail for Local Journalist," *Far Eastern Economic Review* 156, no. 37 (Sept. 16, 1993): 5.

186. "Satellite Ban to Keep Out 'Foreign' Influence," *South China Morning Post*, Oct. 16, 1993, 10.

187. Patrick Tyler, "Who Makes the Rules for Chinese Films?" *International Herald Tribune*, Oct. 20, 1993, 22.

188. Doerner, "Pirates of the High Cs."

189. To be sure, China's citizenry have increasing opportunities to seek redress through law. A range of cases in which prominent citizens availed themselves of legal remedies are discussed in Alford, "Double-Edged Swords." Less prominent PRC nationals are turning in growing, if still modest (at least relative to the size of China's populace), numbers to the law on administrative litigation (Zhonghua renmin gongheguo xingzheng susongfa), which sets forth procedures by which citizens may appeal administrative determinations to the courts.

Five. As Pirates Become Proprietors

1. Loh, ed., *Kuomintang Debacle.*

2. Although the Taiwanese initially welcomed Nationalist troops for their role in bringing the Japanese colonial period to an end, the brutality with which Guomindang forces moved to consolidate their position even prior to the general Nationalist retreat to Taiwan incurred the native population's enmity. Observers estimate that between 10,000 and 25,000 Taiwanese were killed, leaving a bitterness that persists to the present. See Lai and Myers, *Tragic Beginning*; Chao, "Exorcising Ghosts."

3. Kaser, *Book Pirating*, 31.

4. He Defen, "Comparative Study," 339.

5. Kaser, *Book Pirating*, 40.

6. Benjamin, *U.S. Books Abroad.*

7. Kaser, *Book Pirating*, 31–41. The U.S. Military Assistance Group, which grew from 116 soldiers in 1951 to thousands at its peak, was one audience for pirated versions produced in Taiwan, Japan, and elsewhere.

8. He Defen, "Comparative Study," 335.

9. Kaser, *Book Pirating*, 48.

10. Ibid., 67–70.

11. He Defen, *Zhuzuoquanfa lunwen ji*, 29.

12. Literally speaking, the ROC's pertinent law in this area, the Zhuzuoquanfa, should be translated as "law on author's rights," but ROC publications render it as copyright in English.

13. Shi Wengao, *Zhuzuoquan*; id., *Guoji zhuzuoquan.*

14. See Kaser, *Book Pirating*, passim; *Publisher's Weekly*, May 30, 1966, 58.

15. General Accounting Office, *International Trade.*

16. *Publishing Yearbook of the ROC*, 174, cited in Simone, "Protection of American Copyright," 115.

17. He Defen, "Comparative Study," 339.

18. Ibid., 368. The other three sentences were commuted. As recently as 1983, fewer than 1,000 copyrights were registered annually.

19. See, e.g., Freemantle, *The Steal.* Long before the easing in 1987 of travel and other restrictions on intercourse between Taiwan and the Chinese mainland, there was considerable unauthorized reproduction in each jurisdiction of written material originating in the other (based on direct observation by the author in Taipei and Beijing). Interestingly, for political purposes, the authorities on the mainland have set aside in a special account what they describe as basic payments owed to Taiwan authors whose works are reprinted without permission.

20. Han, "Protection from Commercial Counterfeiters," 64.

21. See, e.g., Maria Shao, "Taiwan Lowers Boom on Counterfeiters," *Asian Wall Street Journal*, 1.

22. Hickman, "Protecting Intellectual Property," 117; C. V. Chen, "Legal Protection."

23. Lohr, "Crackdown on Counterfeiting"; *Asia Magazine*, Dec. 30, 1984; Freemantle, *The Steal*.

24. "Taiwan's Brazen Pirates," *Newsweek*, Nov. 15, 1982; Lohr, "Crackdown on Counterfeiting."

25. U.S. International Trade Commission, *Effect of Foreign Product Counterfeiting*.

26. He Defen, *Zhuzuoquanfa lunwenji*, 29–30.

27. See Alford, "Intellectual Property."

28. To facilitate economic growth in the developing world through tariff preferences, GATT allows developed nations to deviate from the principle of nondiscrimination, which provides that privileges accorded one trading partner be given to all. See Belassa, "Tokyo Round," 93; Dorris, "Very Specialized United States Generalized System of Preferences," 39.

29. 19 U.S.C. §§ 2462(c)(5) and 2464(c)(3)(B)(2).

30. "Can Asia's Four Tigers Be Tamed?" *Business Week*, Feb. 15, 1988, 46.

31. U.S. House, 100th Cong., 2d sess., 1988, "Message from the President of the United States Transmitting Notification of His Intent to Remove . . . Taiwan . . . from the List of Beneficiary Developing Countries Under the GSP" (H.R. Doc. No. 162).

32. Omnibus Trade and Competitiveness Act of 1988, Pub. L. No. 100-418, §§ 1301, 1303, 102 Stat. 1164–76, 1179–81 (1988) (amending the Trade Act of 1974, Pub. L. No. 93-316, §§ 302(b), 182 (1974).

33. Han, "Protection from Commercial Counterfeiters," 650; He Defen, *Zhuzuoquanfa lunwenji*, 29–30. These campaigns are discussed in National Anti-Counterfeiting Committee, *Intellectual Property*.

34. These are discussed in Pow and Lee, "Taiwan's Anti-Counterfeit Measures," 157.

35. Shangbiaofa, Art. 62. This amendment did not limit the possibility of monetary redemption of penalties (of up to three years' imprisonment) that might be imposed for infringing unregistered well-known foreign trademarks.

36. Shangbiaofa, Arts. 66 and 64. See also Shangbiaofa xiuzheng shuoming; Silk, "Legal Efforts," 301.

37. Zhuzuoquanfa, Art. 4 I (14). Programs are defined in Art. 3 I (19). See also Lin Ruey-Long, "Protection."

38. Zhuzuoquanfa, Art. 4.

39. *Public Prosecutor v. Tan Ching Publishing Co.*, Criminal Judgment at the Taipei District Court of Taiwan (1988), Yi-Zi No. 2574, Sept. 20, 1988, discussed in Chiu Hungdah, "Contemporary Practice"; Stone, "Legal Aspects," 210–11.

40. Zhuzuoquanfa, Art. 17 III.

41. Ibid., Art. 40.

42. Zhuanlifa tiaowen xiuzheng caoan shuoming; Taiwan's Patent Law, as amended Dec. 24, 1986, translated and reprinted in *East Asian Executive Reports*, June 15, 1987, Art. 88-1.

43. Shangbiaofa, Art. 62 I.

44. Author's interviews and observations, Taipei, Sept. 1986. See also Freemantle, *The Steal.*

45. N. S. Cheng and M. H. Chao, "Update on Intellectual Property," 19; Silk, "Legal Efforts," 326–27.

46. Cho, "Anti-Counterfeiting Committee," 25. Also U.S. International Trade Commission, *Foreign Protection*, K-33; Wu Wen-ya, "Board of Foreign Trade," 32; Huang Mao-zong, "Assistance and Services," 160.

47. See, e.g., Ye Yuqi, "Shangbiaofa xiuzheng de yinxiang," 69; Silk, "Legal Efforts"; National Anti-Counterfeiting Committee, *Intellectual Property*, 25–29, 160–63.

48. Silk, "Legal Efforts," appendices III–VII; Goldstein, "Parting Gesture," 19.

49. Seng, "Film and Video Piracy" (supplement), vol. 1.

50. Freemantle, *The Steal*, 120, 126.

51. Author's interviews, Taipei, Sept. 1986.

52. International Intellectual Property Alliance Report to the U.S. Trade Representative, "Trade Losses."

53. Alford, "Intellectual Property."

54. Bureau of National Affairs, "USTR Fact Sheet on Special 301."

55. Bello and Holmer, "'Special 301,'" 259.

56. Author's interviews, Taipei, 1989.

57. Y. T. Zhao, *Shijie ribao*, Apr. 21, 1988. Since the United States terminated formal diplomatic relations with the ROC on January 1, 1979, the two nations have carried on quasi-official relations through the AIT and the CCNAA.

58. Winkler, "US–ROC Trade Talks," 14–15; Bello and Holmer, "GATT Uruguay Round," 307.

59. *Jingji ribao*, Jan. 24, 1990, 4.

60. Author's interviews, Taipei, Jan. 1991. Although Wang's resignation was not accepted, he did not participate as fully in subsequent negotiations.

61. Clifford, "Pirates' Lair," 79.

62. Francis S. L. Wang, "Analysis of AIT-CCNAA Understanding."

63. Quoted in Bureau of National Affairs, "Six Parties Comments," 301.

64. Francis Wang, "Taming the Infringers," 527.

65. Clifford, "Pirates' Lair."

66. Ibid.

67. Bureau of National Affairs, "Taiwan Tries."
68. The question of Taipei's GATT application is addressed in Feinerman, "Taiwan and GATT."
69. USTR, "Fact Sheet on AIT–CCNAA Understanding."
70. Shao Chiung-hui, "Internationalization of Copyright Protection in Taiwan," 20.
71. Wang and Young, "Taiwan's New Copyright Regime."
72. Shao Chiung-hui, "Internationalization of Copyright Protection in Taiwan," 26.
73. Parallel importation in this context means the acquisition from abroad of copyrighted works through other than authorized channels. Copyright owners typically object to this both because it undercuts their monopoly position and because of the possibility that someone importing under these circumstances may jeopardize their goodwill through, for example, inattention to servicing requirements.
74. Understanding Between the AIT and the CCNAA, June 5, 1992.
75. The Dunkel draft is discussed in Bello and Holmer, "GATT Uruguay Round."
76. USTR, "Fact Sheet on AIT-CCNAA Understanding."
77. These changes in political life on Taiwan are chronicled in Simon and Kao, eds., *Taiwan: Beyond the Economic Miracle.*
78. Author's interviews, Cambridge, Mass., June 1992.
79. Shao Chiung-hui, "Internationalization of Copyright Protection in Taiwan," 68. The Berne Convention, for example, does not require nations to bar parallel importation.
80. Susan Yu, "US Retaliation Fear."
81. Author's interviews, Cambridge, Mass., June 1993.
82. *Lifayuan gongbao,* Jan. 15, 1993.
83. Francis Wang, "Taming the Infringers," S 27.
84. Susan Yu, "ROC Avoids US Trade Sanctions," *Free China Journal* 10, no. 32 (May 4, 1993): 1.
85. Susan Yu, "US Ratification Fear," 2; Shao Chiung-hui, "Internationalization of Copyright Protection in Taiwan," 59.
86. Daisy Wong, "Comprehensive Action Plan for the Protection of Intellectual Property Rights Approved," *IP Asia,* no. 6 (Aug. 16, 1993): 19–20.
87. See, e.g., "U.S. Sees Progress in Thai, Taiwan, Hungarian Intellectual Property Efforts," *Agence France Presse,* Aug. 3, 1993.
88. Alford, "Intellectual Property."
89. Taiwan's "economic miracle" is discussed in Cal Clark, *Taiwan's Development*; Haggard, *Pathways from the Periphery*; and Vogel, *Four Little Dragons.*

90. Liu, "Tougher Laws Make Better Software," 42. See also Chin, "From Imitation to Innovation."

91. Simon, "Taiwan's Emerging Technological Trajectory"; Chang Yuwen, "Single Digit Growth," 46; Liu, "Tougher Laws Make Better Software"; Zhang Jing, "Dalu chubanpin falü wenti tantao," 26; "Cross-Strait Symposium"; "CPA v. NPA," 39; Winkler, "Taiwan," 22; and "Legal Cable TV One Step Away: Proposed Law Sets 48 Districts," *Free China Journal*, Feb. 11, 1992, 4. Cross-Straits collaboration now seems to embrace a good deal of infringement, ranging from high-tech fields (Clifford, "Pirate's Lair") to the sale of unpublished master's theses.

92. Douglas Sease, "Taiwan's Export Boom to the U.S. Owes Much to American Firms," *Wall Street Journal*, May 27, 1987, 1.

93. David Chen, " 'Made in Taiwan' Makes the Grade," *Free China Journal*, June 15, 1993, 7; Maria Shao, "Stan Shih Wants 'Made in Taiwan' to Mean First-Rate," *Business Week*, June 8, 1987, 109; "Headway for Computer Firms, Brand names, OEM Mode," *Free China Journal*, Feb. 11, 1992, 8.

94. Philip Liu, "Rejecting the Old Boy Network," 18.

95. See, e.g., "Taiwan: Oiling Palms," *The Economist*, June 12, 1993, 83; "Taiwan Cabinet to Oppose Anti-Corruption Bill," Reuters, June 9, 1993; "27 Convicted in Taiwan Election Scandal," Reuters, Apr. 16, 1992.

96. Berman, *Words Like Colored Glass*, 122–69. The "three limitations" required that newspapers register with the government prior to commencing publication, locate their presses within the distribution areas, and print no more than the number of pages authorized by the government.

97. See, e.g., Shin Jae Hoon, "Freer to Speak Out," 12.

98. Mark Cohen, *Taiwan at the Crossroads*, 309–51. See also Lawrence Liu, "A Lesson in Persuasion."

99. Mendel, "Judicial Power and Illusion," 157–90.

100. See, e.g., Jeremy Mark, "Taiwan Finds Diplomatic Gold Mine in Relations with New C.I.S. States," *Wall Street Journal*, Feb. 7, 1992, 5.

101. The GATT is becoming increasingly involved in intellectual property issues, as evidenced by the Uruguay Round Trade Related Intellectual Property (TRIPS) agreement. Alford, "Intellectual Property."

102. See Wu Xianxiang, "Bu zhongshi zhuzuoquan," 13. The issues of copyright and the ROC's standing in the world community have come together in a somewhat novel manner in the case of *New York Chinese TV Programs v. U.E. Enterprises* (Civil Action No. 88 Civ. 4170 [JMW]), U.S. Dist. Ct., S.D., N.Y., Mar. 8, 1989. In that case, an alleged infringer of videotapes copyrighted in Taiwan used as a defense the argument that the plaintiff did not hold a copyright enforceable in the United States. First, the defendant contended that the 1946 Friendship, Commerce and Navigation (FCN) Treaty between the United States and the ROC did not apply

to Taiwan. Second, the defendant argued that even if the FCN Treaty did apply to Taiwan, the Taiwan Relations Act could not constitutionally have continued such copyright relations as may have existed between the United States and the ROC prior to the termination of American recognition of Taipei on December 31, 1978. Notwithstanding the defendant's reliance on a memorandum of law prepared by Professor Laurence Tribe of the Harvard Law School, the court rejected the defendant's arguments and entered a permanent injunction against its infringing behavior. The Federal Court of Appeals for the Second Circuit affirmed the District Court's judgment on January 24, 1992 (*New York Chinese TV Programs v. U.E. Enterprises*, 954 F. 2d 847 [1992]).

Six. No Mickey Mouse Matter

1. Alford, "Seek Truth from Facts," 177.
2. Mao Lei and Zhang Zhiyu, "Wang Zhengfa: China Can Effectively Stop Infringement on Protection of Intellectual Property Rights." *Renmin ribao (haiwaiban)*, May 7, 1990, 4, translated and reprinted in *Foreign Broadcast Information Service* CHI-90-095 (May 16, 1990), 34; Bureau of National Affairs, "China Agrees." My repeated efforts to secure background materials regarding these negotiations from the Office of the United States Trade Representative (USTR) under the Freedom of Information Act have been unavailing. Indeed, the USTR's office has failed even to comply with its legal obligation to explain its refusal to provide such materials.
3. Martial law was declared on May 19, 1989, effective 12:00 A.M. on May 20. For the declaration, see "Li Peng zongli qianshu guowuyuan ling Beijing bufen diqu shixing jianyan" (Premier Li Peng Signs the State Council's Order to Impose Martial Law on Certain Districts of Beijing), *Renmin ribao (haiwaiban)*, May 21, 1991, 1.
4. Nicholas Kristof, "Visit to China: Vexing Ritual: Baker's Trip Hindered by Misunderstandings," *New York Times*, Nov. 19, 1991, A9. The joining of intellectual property issues with concerns over nuclear weapons proliferation and arms control was also evident in late February 1992 when the United States lifted sanctions imposed on China for sale of "missile technology to Syria, Iran and Pakistan and nuclear technology to Iran." As the *New York Times* put it, "In explaining the reasons, Lawrence Eagleburger, the Under Secretary of State . . . argued . . . that [Chinese] adherence to the missile control regime [in exchange of a lifting of sanctions] 'was an important first step toward achieving similar concessions in other contentious areas such as the transfer of nuclear technology and intellectual property rights'" (Elaine Sciolino, "U.S. Lifts Its Sanctions on China over High-Technology Transfers," *New York Times*, Feb. 22, 1992, A1).

5. Bureau of National Affairs, "USTR Sets January 16 Deadline."
6. Michael Chugari, "PRC Not to 'Keep Silent' on Tariffs," *South China Morning Post*, Jan. 11, 1992, 1; Alford, "Perspective on China." MFN status is something of a misnomer, as the preferential tariff rates it provides under U.S. law are available to virtually all noncommunist nations. The so-called Jackson-Vanik amendment to the 1974 Trade Act further provides that even communist nations may receive MFN status if they permit their nationals to emigrate or the president waives this condition (as U.S. presidents have done annually since 1980 with respect to China). For more on MFN, see Alford, "Both Democrats and Republicans"; id., "Underestimating a Complex China."

7. "Memorandum of Understanding . . . on the Protection of Intellectual Property," Jan. 17, 1992; "Chinese Checkers," *National Journal* 24 (Jan. 25, 1992): 226; Richard Katz, "Settlement of Copyright Dispute Staves Off Tension," *Nikkei Weekly*, Feb. 1. 1992, 20; Lachica, "China Settles Dispute"; "One Clear Round, but More Hurdles to Come," *South China Morning Post*, Jan. 18, 1992, 12.

8. Kaye and Awanohara, "Down to the Wire."

9. Thomas Friedman, "China Faces U.S. Sanctions in Electronic Copyright Piracy," *New York Times*, July 1, 1994, D2. The shift in the Clinton administration's China policy has been stunning. Lincoln Kaye, "One-Way Street," 11. Although there are certainly good arguments to be made for its current (at least as of this writing) policy of "constructive engagement" (to borrow a term left over from a previous administration), the Clinton administration's initial policy also had a very serious rationale. As Lincoln Kaye of the *Far Eastern Economic Review* wrote after interviewing the leading Chinese dissident Wei Jingsheng following Wei's release from some fourteen years' imprisonment: "He [Wei] scorns the Clinton administration's de-emphasis on human rights in its overall China policy. Confrontation over most-favored-nation trading status might not have been the most effective US strategy to begin with, he admits. But, having come this far with it, Washington would now be 'foolish' to throw away that card 'just as it seems on the verge of winning' more prisoner releases and other concessions" (Kaye, "Learning New Rules," 21).

Ironically, in moving from a China policy that initially made much rhetorically of human rights to one more focused on economic and strategic considerations, Bill Clinton is unwittingly emulating a similar, if less publicized, shift by George Bush in the first year of his presidency. Although it was subsequently obscured by his reaction to the Beijing Spring of 1989, Bush's first consequential action toward China as president was to invite the dissident physicist Fang Lizhi to the state dinner he was hosting for the Chinese leadership, much to its consternation, in order to make a symbolic gesture about the importance of human rights considerations in American China policy.

10. This linkage is discussed in Alford, "Intellectual Property."

11. Memorandum of Understanding on the Protection of Intellectual Property, Jan. 17, 1992.

12. Li Ying, "International Copyright Treaties and Chinese Implementation Rules."

13. Eduardo Lachica, "U.S. Plans Tariffs for Chinese Imports as Beijing Fails to Move on Patent Issues," *Wall Street Journal*, Nov. 27, 1991, A10.

14. Although actions such as those taken by the USTR are said to have as an objective bringing China into the world community, their largely unilateral nature—and the comparable actions that they evoke among our trading partners anxious not to be left behind—at times result in China (and other similarly situated nations) being pulled in a variety of directions by different members of the world community. See, e.g., Islam and Karp, "Grab that Rolex," 63.

15. The ways in which dissidents and others are seeking to use the law to call the Communist party to task for not adhering to its own standards are the subject of Alford, "Double-Edged Swords."

16. A cynic might suggest that the Bush administration was relatively indifferent to the question of how effectively these laws might take hold, arguing that the administration's principal objective was to conclude an agreement securing seeming concessions from China that might defuse objections to its China policy in general and its advocacy of continued MFN status in particular. This had the advantage, so the argument goes, of enabling the president to claim that his attention to foreign affairs was, indeed, opening up economic opportunities abroad (and, with them, jobs for American workers) while also earning the gratitude (and campaign support) of leaders of the entertainment, pharmaceutical, and computer industries.

17. There is surprisingly little academic literature in the West (or, for that matter, in the Chinese world) on what Alan Watson has termed "legal transplantation," whether with reference to particular nations (such as China) or in general. This may in part be a lingering after-effect of the unsuccessful efforts of the so-called law and development movement, undertaken chiefly during the 1950's and 1960's, to encourage Latin American, African, and Asian nations to promulgate laws modeled on those of Western liberal democracies in order to expedite their "modernization." See, e.g., Trubek and Galanter, "Scholars in Self-Estrangement," and Merryman, "Comparative Law."

Watson himself has remained quite sanguine about the ease with which law might be transplanted between societies, but his findings are largely inapplicable to the PRC for two principal reasons. First, for all their differences, the societies Watson studied were far closer legally, politically, culturally, and economically than are the PRC and the major industrialized democracies. Second, Watson tends to treat transplantation as successful so long as the adopting society has taken on the foreign forms in question, irrespective of whether said forms yield the results their adopters desired. While the study of the unexpected ways in which transplanted forms grow in their new soil is interesting in its own right, that is a rather different endeavor from assessing the workings of a highly instrumental effort at legal development of the type the PRC has been undergoing. For a representative example of Watson's writing on this subject, see Watson, *Legal Transplants*. I further discuss the problems of transplantation in "Inscrutable Occidental" and "On the Limits of 'Grand Theory.'" One of the best studies of the transplantation of foreign legal forms to China is Edward Epstein, "Theoretical System of Property Rights."

18. Intellectual property has not been the only trade front on which the USTR has brought extensive pressure to bear on the Chinese world. The USTR has utilized the threat of a Section 301 action against Taiwan (and a number of other Asian nations) in order to secure better market access for American tobacco exports. To at least some observers, both in the United States and on Taiwan, this has been all too reminiscent of the Opium War a century and a half earlier. See, e.g., Sesser, "Opium War Redux."

19. It should be noted that some scholars are of the view that copyright, and, with it, the increasing commercialization of knowledge, at least in liberal democratic societies, work to curtail the marketplace of ideas. See Boyle, "Theory of Law and Information."

Readers may wonder whether my suggestion that the rise of a constituency with an economic interest is of consequence in securing effective copyright protection constitutes an implicit endorsement of the work of Adelstein and Peretz and North and Thomas, discussed in chapter 2. As I believe the ROC example indicates, economic considerations are significant variables. Neither Adelstein and Peretz nor North and Thomas, however, pay adequate heed to the impact of the type of cultural, social, political, and diplomatic considerations on which this study has focused. Nor do they provide us with a means of isolating the impact of these many variables—unless one starts with their assumption that economic factors are paramount.

20. One of the failings of the law and development movement may have been that it overestimated the power of law to lead social transformation and did not adequately heed the degree to which a society's law is intertwined with other dimensions of its political, institutional, and cultural life.

21. Challenges posed by the effort to reconcile international human rights norms with cultures not actively represented in the initial formula-

tion of such norms are addressed in Alford "Making a Forum of Democracy."

22. Alford, "Both Democrats and Republicans"; id., "Seek Truth from Facts"; id., "Double-Edged Swords"; id., "Underestimating a Complex China."

23. I discuss this phenomenon in a forthcoming essay on the rise of *hezuozhi* (cooperative or quasi-private) law firms in the PRC. Alford, "Tasselled Loafers."

24. See, e.g., Louise Lucas, "US Threatens Action Against China Over Textile Exports," *South China Morning Post*, Nov. 18, 1993, Business Section, 1; Stross, *Bulls in the China Shop*, 88–89. To make this point is not to condone the fraudulent mislabeling of textiles in which some Chinese enterprises are said to be engaged. It should be noted that some reputable commentators believe that the U.S. government has wildly exaggerated the mislabeling problem. James Bovard, "Trade Quotas Build New Chinese Wall," *Wall Street Journal*, Jan. 10, 1994, A12.

Bibliography

Adelstein, Richard, and Steven Peretz. "The Competition of Technologies and Market for Ideas: Copyright and Fair Use—An Evolutionary Perspective." *International Review of Law & Economics* 5, no. 2 (1985): 210–38.

Adikibi, Owen. "The Multinational Corporation and Monopoly of Patents in Nigeria." *World Development* 16, no. 4 (1988): 511–26.

Alford, William. "Both Democrats and Republicans Miss the Point on China." *Boston Globe*, Nov. 13, 1991, 17.

———. "Don't Stop Thinking About . . . Yesterday: Why There Was No Indigenous Counterpart to Intellectual Property Law in Imperial China." *Journal of Chinese Law* 7, no. 1 (1993): 3–34.

———. "Double-Edged Swords Cut Both Ways: Law and Legitimacy in the People's Republic of China." *Dædalus* 122, no. 2 (1993): 45–70.

———. "Intellectual Property, the General Agreement on Tariffs and Trade, and Taiwan: A GATT-fly's View." *Columbia Business Law Review* 1992, no. 1: 97–107.

———. "The Inscrutable Occidental: Roberto Unger's Uses and Abuses of the Chinese Past." *Texas Law Review* 64, no. 5 (1986): 915–72.

———. "Law, Law, What Law?: Why Historians and Social Scientists of China Ignore Its Law." Forthcoming in James Feinerman, Kent Guy, and Karen Turner, eds., *Justice and Discretion in Chinese Law*, 1995.

———. "Making a Goddess of Democracy from Loose Sand: Observations on Human Rights in China." In Abdullahi An-Na'iem, ed., *Human Rights in Cross-Cultural Perspectives*. Philadelphia: University of Pennsylvania Press, 1992.

———. "Of Arsenic and Old Laws: Looking Anew at Criminal Justice in Late Imperial China." *California Law Review* 72, no. 6 (1984): 1180–1256.

———. "On the Limits of 'Grand Theory' in Comparative Law." *Washington Law Review* 61, no. 3 (1986): 945–56.

———. "Perspective on China: Pressuring the Pirate." *Los Angeles Times*, Jan. 12, 1992, D5.

―――. "The Role of Law in Chinese Society." Course materials, Harvard Law School, 1991.

―――. " 'Seek Truth from Facts'—Especially When They Are Unpleasant: America's Understanding of China's Efforts at Law Reform." *UCLA Pacific Basin Law Journal* 8, nos. 1–2 (1990): 177–96.

―――. "Tasselled Loafers for Barefoot Lawyers: Tensions and Transformations in the Chinese Legal World." Forthcoming, *China Quarterly,* 1995.

―――. Underestimating a Complex China." *Chicago Tribune,* May 24, 1994, 23.

―――. "When Is China Paraguay? An Examination of the Application of the Antidumping and Countervailing Duty Laws of the United States to Non-Market Economy Nations." *Southern California Law Review* 61, no. 1 (1987): 79–135.

Alford, William, and David Birenbaum. "Ventures in the China Trade: An Analysis of China's Emerging Legal Framework for the Regulation of Foreign Investment." *Northwestern Journal of International Law and Business* 3, no. 1 (1981): 56–102.

Alford, William, and Shen Yuanyuan. " 'Law Is My Idol': John C. H. Wu and the Role of Legality and Spirituality in the Effort to 'Modernise' China." In Ronald Macdonald, ed., *Essays in Honour of Wang Tieya,* pp. 43–53. Dordrecht: Martinus Nijhoff, 1993.

Alford, William, and Henry Steiner, eds. *Human Rights and Foreign Policy.* Cambridge: Harvard Law School, 1994.

Allen, George, and Audrey Donnithorne. *Western Enterprise in Far Eastern Economic Development.* New York: Macmillan, 1954.

Allman, Norwood. *Protection of Trademarks, Patents, Copyrights and Trade-names in China.* Shanghai: Kelly & Walsh, 1924.

Andrews, John. "A Survey of Taiwan: A Change of Face." Supplement to *The Economist,* Oct. 10, 1992.

"The Announcement About Drunkenness." In *The Book of Documents.* Trans. Bernhard Karlgren. *Museum of Far Eastern Antiquities Bulletin* (Stockholm) 22, no. 1 (1950): 1–81.

Arnold, Julian. *China: A Commercial and Industrial Handbook.* Shanghai: Kelly & Walsh, 1926.

Awanohara Susumu and Lincoln Kaye. "Patently Hostile." *Far Eastern Economic Review* 153, no. 36 (Sept. 5, 1991): 69–70.

Bai Shouyi, ed. *An Outline History of China.* Beijing: Foreign Language Press, 1982.

Balassa, Bela. "The Tokyo Round and the Developing Countries." *Journal of World Trade Law* 14, no. 2 (1980): 93–118.

"Baozhang famingquan yu zhuanliquan zanxing tiaoli" (Provisional Regulations on the Protection of Invention Rights and Patent Rights). Promulgated on and effective from Aug. 17, 1950. In *Zhongyang renmin zhengfu faling huibian* (The Collected Laws and Decrees of the Central People's Government), 2 (1949–50): 359–62. Beijing: Renmin chuban she, 1952.

Barnes, Denny. "Cantonese Consumer." *China Business Review* 19, no. 6 (1992): 28–35.

Baum, Julian. "Taipei on a Tightrope—US: Copyright Laws or Trade Sanctions." *Far Eastern Economic Review* 155, no. 19 (May 14, 1992): 45–46.

Baum, Richard. *China's Four Modernizations: The New Technological Revolution*. Boulder, Colo.: Westview Press, 1980.

Baum, Richard, and Frederick Teiwes. *Ssu-ch'ing: The Socialist Education Movement, 1962–1966*. Berkeley: Center for Chinese Studies, 1968.

Beale, Louis, and G. C. Pelham. *Trade and Economic Conditions in China, 1931–1933*. Reprint. San Francisco: Chinese Materials Center, 1975.

Beasley, William, and Edward Pulleyblank, eds. *Historians of China and Japan*. London: Oxford University Press, 1961.

Bello, Judith, and Alan Holmer. "The GATT Uruguay Round: Its Significance for U.S. Bilateral Trade with Korea and Taiwan." *Michigan Journal of International Law* 11, no. 2 (1990): 307–25.

———. "'Special 301': Its Requirements, Implementation and Significance." *Fordham International Law Journal* 13, no. 3 (1989–90): 259–75.

Benjamin, Curtis. *U.S. Books Abroad: The Neglected Ambassadors*. Washington, D.C.: Library of Congress, 1984.

Bernhardt, Kathryn. "Women and the Law: Divorce in the Republican Era." In Kathryn Bernhardt and Philip Huang, eds., *Civil Law in Qing and Republican China*. Stanford: Stanford University Press, 1994.

Bernstein, Thomas. *Up to the Mountains and Down to the Villages: The Transfer of Youth from Urban to Rural China*. New Haven: Yale University Press, 1977.

Berman, Daniel. *Words Like Colored Glass; The Role of the Press in Taiwan's Democratization Process*. Boulder, Colo.: Westview Press, 1992.

Blass, Anthony. "Case for Sherlock Holmes." *Far Eastern Economic Review* 155, no. 48 (Dec. 3, 1992): 58.

———. "Learning the Soft Way." *Far Eastern Economic Review* 155, no. 48 (Dec. 3, 1992): 54–58.

Blaustein, Albert, ed. *Fundamental Legal Documents of Communist China*. South Hackensack, N.J.: F. B. Rothman, 1962.

Bodde, Derk. *China's First Unifier: A Study of the Ch'in Dynasty as Seen in the Life of Li Ssü, 280?–208*. Reprint. Hong Kong: Hong Kong University Press, 1967.

Bodde, Derk, and Clarence Morris. *Law in Imperial China.* Cambridge, Mass.: Harvard University Press, 1967.

Boyle, James. "A Theory of Law and Information: Copyright, Spleens, Blackmail and Insider Trading." *California Law Review* 80, no. 6 (1992): 1413–1540.

Brauchli, Marcus. "Fake CDs Are a Growth Industry in China." *Wall Street Journal,* Feb. 11, 1994, B1.

Breyer, Stephen. "The Uneasy Case for Copyright: A Study of Copyright in Books, Photocopies, and Computer Programs." *Harvard Law Review* 84, no. 2 (1970–71): 281–351.

Brown, Chris. "Taiwan Nurtures Biotech." *Far Eastern Economic Review* 150, no. 45 (Nov. 8, 1990): 70.

Brown, Francis, and Carole Ganz Brown, eds. *Intellectual Property Rights in Science, Technology, and Economic Performance.* Boulder, Colo.: Westview Press, 1990.

Bureau of National Affairs. "China Agrees to Push for Copyright Protection of Computer Software." *International Trade Reporter* 6, no. 25 (June 21, 1989): 818.

———. "Hills Removes Taiwan, Korea, and Singapore from Priority List: Six Countries Remain." *International Trade Reporter* 6, no. 44 (Nov. 8, 1989): 1436–37.

———. "Six Parties Comment on 17 Countries in Second Round Under Special 301 Provision." *International Trade Reporter* 7, no. 9 (Feb. 28, 1990): 300–301.

———. "Taiwan, Poland and Philippines Cited for Alleged Copyright Problems." *International Trade Reporter* 9, no. 9 (Feb. 26, 1992): 353.

———. "Taiwan Tries to Avert U.S. Trade Action on Intellectual Property After Talks Fail." *International Trade Reporter* 9, no. 16 (Apr. 15, 1992): 667–68.

———. "US and Taiwan Fail to Reach Agreement in Intellectual Property Dispute Talks." *International Trade Reporter* 9, no. 50 (Dec. 16, 1992): 2128–29.

———. "USTR Fact Sheet on Special 301 on Intellectual Property, Released May 25, 1989." *International Trade Reporter* 6, no. 22 (May 31, 1989): 715–21.

———. "USTR Sets January 16 Deadline for Decision on Sanctions Against Chinese Imports." *International Trade Reporter* 8, no. 50 (Dec. 18, 1991): 1837.

———. "Valid Copyright Treaty Exists Between the United States and Taiwan." *International Trade Reporter* 9, no. 7 (Feb. 12, 1992): 268–69.

Bush, Susan. *The Chinese Literati on Painting: Su Shih (1037–1101) to Tung Ch'i-ch'ang (1555–1636).* Cambridge, Mass.: Harvard University Press, 1971.

Cahill, James. *The Compelling Image*. Cambridge, Mass.: Harvard University Press, 1982.

———. "The Orthodox Movement in Early Ch'ing Painting." In Christian Murck, ed., *Artists and Traditions: Uses of the Past in Chinese Culture*. Princeton, N.J.: The Art Museum, Princeton University, 1976.

Carter, Thomas. *The Invention of Printing in China and Its Spread Westward*. Revised by L. Carrington Goodrich. 2d ed. New York: Ronald Press, 1955.

Chan Hok-lam. "Control of Publishing in China, Past and Present." Presented in the G. E. Morrison Lecture Series at the Australian National University, Canberra, in 1983.

———. *Legitimation in Imperial China*. Seattle: University of Washington Press, 1984.

Chang Hsin-pao. *Commissioner Lin and the Opium War*. Cambridge, Mass.: Harvard University Press, 1964.

Chang, T. K. "The Making of the Chinese Bankruptcy Law: A Study in the Chinese Legislative Process." *Harvard International Law Journal* 28, no. 2 (1987): 333–72.

Chang Wejen. "Chuantong guannian yu xianxing falü weishenma yao xue zhongguo fazhi shi" (The Traditional Perspective and the Contemporary Chinese Legal System: Why Study Chinese Legal History?). *Guoli Taiwan daxue faxue luncong* (National Taiwan University Law Review) 17 (Dec. 1987): 1–64.

———. "Traditional Chinese Legal Thought." *Guoli Taiwan daxue faxue luncong* (National Taiwan University Law Review) 20, no. 2 (1991): 1–43.

Chang Wejen and William Alford. "Major Issues in Chinese Legal History." Course materials, 1992.

Chao, Gene. "Exorcising Ghosts: Taiwan's 2–28 Incident of 1947." *UCLA Pacific Basin Law Journal* 8, no. 2 (1990): 368–89.

Chaves, Jonathan. "The Panoply of Images: A Reconsideration of the Literary Theory of the Kung-an School." In Susan Bush and Christian Murck, eds., *Theories of the Arts in China*. Princeton, N.J.: Princeton University Press, 1983.

Chen, Albert. *An Introduction to the Legal System of the People's Republic of China*. Singapore: Butterworths, 1992.

Chen, C. V. "The Legal Protection of Industrial and Intellectual Property Rights in China (Taiwan)." In *Proceedings of the Manila Symposium on Counterfeiting and Infringement and Licensing*, Nov. 1984.

Ch'en, Jerome. *China and the West: Society and Culture, 1815–1937*. Bloomington: University of Indiana Press, 1979.

Chen Jiajun and Lu Yinghai. *Diannau ruanti zhuzuoquan* (Computer Software Copyright). Taipei: Weili falü chuban she, 1987.

Chen Jinquan. "CPA v. NPA: Xianggang liangjia dalu zhuanli shangbiao daili jigou jieshao" (The CPA v. the NPA: Introducing the Two Hong Kong Entities That Serve as Patent and Trademark Agents on the Mainland). *Zixunfawu touxi* (Analysis of Legal Information), Jan. 1991.

Chen Xiaoyi. "Kan zhishicanquan de baohu dui guoji maoyi de yingxiang" (Looking at the Influence of the Protection of Intellectual Property on International Trade).

Chen Yi. "Publishing in China in the Post-Mao Era." *Asian Survey* 32, no. 6 (1992): 568–82.

Cheng, Joseph K. H. "Chinese Law in Transition: The Late Ch'ing Law Reform, 1901–1911." Ph.D. diss., Brown University 1977.

Cheng Kaiyuan. "Yibu juyou zhongguo tese de zhuanli fa" (A Patent Law with Chinese Characteristics). *Faxue jikan* (Legal Quarterly), no. 1 (1985): 42 (4 pp.).

Cheng, Lucie, and Arthur Rosett. "Contract with a Chinese Face, Socially Embedded Factors in the Transformation from Hierarchy to Market, 1978–1989." *Journal of Chinese Law* 5, no. 2 (1991): 143–244.

Cheng, N. S., and M. H. Chao. "Update on the Intellectual Property Rights Protection in Taiwan." *East Asian Executive Reports* 9, no. 6 (June 15, 1987): 7 (3 pp.).

Chiang Kai-shek. *Soviet Russia in China: A Summing Up at Seventy.* New York: Farrar, Straus & Cudahy, 1957.

Chiang, P. K. "The Impact of United States Trade Law Actions on Business Decisions in Taiwan." *Michigan Journal of International Law* 11 (1990): 279–87.

Ch'ien Ts'un-shun (T. H. Tsien). *Paper and Printing.* Part 1. Vol. 5 of *Science and Civilization in China,* Joseph Needham, ed. Cambridge: Cambridge University Press, 1986.

Chin Chun-tsung. "From Imitation to Innovation: East Asia's Experience in Protecting Intellectual Property." Paper delivered at the annual meeting of the International Studies Association, Vancouver, B.C., March 21, 1991.

China Law Review. Vols. 1–10. 1922–40.

Chiu Hanping, ed. *Lidai xingfa zhi* (The Legal Treatise of the Successive Dynasties). Reprint. Beijing: Xinhua shudian, 1988.

Chiu Hungdah. "Contemporary Practice and Judicial Decisions of the Republic of China Relating to International Law, 1986–1988." *Chinese Yearbook of International Law and Affairs* 7 (1987/88): 225–302.

Cho Tsung-shun. "The Anti-Counterfeiting Committee (ACC) Investigation to Prevent Counterfeiters from Being Exporters." In National Anti-Counterfeiting Committee, *Intellectual Property Rights Enforcement Seminar.* Taipei: National Anti-Counterfeiting Committee, 1987.

Chou Ju-hsi. "Through the Disciples' Eyes." In *Heritage of the Brush*. Phoenix: Phoenix Art Museum, 1991.

Chow Tse-tsung. *The May Fourth Movement*. Cambridge, Mass.: Harvard University Press, 1960.

Ch'ü T'ung-tsü. *Law and Society in Traditional China*. Paris: Moulton, 1961.

Chwang Tek Ling and Richard Thurston. "Technology Takes Command: The Policy of the People's Republic of China with Respect to Technology Transfer and Protection of Intellectual Property." *International Lawyer* 21, no. 1 (1987): 129–67.

Clark, A. M., and William Clark. *Analytic Summaries of the Patents, Designs, and Trademarks Act, 1883, and the Patent Laws of All European Countries and British Colonies*. London: A. M. and Wm. Clark, 1884.

Clark, Aubert. *The Movement for International Copyright in 19th Century America*. Washington, D.C.: Catholic University, 1960.

Clark, Cal. *Taiwan's Development: Implications for Contending Political Economy Paradigms*. New York: Greenwood Press, 1989.

Clifford, Mark. "Pirates' Lair: Taiwan Software Copiers Perfect the Hologram." *Far Eastern Economic Review* 155, no. 40 (Oct. 8, 1992): 79–80.

Cochran, Sherman. *Big Business in China: Sino-American Rivalry in the Tobacco Industry. 1896–1930*. Cambridge, Mass: Harvard University Press, 1975.

———. "Commercial Penetration and Economic Imperialism in China: An American Cigarette Company's Entrance into the Market." In Ernest May and John King Fairbank, eds., *America's China Trade in Historical Perspective: The Chinese and American Performance*, 151–203. Cambridge, Mass.: Council on East Asian Studies, Harvard University Press, 1986.

Cohen, Jerome. "The Chinese Communist Party and 'Judicial Independence,' 1949–1959." *Harvard Law Review* 82, no. 5 (1968–69): 967–1006.

———. "Law and Leadership in China." *Far Eastern Economic Review* 145, no. 28 (July 13, 1989): 23–24.

Cohen, Jerome, and Chiu Hungdah. *People's China and International Law*. Princeton, N.J.: Princeton University Press, 1974.

Cohen, Mark. *Taiwan at the Crossroads: Human Rights, Political Development and Social Change on the Beautiful Island*. Washington, D.C.: Asia Research Center, 1988.

Conger, F. H. "Letter to Secretary of State John Hay, Oct. 13, 1904." Reprinted in *Foreign Relations of the United States* (1906), item no. 1724, 242. Washington, D.C.: Government Printing Office, 1906.

Conner, Alison. "To Get Rich Is Precarious: Regulation of Private Enterprise in the People's Republic of China." *Journal of Chinese Law* 5, no. 1 (1991): 1–57.

Coolidge, John. "Letter to Secretary of State John Hay, Jan. 7, 1905." Reprinted in *Foreign Relations of the United States* (1906), item no. 1788, pp. 245–46. Washington, D.C. Government Printing Office, 1906.

Cornish, William. *Intellectual Property: Patents, Copyrights, Trademarks and Allied Rights*. London: Sweet & Maxwell, 1989.

"Cross-Strait Symposium on Patent Trademark and Copyright Held in Zhuhai." *China Patents & Trademarks*, no. 1 (1992): 119–20.

Crothall, Geoffrey. " 'Pirated' Products Said Still Widely Available." *South China Morning Post*, Dec. 29, 1991, 3.

Crow, Carl. *400 Million Customers. The Experiences, Some Happy, Some Sad, of an American in China, and What They Taught Him*. London: Harper & Bros., 1937.

Darnton, Robert. *The Literary Underground of the Old Regime*. Cambridge, Mass.: Harvard University Press, 1982.

De Bary, William T., et al., trans. Sima Qian, *Shi ji*. In *Sources of Chinese Tradition*. New York: Columbia University Press, 1960.

Da Qing huidian (Collected Institutes of the Great Qing Dynasty). Reprint of the 1899 edition, Beijing: Zhonghua shu ju, 1991.

Da Qing huidian shili (Supplement to the Collected Institutes of the Great Qing Dynasty). Vols. 1–12. Reprint of the 1899 edition. Beijing: Zhonghua shu ju, 1991.

"Disclosure of Timetable to Evidence ROC's Sincerity Toward Copyrights." *Free China Journal* 9, no. 27 (Apr. 21, 1992): 3.

Doerner, William. "Pirates of the High Cs." *Time*, Nov. 15, 1993, 42.

Dongfang zazhi (Orient Magazine). Shanghai: Shanghai yinshu guan: 1901–8.

Dong Baolin. "A Decade of Mighty Advance: Celebrating the Tenth Anniversary of Implementation of the Trademark Law of the PRC." *China Patents & Trademarks*, no. 2 (1993).

Doolittle, Justus. *Social Life of the Chinese*. Reprint. Taipei: Chengwen Publishers, 1966.

Dorris, Gregory. "The Very Specialized United States Generalized System of Preferences: An Examination of Renewal Changes and Analysis of Their Legal Effects." *Georgia Journal of International and Comparative Law* 15, no. 1 (1985): 39–81.

Dregé, Jean Pierre. "La Commercial Press de Shanghai, 1897–1949." Ph.D. diss., University of Paris, 1976.

Duan Ruilin. *Zhuanlifa shangbiaofa gailun* (An Introduction to Patent and Trademark Law). Jilin: Jilin daxue chuban she, 1985.

Duan Xuanwu. *Songdai banke fazhi yanjiu* (A Study of the Legal System for Publication in the Song Dynasty). Taipei: Shishi yanjiu, 1976.

Eastman, Lloyd. *The Abortive Revolution: China Under Nationalist Rule, 1927–1937*. Cambridge, Mass.: Harvard University Press, 1974.

————. *Family, Field and Ancestors: Constancy and Change in China's Social and Economic History, 1550–1949.* New York: Oxford University Press, 1988.

Edwards, R. Randle. "The Canton System." In Victor Li, ed., *Law and Policy in China's Foreign Trade.* Seattle: University of Washington Press, 1977.

————. "Ch'ing Legal Jurisdiction over Foreigners." In Jerome Cohen, R. Randle Edwards, and Fu-mei Chen, eds., *Essays on China's Legal Tradition.* Princeton, N.J.: Princeton University Press, 1980.

————. "Imperial China's Border Control Law." *Journal of Chinese Law* 1, no. 1 (1987): 33–62.

Edwards, R. Randle, Louis Henkin, and Andrew Nathan, eds. *Human Rights in Contemporary China.* New York: Columbia University Press, 1986.

Eisenstein, Elizabeth. *The Printing Press as an Agent of Change.* Cambridge: Cambridge University Press, 1979.

Eliot, T. S. *Notes Toward a Definition of Culture.* London: Faber & Faber, 1948.

Elvin, Mark. *The Pattern of the Chinese Past: A Social and Economic Interpretation.* Stanford: Stanford University Press, 1973.

Epstein, Edward. "The Theoretical System of Property Rights in China's *General Principles of Civil Law*: Theoretical Controversy in the Drafting Process and Beyond." *Law and Contemporary Problems* 52, no. 2 (1989): 177–216.

Epstein, Richard. "*International News Services v. Associated Press*: Custom and Law as Sources of Property Rights." *Virginia Law Review* 78, no. 1 (1992): 85–128.

Fairbank, John King. *The Great Chinese Revolution, 1800–1985.* New York: Harper & Row, 1986.

————. *Trade and Diplomacy in the China Coast: The Opening of the Treaty Ports, 1842–1854.* Cambridge, Mass.: Harvard University Press, 1953.

Fairbank, John King, and Teng Ssu-yü, eds. *China's Response to the West.* Cambridge, Mass.: Harvard University Press, 1954.

"Faming jiangli tiaoli" (Regulations to Encourage Invention). Effective from Nov. 3, 1963. In *Zhonghua renmin gongheguo fagui huibian* (The Collected Laws and Regulations of the People's Republic of China), 13 (Jan. 1962–Dec. 1963): 241–46. Beijing: Falü chuban she, 1964.

Fang Yangchun. "Bocai ta guo zhi chang, zou Zhongguo ziji de daolu" (Assimilate the Strong Points of Other Countries, Take China's Own Road). *Gongye chanquan* (Industrial Property), no. 1 (1988).

Fei Zongyi. "Protection for Intellectual Property by the People's Courts in China." *China Patents & Trademarks*, no. 3 (1992): 17–21.

Feinerman, James. "Taiwan and the GATT." *Columbia Business Law Review* 1992, no. 1: 39–60.

Feuerwerker, Albert. *China's Early Industrialization: Sheng Hsuan-huai (1844–*

1916) and Mandarin Enterprise. Cambridge, Mass.: Harvard University Press, 1958.

Fishel, Wesley. *The End of Extraterritoriality in China.* Berkeley and Los Angeles: University of California Press, 1952.

Fisher, William. "Reconstructing the Fair Use Doctrine." *Harvard Law Review* 101, no. 8 (1988): 1659–1759.

Foreign Relations of the United States. 1899–1908. Washington, D.C.: Government Printing Office, 1901–1912.

Foucault, Michel. *Discipline and Punish: The Birth of the Prison.* Trans. A. Sheridan. New York: Pantheon Books, 1977.

Freemantle, Brian. *The Steal: Counterfeiting and Industrial Espionage.* London: Michael Joseph, 1986.

Gadbaw, Michael, and Timothy Richards. *Intellectual Property Rights: Global Consensus, Global Conflicts.* Boulder, Colo.: Westview Press, 1989.

"Gaiding shangbiao tiaoli" (Revised Trademark Regulations). In *Da Qing Guangxu xin faling* (New Laws and Ordinances of Emperor Guangxu of the Great Qing Dynasty), ch. 16, 1909.

Gale, Barden. "The Concept of Intellectual Property in the People's Republic of China: Inventors and Inventions." *China Quarterly* 74, no. 2 (June 1978): 334–55.

Gao Lulin. "On the Revision of the Current Patent Law in China." *China Patents & Trademarks,* no. 4 (1992): 7–13.

Gardella, Robert. "The Boom Years of the Fukien Tea Trade, 1842–1888." In Ernest May and John King Fairbank, eds., *America's China Trade in Historical Perspective: The Chinese and American Performance,* 33–76. Cambridge, Mass.: Council on East Asian Studies, Harvard University, 1986.

Ge Gongzhen. *Zhongguo baoxue shi.* Beijing: Sanlian chuban she, 1955.

Gelatt, Timothy "The Foreign Exchange Quandary." *China Business Review* 13, no. 3 (May–June 1986): 28–32.

General Accounting Office. *International Trade: Strengthening Worldwide Protection of Intellectual Property Rights.* GAO Report NSIAD-87-65. Washington, D.C.: Government Printing Office, 1987.

Goldman, Merle. *Literary Dissent in Communist China.* Cambridge, Mass.: Harvard University Press, 1971.

Goldstein, Carl. "A Parting Gesture." *Far Eastern Economic Review* 139, no. 4 (Jan. 28, 1988): 19–24.

Gong Xuanwu. "Wubai nian lai di yi ren, jifan huadu xiao wang shu: Zhang Daqian de liu fa yishi" (Anecdotes of Zhang Daqian's Travels in France: The Adventures in Paris of the Most Famous [Chinese] Artist of the Past 500 years). *Xin xinwen zhoukan* (New Journalism Weekly) 264 (Mar. 29–Apr. 4, 1992): 82–87.

Goodrich, L. Carrington. *The Literary Inquisition of Ch'ien-lung*. 1935. Rev. ed. New York: Paragon, 1966.

Goonatilake, Susantha. *Aborted Discovery: Science and Creativity in the Third World*. London: Zed Books, 1984.

Gordon, Wendy. "An Inquiry into the Merits of Copyright: The Challenge of Consistency, Consent, and Encouragement Theory." *Stanford Law Review* 41 (1989): 1343–1469.

"Guanli shukan chubanye yinshuaye faxingye zanxing tiaoli" (Provisional Regulations on the Management of Book and Periodical Publishing, Printing, and Distribution). Effective from Aug. 15, 1952. In *Zhongyang renmin zhengfu faling huibian* (The Collected Laws and Decrees of the Central People's Government), 203–5. Beijing: Renmin chuban she, 1954.

"Guanyu guoying chuban bianji jigou ji gongzuo zhidu de guiding" (Rules on the Editorial Organization and Work System of State Publishing Entities). Issued in 1951.

"Guanyu jiaqiang zhuanli guanli gongzuo tongzhi" (Circular Concerning the Strengthening of Patent Administration). Feb. 2, 1990. In *Zhuanli fagui huibian* (Collected Laws and Regulations Concerning Patent Matters). 1984–90. Beijing: Zhuanli wenxian chuban she, 1991.

"Guanyu jiuzheng renyi fanyin tushu xianxiang de guiding" (Regulations on the Redress of the Phenomenon of Willful Reproduction of Books). Issued in Nov. 1953.

"Guanyu qinfan shangbiao zhuanyong ruhe jisuan sunshi peichang ho qinquan qijian wenti de pifu" (Reply from the Supreme People's Court to Questions of How to Calculate the Amount of Damages and the Period of Infringement of the Exclusive Right to Use a Trademark). *Zhonghua renmin gongheguo zuigao renmin fayuan gongbao* (Gazette of the Supreme People's Court of the People's Republic of China) 4, no. 4 (1985): 24. Beijing: Zhonghua renmin gonghe guo zuigao renmin fayuan bangongting, 1985.

"Guanyu shuji gaofei de zanxing guiding" (The Provisional Regulations on Basic Payments for Books). Effective from July 1, 1980.

"Guanyu zhengdun luyin, luxiang zhipin shichang, zhizhi weizhang fanlu xiaoshou huodong de tongzhi" (Circular on Rationalizing Audio-Video Markets and Prohibiting the Illegal Copying of Such Products). Issued on Feb. 4, 1986. In *Zhonghua renmin gongheguo fagui huibian* (The Collected Laws and Regulations of the People's Republic of China), Jan.–Dec. 1986: 809–11. Beijing: Falü chuban she, 1987.

"Guanyu zhixing xinwen chuban gaofei ji butie banfa de tongzhi" (The Trial Circular Concerning Basic and Supplemental Payments for News Publications). Issued in Oct. 1977.

Guojia dang'anju Ming-Qing dang'an guan, comp. *Wuxu bianfa dang'an shiliao* (Source Materials Concerning the Reform Movement of 1898). Beijing: Zhonghua shu ju, 1958.

Guojia kexue jishu weiyuanhui, ed. *Zhongguo de zhishicanquan zhidu* (The Intellectual Property System of China). Beijing: Zhongguo kexue jishu wenjian chuban she, 1992.

Guo Shoukang. "The Common Rules of Civil Law and Intellectual Property." *China Patents & Trademarks*, no. 3 (1987): 96–101.

Guomin zhengfu gongbao (The Gazette of the Republic of China Government). Taipei: Guomin zhengfu wenguan chu yinzhu ju, 1985–93.

Gutzlaff, Karl. *Sketch of Chinese History*. Reprint. Taipei: Chengwen Publishers, 1968.

Habermas, Jürgen. *Legitimation Crisis*. Trans. T. McCarthy. Cambridge: Polity Press, 1976.

Haeusser, Erich. "Industrial Property in the People's Republic of China—Justified Expectations (I)." *China Patents & Trademarks*, no. 4 (1986): 4–12.

Haggard, Stephan. *Pathways from the Periphery: The Politics of Growth in Newly Industrializing Countries*. Ithaca, N.Y.: Cornell University Press, 1990.

Hall, W. S. "Pirating of American Books Booms in China." *Publishers' Weekly* 136, no. 21 (Nov. 18, 1939): 1914–18.

Hall, Donald, and Roger Ames. *Thinking Through Confucius*. Albany: State University of New York Press, 1987.

Hamilton, Gary, and Lai Zhigong. "Jinshi zhongguo shangbiao yu quanguo dushishichang" (Trademarks and the National Urban Market in Late Imperial China). In *Proceedings of the Conference on Regional Studies of Modern China*. Taipei: Academia Sinica, 1986.

Han, Edward. "Protection from Commercial Counterfeiters in Taiwan for U.S. Firms." *Law & Policy in International Business* 16, no. 2 (1984): 641–61.

Hao Yen-p'ing. *The Commercial Revolution in Nineteenth-Century China: The Rise of Sino-Western Mercantile Capitalism*. Berkeley and Los Angeles: University of California Press, 1986.

Hao Yen-p'ing and Wang Erh-min. "Changing Chinese Views of Western Relations, 1840–95." In John King Fairbank and K. C. Liu, eds., *The Cambridge History of China*, vol. 11, *Late Ch'ing, 1800–1911*, pt. 2. Cambridge: Cambridge University Press, 1980.

Harding, Harry. *China's Second Revolution*. Washington, D.C.: Brookings Institution, 1987.

Hazard, John. *Communists and Their Laws*. Chicago: University of Chicago Press, 1969.

He Defen. "A Comparative Study of the Copyright Protection in the United States and the Republic of China." *Journal of Social Science* 28 (1980): 303–412.

————. *Zhuzuoquanfa lunwenji* (Collected Essays on Copyright Law). Taipei: Sanmin shu ju, 1986.

————. *Zhuzuouqan mianmianguan* (Looking at All Sides of Copyright Law). Taipei: Youshi wenhua shiye gongsi, 1987.

Heuser, Robert. "The Chinese Trademark Law of 1904: A Preliminary Study in Extraterritoriality of Competition and Late Ch'ing Law Reform." *Oriens Extremus* 22, no. 2 (Dec. 1975): 183–210.

Hickman, Michael. "Protecting Intellectual Property Rights in Taiwan—Non-Recognized U.S. Corporations and Their Treaty Rights to Access to Courts." *Washington Law Review* 60, no. 1 (1984): 117–40.

Ho Wai-kam. *Eight Dynasties of Chinese Painting*. Cleveland: Cleveland Museum of Arts, 1980.

Holm, Bill. *Coming Home Crazy*. Minneapolis: Milkweed Press, 1990.

Hoon Shim Jae. "Freer to Speak Out." *Far Eastern Economic Review* 139, no. 6 (Feb. 11, 1988): 12–13.

Horsley, Jamie. "Protecting Intellectual Property: A Basic Legal Framework Is Emerging, but Companies Still Tread Warily." *China Business Review* 13, no. 6 (Nov.–Dec. 1986): 17–22.

Hou Chi-ming. *Foreign Investment and Economic Development in China, 1840–1937*. Cambridge, Mass.: Harvard University Press, 1965.

Howson, Nicholas. "Cao Siyuan: A Responsible Reformer Silenced." *UCLA Pacific Basin Law Journal* 7, nos. 1–2 (1990): 267–302.

Hsia Ching-lin. *The Status of Shanghai*. 1929. Reprint. Taipei: Chengwen Publishers, 1971.

Hsia Tao-tai. "China's New Patent Law and Other Recent Legal Developments." Report Prepared for the Special Subcommittee on U.S. Trade with China of the Committee on Energy and Commerce of the U.S. House of Representatives, July 1984. Washington, D.C.: Government Printing Office, 1984.

Hsiao Kung-ch'uan. *From the Beginning to the Sixth Century* A.D.. Vol. 1 of *A History of Chinese Political Thought*. Trans. Frederick Mote. Princeton, N.J.: Princeton University Press, 1978.

————. *Rural China: Imperial Control in the Nineteenth Century*. Seattle: University of Washington Press, 1960.

Hsü, Immanuel. *The Rise of Modern China*. 3d ed. London: Oxford University Press, 1970.

Huang Kunyi. "China's Patent System Takes Shape." *Intertrade*, Feb. 1984.

————. "Guanyu zhonghua renmin gongheguo zhuanlifa (caoan) de shuoming" (An Explanation of the [Draft] Patent Law of the People's Republic of China). *Guowuyuan gongbao* (State Council Gazette) 427, no. 6 (1984): 176–82.

Huang Mao-zong. "Assistance and Services Provided by the National Anti-

Counterfeiting Committee." In National Anti-Counterfeiting Committee, *Intellectual Property Rights Enforcement Seminar*. Taipei: National Anti-Counterfeiting Committee, 1987.

Huang, Philip. "Codified Law and Magisterial Adjudication in the Qing." In Kathryn Bernhardt and Philip Huang, eds., *Civil Law in Qing and Republican China*. Stanford: Stanford University Press, 1994.

Huang, Ray. *1587: A Year of No Significance—The Ming Dynasty in Decline*. New Haven, Conn.: Yale University Press, 1981.

Huang Zhuhai. "Guanyu wo guo zhuzuoquan lifa de tedian sikao" (Deliberations Regarding the Special Points of Our Nation's Drafting of a Copyright Law). *Chuban cankao ziliao* (Reference Materials on Publishing), vol. 1. Beijing: 1990.

Hucker, Charles. *The Ming Dynasty: Its Origins and Evolving Institutions*. Ann Arbor: Center for Chinese Studies, 1978.

Hunt, Michael. *The Making of a Special Relationship*. New York: Columbia University Press, 1984.

"IBM v. Six Shenzhen Companies." *Chinese Law and Practice* 3, no. 5 (1985): 32–33.

Ichiko Chuzo. "Political and Institutional Reform, 1901–11." In John King Fairbank and K. C. Liu, eds., *The Cambridge History of China*, vol. 11, *Late Ch'ing, 1800–1911*, pt. 2. Cambridge: Cambridge University Press, 1980.

"Implementing Rules Under the Regulations Governing Trademarks." Promulgated by the State General Administration for Industry and Commerce of the PRC, Apr. 25, 1963.

"Inclosure to Letter of U.S. Minister Conger to Secretary of State Hay, Dec. 8, 1904." Reprinted in *Foreign Relations of the United States* (1906), item no. 1762, pp. 243–44. Washington, D.C.: Government Printing Office, 1906.

"Infringement of American Trade-marks in China—Vaseline Trade-mark Case: The Cheesebrough Manufacturing Co. v. Yung Ch'i-Hsiang et al." In *Foreign Relations of the United States* (1915): 231–56. Washington, D.C.: Government Printing Office, 1924.

"Infringement of the Exclusive Right to Use the Designs of the Registered Trademarks 'Mickey Mouse' & 'Donald Duck' Penalized in Hangzhou." *China Patents & Trademarks*, no. 2 (1990): 70.

International Intellectual Property Alliance. "Trade Losses Due to Piracy and Other Market Access Barriers Affecting United States Copyright Industries." Report to the U.S. Trade Representative. Washington, D.C., 1989.

Islam, Shada, and Jonathan Karp. "Grab That Rolex." *Far Eastern Economic Review* 156, no. 31 (Aug. 5, 1993): 63.

Jaszi, Peter. "Towards a Theory of Copyright: The Metamorphoses of 'Authorship.'" *Duke Law Journal* 1991, no. 2: 455–502.

Jernigan, Thomas. *China in Law and Commerce.* Shanghai: Kelly & Walsh, 1905.

Jernow, Alison Liu. "Amicable Divorce." *Index on Censorship* 21, no. 8 (1992): 12–14.

Jiang Ping and Shen Ren'gan. *Zhonghua renmin gongheguo zhuzuoquanfa jiangxi* (Talks on the Copyright Law of the People's Republic of China). Beijing: Zhongguo guoji guangbo chuban she, 1991.

Jiang Ying. "Looking Back and Looking Ahead." *China Patents & Trademarks,* no. 2 (1993): 5–9.

Jilin sheng gongshang xingzheng guanliju. *Zhonghua renmin gonghehuo shangbiaofa tushi* (An Illustrated Explanation of the Trademark Law of the People's Republic of China). Beijing: Gongshang chuban she, 1985.

"Jishu gaijin jiangli tiaoli" (Regulations to Encourage Technical Improvements). Effective from Nov. 3, 1963. In *Zhonghua renmin gongheguo fagui huibian* (The Collected Laws and Regulations of the People's Republic of China), 13 (Jan. 1962–Dec. 1963): 246–51. Beijing: Falü chuban she, 1964.

"Jisuanji ruanjian baohu tiaoli" (Regulations on the Protection of Computer Software). Promulgated on June 4, 1991. Effective Oct. 1, 1991.

"Jisuanji ruanjian zhuzuoquan dengji banfa" (Measures for the Registration of Copyrights in Computer Software). Original Chinese and English translation. Reprinted in *China Patents & Trademarks,* no. 3 (1992): 86–88.

Johnson, Wallace. *The T'ang Code.* Princeton, N.J.: Princeton University Press, 1979.

Jones, William. "Some Questions Regarding the Significance of the General Principles of the Civil Law in the People's Republic of China." *Harvard International Law Journal* 28 (1987): 309–31."

———, trans. *The Great Qing Code.* Oxford: Clarendon Press, 1994.

"Jurisprudence and Jurisdiction." In *Opinions, VII Attorneys-General* (Sept. 19, 1915). Reprinted in Charles Lobingier, *Extraterritorial Cases.* Manila: Bureau of Printing, 1920.

Kang, Youwei. *Xinxue weijing kao* (A Study of the Forged Classics of the Xin Period). In Jiang Yihua and Wu Genliang, comps., *Kang Youwei quanji* (The Collected Works of Kang Youwei). Shanghai: Shanghai guji chuban she, 1987.

Kaplan, Benjamin. *An Unhurried View of Copyright.* New York: Columbia University Press, 1967.

Kaser, David. *Book Pirating in Taiwan.* Philadelphia: University of Pennsylvania Press, 1969.

Katz, Richard. "U.S., China Reach Uneasy Compromise: Settlement of

Copyright Dispute Staves off Tension." *Nikkei Weekly* 30, no. 1502 (Feb. 1, 1992): 20.

Kaufer, Erich. *The Economics of the Patent System.* New York: Harwood, 1989.

Kaufman, Deborah. "Intellectual Property and Political Change in the People's Republic of China." Third-year paper, Harvard Law School, 1992.

Kay, David. "The Patent Law of the People's Republic of China in Perspective." *UCLA Law Review* 33, no. 1 (1985): 331–67.

———. "PRC: Regulations for the Protection of Computer Software." *IP ASIA* 1991, no. 6: 22–30.

Kay, David, and Lee Green. *Chinese Trademarks.* Hong Kong: Shomei, 1988.

Kaye, Lincoln. "Learning New Rules." *Far Eastern Economic Review* 156, no. 44 (Nov. 4, 1993): 20–22.

———. "One Way Street." *Far Eastern Economic Review* 156, no. 45 (Nov. 11, 1993): 12–13.

Kaye, Lincoln, and Susumu Awanohara. "Down to the Wire." *Far Eastern Economic Review* 155, no. 4 (Jan. 24, 1992): 37 (2 pp.).

Ke Tongzhen. *Zhongguo baoxue shi* (A History of the Chinese Press). Beijing: Sanlian chuban she, 1955.

Keeton, George. *The Development of Extraterritoriality in China.* 2 vols. London: Longman's Green, 1928.

Keightley, David. "The Religious Commitment: Shang Theology and the Genesis of Chinese Political Culture." *History of Religions* 17, nos. 3–4 (1978): 211–25.

King, Frank. *Money and Monetary Policy in China, 1845–1895.* Cambridge, Mass.: Harvard University Press, 1965.

Kirim, Arman. "Reconsidering Patents and Economic Development: A Case Study of the Turkish Pharmaceutical Industry." *World Development* 13, no. 2 (1985): 219–36.

Kitch, Edmund. "The Nature and Function of the Patent System." *Journal of Law & Economics* 20, no. 2 (1977): 265–90.

———. "Patents, Prospects and Economic Surplus: A Reply." *Journal of Law and Economics* 23, no. 1 (1980) 205–7.

Klemm, Friedrich. *A History of Western Technology.* Trans. Dorothea Waley Singer. Cambridge, Mass.: MIT Press, 1964.

Kotenev, Anatol. *Shanghai and Its Mixed Court and Council.* 1925. Reprint. Taipei: Chengwen Publishers, 1968.

Ku Chieh-gang. "A Study of the Literary Persecution During the Ming Dynasty." Trans. L. Carrington Goodrich. *Harvard Journal of Asiatic Studies* 3, nos. 3–4 (1938): 254–311.

Kuhn, Philip. "The Taiping Rebellion." In John King Fairbank and K. C. Liu, eds., *The Cambridge History of China,* vol. 10, *Late Ching, 1800–1911,* pt. 1. Cambridge: Cambridge University Press, 1978.

Kuo Ting-yee and K. C. Liu. "Self-Strengthening: The Pursuit of Western Technology." In John King Fairbank and K. C. Liu, eds., *The Cambridge History of China*, vol. 10, *Late Ch'ing, 1800–1911*, pt. 1. Cambridge: Cambridge University Press, 1978.

Lachica, Eduardo. "China Settles Dispute over U.S. Patents, Copyrights, Heading off Threat." *Wall Street Journal*, Jan. 17, 1992, A2.

Lai Tse-han and Ramon Myers. *A Tragic Beginning: The Taiwan Uprising of February 28, 1947.* Stanford: Stanford University Press, 1991.

Landes, William. "An Economic Analysis of Copyright Law." *Journal of Legal Studies* 18, no. 2 (1989): 325–63.

Lee, Benny, and Xavier Delmar. "Welcome Changes to the Trade Mark Law of the People's Republic of China." *European Intellectual Property Review* 14, no. 2 (Feb. 1992): 67–69.

Lee, Thomas. *Government Education and Examinations in Sung China.* Hong Kong: Chinese University of Hong Kong Press, 1985.

Levenson, Joseph. *Confucian China and Its Modern Fate: A Trilogy.* Berkeley and Los Angeles: University of California Press, 1968.

Levin, Richard. "Appropriability, R & D Spending and Technological Performance." *American Economic Review (Paper & Proceedings)* 78, no. 2 (1988): 424–28.

Levin, Richard, Alvin Klevorick, Richard Nelson, and Sidney Winter. "Appropriating the Returns from Industrial R & D." *Brookings Papers on Economic Activity* 1987, no. 3: 783–831.

Levitsky, Serge. *Copyright, Defamation, and Privacy in Soviet Civil Law.* Germantown, Md.: Sijthoff & Noordhoff, 1979.

Leys, Simon. *Chinese Shadows.* New York: Viking, 1977.

Li Cang. "The Similarities and Dissimilarities Between the Patent Laws of the PRC & USA." *China Patents & Trademarks*, no. 3 (1987): 30–35.

Lifayuan gongbao (The Gazette of the Legislative Yuan). Taipei: Legislative Yuan Secretariat, 1985–93.

Li Guilian. *Shen Jiaben yu zhongguo falü xiandaihua* (Shen Jiaben and the Modernization of Chinese Law). Beijing: Guangming ribao chuban she, 1989.

Li Xiangsheng. "Waiting for Supplements: Comments on China's Copyright Law." *European Intellectual Property Review* 13, no. 5 (1991): 171–77.

Li Ying. "International Copyright Treaties and Chinese Implementation Rules." *China Patents & Trademarks*, no. 1 (1993): 66–69.

Liang Qichao. *Yinbingshi heji* (Collected Essays from the Ice Drinker's Studio). 1902. Reprint. Beijing: Zhonghua shu ju, 1989.

Libecap, Gary. "Property Rights in Economic History: Implications for Research." *Explorations in Economic History* 23, no. 3 (1986): 227–52.

Lin Ruey-Long. "Protection of Intellectual Property in the Republic of China." *Chinese Yearbook of International Law and Affairs* 6 (1986–87): 120–60.

Lin Shuen-fu. "Chiang K'uei's Treatises on Poetry and Calligraphy." In Susan Bush and Christian Murck eds., *Theories of the Arts in China.* Princeton, N.J.: Princeton University Press, 1983.

Link, Perry. *Mandarin Ducks and Butterflies: Popular Fiction in Early Twentieth-Century Chinese Cities.* Berkeley and Los Angeles: University of California Press, 1981.

————. *Evening Chats in Beijing: Probing the Chinese Predicament.* New York: Norton, 1992.

Liu Chuntian. "The Current Situation of China's Copyright Related Legal System Viewed Through Cases." *China Patents & Trademarks,* no. 2 (1993): 77–80.

Liu Gushu. "The Practice and Development of the Chinese Industrial Property System." *China Patents & Trademarks,* no. 4 (1990): 3–15.

————. "Questions of World-wide Interest in Connection with the Chinese Copyright Law." *China Patents & Trademarks,* no. 4 (1991): 19–24.

Liu, Lawrence Shao-Liang. "Judicial Review and Constitutionalism: The Uneasy Case for the Republic of China on Taiwan." *American Journal of Comparative Law* 39, no. 3 (1991): 509–58.

————. "Legal and Policy Perspectives on U.S. Trade with and Economic Liberalization in the Republic of China." *Michigan Journal of International Law* 11, no. 2 (1990): 326–67.

————. "A Lesson in Persuasion." *Far Eastern Economic Review* 150, no. 46 (Nov. 15, 1990): 26.

Liu Li. "On the Legal System of China Governing Trademarks." *China Patents & Trademarks,* no. 3 (1992): 51–57.

Liu, Paul. "A Review of the Intellectual Property Laws in Taiwan: Proposals to Curb Piracy and Counterfeiting in a Developing Country." *Brigham Young University Law Review* 1988, no. 3: 619–42.

Liu, Philip. "Rejecting the Old Boy Network." *Free China Review* 41, no. 7 (1991): 18–25.

Liu Song. "The Role of the Chinese Government in the Protection of Copyright." *China Patents & Trademarks,* no. 4 (1992): 64–66.

Liu Wang Hui-chen. *Traditional Chinese Clan Rules.* Locust Valley, N.Y.: J.J. Augustin, 1959.

Lobingier, Charles. "American Courts in China." Second Inaugural Address of Judge Charles Lobingier as president of the Far Eastern Bar Association. Bar Association Publications, no. 2. Far Eastern Bar Association, n.d.

Loh Pin-chon, ed. *The Kuomintang Debacle of 1949: Conquest or Collapse?* Boston: D. C. Heath, 1965.

Lohr, Steven. "Crackdown on Counterfeiting." *New York Times,* May 7, 1984, 12.

Lu Guang and Pan Xianmou. *Zhongguo xinwen falü gailun* (A General Survey of Press Law in China). Taipei: Zhengzhong shu ju, 1956.

Lu Guangcan. "The Second National Conference on Patent Law." *China Patents & Trademarks*, no. 1 (1987): 106–8.

Lu Xun. *Selected Stories of Lu Hsün*. Trans. Yang Hsien-yi and Gladys Yang. New York: Oriole Editions, n.d. 3d ed. Beijing: Foreign Language Press, 1972.

Lubman, Stanley. "Emerging Functions of Formal Legal Institutions in China's Modernization." *China Law Reporter* 2, no. 4 (1983): 195–266.

"Lun shangbiao zhuce buying zhanqi" (Discussion of the Unwillingness to Extend the Period for Trademark Registration). *Dongfang zazhi* (Orient Magazine) (The Twelfth Period), Guangxu 30th year, 12th month, 25th day (1904): 143–45.

"Luyin, luxiang chubanwu chuban baohu zanxing tiaoli" (The Provisional Regulations Concerning Protection for Audio-Video Publications). Issued in Sept. 1986.

"Luyin, luxiang chuban gongzuo zanxing tiaoli" (The Provisional Regulations on the Administration of Audio-video Publications). In *Zhonghua renmin gongheguo xianxing xinwen chuban fagui huibian* (The Current Collected Laws and Regulations of the People's Republic of China Concerning Press and Publication), 1949–90: 294–97. Beijing: Renmin chuban she, 1991.

"Luyin, luxiang zhipin guanli zanxing guiding" (The Provisional Regulations on the Manufacture of Audio-visual Products). In *Zhonghua renmin gongheguo xianxing chuban fagui huibian* (The Current Collected Laws and Regulations of the People's Republic of China Concerning Press and Publication Matters), 1949–90: 272–76. Beijing: Renmin chuban she, 1991.

Lynn, Richard. "Alternative Routes to Self-Realization in Ming Theories of Poetry." In Susan Bush and Christian Murck, eds., *Theories of the Arts in China*. Princeton, N.J.: Princeton University Press, 1983.

"M&Ms v. W&Ws." *Chinese Law and Practice* 4, no. 5 (1990): 24–27.

MacFarquhar, Roderick. *The Origins of the Culture Revolution*. Vol. 1. London: Oxford University Press, 1974.

MacGowan, John. *Sidelights on Chinese Life*. Philadelphia: Lippincott, 1907.

Machlup, Fritz, "Patents." In David Sills, ed., *The International Encyclopedia of the Social Sciences*, 11: 468–71. New York: Macmillan, 1968.

Machlup, Fritz, and Edith Penrose. "The Patent Controversy in the Nineteenth Century." *Journal of Economic History* 10, no. 1 (1950): 1–29.

MacMurray, J., ed. *Treaties and Agreements with and Concerning China, 1894–1919*. Vols. 1 and 2. New York: 1921.

Mandich, Guilo. "Venetian Patents, 1450–1550." *Journal of the Patent Office Society* 30, no. 3 (1948): 166–223.

Mann, Susan. *Local Merchants and the Chinese Bureaucracy*. Stanford: Stanford University Press, 1987.
Mansfield, Edwin. "Intellectual Property, Technology, and Economic Growth." In Charls Walker and Mark Bloomfield eds., *Intellectual Property Rights and Capital Formation in the Next Decade*. Washington, D.C.: University Press of America, 1988.
———. "Patents and Innovation: An Empirical Study." *Management Science* 32, no. 2 (1986): 173–81.
Mao Zedong. "On the Tactics of Fighting Japanese Imperialism." In *Selected Works of Mao Zedong*, vol. 1. Beijing: Foreign Language Press, 1961–77.
Marx, Karl. *Early Writings*. Trans. and ed. T. Bottomore. London: Watts, 1963.
———. "Revolution in China and Europe." *New York Daily Tribune*, June 14, 1853.
Massey, Joseph. "301: The Successful Resolution." *China Business Review* 19, no. 6 (Nov.–Dec. 1992): 9–11.
May, Ernest, and John King Fairbank, eds. *America's China Trade in Historical Perspective: The Chinese and American Performance*. Cambridge, Mass.: Council on East Asian Studies, Harvard University Press, 1986.
Mayers, W. F., ed. *Treaties Between the Empire of China and Foreign Powers*. Shanghai: Kelly & Walsh, 1897.
McCarthy, Thomas, Jr. *Trademarks and Unfair Competition*. 2d ed. San Francisco: Bancroft-Whitney, 1984–.
Mckee, Delber. *Chinese Exclusion Versus the Open Door Policy, 1900–1908*. Detroit: Wayne State University Press, 1977.
McKnight, Brian. *Law and Order in Sung China*. Cambridge: Cambridge University Press, 1992.
Meijer, Marinus. *The Introduction of Modern Criminal Law in China*. Batavia: Koninklijke Drukkerij Unie, 1950.
"Meixu chubanwu gaofei shixing banfa" (The Trial Measures on Basic Payments for Works of Art). In *Zhonghua renmin gongheguo xianxing xinwen chuban fagui huibian* (The Current Collected Laws and Regulations of the People's Republic of China Concerning Press and Publication Matters) (1949–90): 33–41. Beijing: Renmin chuban she, 1991.
"Memorandum of Understanding Between the Government of the People's Republic of China and the Government of the United States on Market Access." Signed on Oct. 10, 1992, in Washington, D.C. Mimeo.
"Memorandum of Understanding Between the Government of the People's Republic of China and the Government of the United States on the Protection of Intellectual Property." Signed on Jan. 17, 1992, in Washington, D.C. Mimeo.
Mendel, F. Fraser. "Judicial Power and Illusion: The Republic of China's

Council of Grand Justices and Constitutional Interpretation." *Pacific Rim Law and Policy Journal* 2, no. 1 (1993): 157–90.

Merges, Robert. "Commercial Success and Patent Standards: Economic Perspectives on Innovation." *California Law Review* 76, no. 4 (1988): 803–76.

Merryman, John Henry. "Comparative Law and Social Change: On the Origins, Style, Decline, and Revival of the Law and Development Movement." *American Journal of Comparative Law* 25, no. 3 (1977): 457–91.

Metzger, Thomas. "Foreword." In Richard Wilson, Sidney Greenblatt, and Amy Wilson, eds., *Moral Behavior in Chinese Society*. New York: Praeger, 1981.

Morse, Hosea B. *The International Relations of the Chinese Empire: The Period of Subjection, 1894–1911*. 3 vols. London: Longman's Green, 1918.

Moser, Michael, and David Ho. "Registration and Protection of Patent in China." In Michael Moser, ed., *Foreign Trade, Investment and the Law in the People's Republic of China*. 2d ed. Hong Kong: Oxford University Press, 1987.

Mote, Frederick. "The Arts and the 'Theorizing Mode' of Chinese Civilization." In Christian Murck, ed., *Artists and Traditions*. Princeton, N.J.: Princeton University Press, 1976.

Munro, Donald. *The Concept of Man in Early China*. Stanford: Stanford University Press, 1969.

Murck, Christian, ed. *Artists and Traditions: Uses of the Past in Chinese Culture*. Princeton, N.J.: The Art Museum, Princeton University, 1976.

Murphy, Kevin. "CD Pirates Make China Home Port as Sales Soar." *International Herald Tribune*, Oct. 30–31, 1993, 17.

National Anti-Counterfeiting Committee. *Intellectual Property Rights Enforcement Seminar*. 2 vols. Taipei: National Anti-Counterfeiting Committee, 1987.

National Foreign Trade Council. Subcommittee on Intellectual Property. *The Protection of Industrial and Intellectual Property in China*. New York: National Council on Foreign Trade, 1945. Pamphlet.

Needham, Joseph. *Science and Civilization in China*. Vol. 2. Cambridge: Cambridge University Press, 1954.

———. "Science and Society in East and West." In Joseph Needham, *The Grand Titration*. London: Allen & Unwin, 1969.

Niida Noboru. *Chūgoku hōseishi kenkyū* (The Legal History of China). Vol. 4. Tokyo: Tokyo University Press, 1964.

Nimmer, Melville, and David Nimmer. *Nimmer on Copyright: A Treatise on the Law and Literary, Musical and Artistic Property*. New York: Matthew Bender, 1978–.

Noble, David. *America by Design: Science, Technology, and the Rise of Corporate Capitalism*. New York: Knopf, 1977.

North, Douglass, and Robert Paul Thomas. *The Rise of the Western World: A New Economic History*. Cambridge: Cambridge University Press, 1973.

Oddi, Samuel. "The International Patent System and Third World Development: Reality or Myth?" *Duke Law Journal* 1987, no. 5: 831–78.

Olsen, Frances. "The Family and Market: A Study of Ideology and Legal Reform." *Harvard Law Review* 96, no. 7 (1983): 1497–1578.

"Oppose the Black Line of Peng [Dehuai] and Luo [Ruiqing] (Fan Peng, Luo hei hsien)." Translated and reprinted in *Chinese Law and Government* 2, no. 4 (1969–70): 3–41.

Owen, Stephen. *Remembrances: The Experience of the Past in Chinese Literature*. Cambridge, Mass.: Harvard University Press, 1986.

Parker, John. "Bargaining Positions." In "China's Economy: Survey." Supplement to *The Economist*, Aug. 1, 1987.

"Patent Law of the Republic of China." Amended Dec. 24, 1986. Translated and reprinted in *East Asian Executive Reports* 9, no. 6 (June 15, 1987): 20–23.

Patterson, Lyman. *Copyright in Historical Perspective*. Nashville, Tenn.: Vanderbilt University Press, 1968.

———. "Free Speech, Copyright, and Fair Use." *Vanderbilt Law Review* 40, no. 1 (1987): 1–66.

Pelliot, Paul. *Les Debuts de l'imprimerie en Chine*. In *Oeuvres posthumes de Paul Pelliot*, ed. Robert des Rotours, vol. 4. Paris: Impr. Nationale, 1953.

Pendleton, Michael. *Intellectual Property in the People's Republic of China*. Singapore: Butterworth, 1986.

———. *The Law of Intellectual and Industrial Property in Hong Kong: A Guide*. Singapore: Butterworth, 1984.

Peng Haiqing. *Zhuanli wenjian shiyong zhinan* (A Practical Guidebook to Patent Documents). Tianjin: Tianjin daxue chuban she, 1987.

Peng, Tammy. "Lee Bemoans Shadow of Sadness." *Free China Journal* 9, no. 3 (Feb. 28, 1992): 1.

People's Republic of China. Information Office of the State Council of the PRC. "White Paper on the Human Rights Situation in China." Translated and reprinted in *Beijing Review* 34, no. 44 (Nov. 4, 1991): 8–45.

Poon Ming-sun. "Books and Printing in Sung China (960–1279)." Ph.D. diss., University of Chicago Graduate Library School, 1979.

———. "The Printer's Colophon in Sung China, 960–1279." *Library Quarterly* 43 (1973): 39–52.

Potter, Pitman. *The Economic Contract Law of China: Legitimation and Contract Autonomy in the PRC*. Seattle: University of Washington Press, 1992.

Pow, Elson, and John Lee. "Taiwan's Anti-Counterfeit Measures: A Hazard for Trademark Owners." *Trademark Report* 72, no. 2 (1982): 157–67.

Priest, George. "What Economists Can Tell Lawyers About Intellectual Property." *Research in Law and Economics* 8 (1986): 19–24.

Pulleyblank, Edward. "Chinese Historical Criticism: Liu Chih-chi and Ssu-ma Kuang." In William Beasley and Edward Pulleyblank, eds., *Historians of China and Japan*. London: Oxford University Press, 1961.

————. "The Historiographical Tradition." In Raymond Dawson, ed., *The Legacy of China*. London: Oxford University Press, 1964.

Qi Shaofu. "Zhongguo gudai de chuban he danxing de chuban faling" (Ancient Chinese Publishing and Pertinent Laws of That Time). *Shanghai chuban gongzuo* (Publishing Work in Shanghai), Aug. 1980.

Qian Duansheng. *The Government and Politics of China*. Cambridge, Mass.: Harvard University Press, 1967.

"Qikan guanli zanxing guiding" (The Provisional Regulations on the Administration of Periodicals). Effective from Nov. 24, 1988. Original Chinese and English translation reprinted in *Chinese Law and Practice* 3, no. 8, Sept. 25, 1989, 36–49.

"Qiye zhuanli gongzuo banfa (shixing)" (Trial Measures Concerning Enterprise Patent Work). Effective from March 22, 1990. In *Zhuanli fagui huibian* (The Collected Laws and Regulations Concerning Patent Matters), 1984–90. Beijing: Zhuanli wenxian chuban she, 1991.

"Quanguo renmin daibiao dahui changwu weiyuanhui guanyu chengzhi jiamao juce shangbiao fanzui de buchong guiding" (The Supplementary Provisions of the Standing Committee of the National People's Congress for the Punishment of Crimes of Passing of Registered Trademarks). Effective from July 1, 1993. Original Chinese and English translation reprinted in *China Patents and Trademarks*, no. 2 (1993): 90–91.

Rakoff, Jed, and Ira Wolff. "Commercial Counterfeiting and the Proposed Trademark Counterfeiting Act." *American Criminal Law Review* 20, no. 2 (1982): 145–225.

Rapp, Richard, and Richard Rozek. "Benefits and Costs of Intellectual Property Protection in Developing Countries." *Journal of World Trade* 24, no. 5 (1990): 75–102.

Ren Jianxin. "China's Judicial System for the Protection of Intellectual Property." *China Patents & Trademarks*, no. 1 (1987): 4–10.

Ren Wei. "Beverage 'Vitasoy' and Its Trademark Registration." *China Patents & Trademarks*, no. 4 (1986): 42–44.

————. "World-Wide Symposium on the International Patent System in the 21 Century." *China Patents & Trademarks*, no. 1 (1990): 9–11.

Republic of China. Government Information Office. *A Brief Introduction to the Book Publishing Industry of the Republic of China*. Taipei: Government Information Office, 1991.

————. Ministry of Economic Affairs. Board of Foreign Trade. *Protection of Intellectual Property Rights in the Republic of China on Taiwan*. Taipei: Ministry of Economic Affairs, 1990.

Richman, Barry. *Industrial Society in Communist China*. New York: Random House, 1969.

Ricketson, Sam. *The Berne Convention for the Protection of Literary and Artistic Works, 1886–1986*. London: Kluwer, 1987.

Rockhill, W. W. "Letter to the Ministers of Great Britain, France, the Netherlands, Belgium, Germany and Italy, Jan. 22, 1906." Reprinted in *Foreign Relations of the United States* (1906), enclosure to item no. 332, 232. Washington, D.C.: Government Printing Office, 1909.

Rohwer, James. "When China Wakes." Special Supplement to *The Economist*, Nov. 28, 1992.

Rosario, Louise do. "Peking's Primary Goal." *Far Eastern Economic Review* 138, no. 46 (Nov. 12, 1987): 66–67.

———. "Publish at Your Peril." *Far Eastern Economic Review* 143, no. 5 (Feb. 2, 1989): 24.

Rose, Mark. *Authors and Owners: Copyright in Eighteenth-Century Britain*. Cambridge, Mass.: Harvard University Press, 1993.

Rosenberg, Nathan, and L. E. Birdzell, Jr. *How the West Grew Rich: The Economic Transformation of the Industrial World*. New York: Basic Books, 1986.

Rosenberg, Peter. *Patent Law Fundamentals*. 2d ed. New York: Clark Boardman, 1983–.

Ross, Frank, Jr. *Oracle Bones, Stars, and Wheelbarrows: Ancient Chinese Science and Technology*. Boston: Houghton Mifflin, 1982.

Rowe, William. *Hankow: Commerce and Society in a Chinese City, 1796–1889*. Stanford: Stanford University Press, 1984.

Saich, Tony. *China's Science Policy in the Eighties*. Manchester: Manchester University Press, 1989.

Santangelo, Paolo. "The Imperial Factories of Suzhou: Limits and Characteristics of State Intervention During the Ming and Qing Dynasties." In Stuart Schram, ed., *The Scope of State Power*. London: School of Oriental and African Studies, University of London, 1985.

Scherer, F. *Industrial Market Structure and Economic Performance*. 3d ed. Boston: Houghton Mifflin, 1990.

Schloss, Peter. "China's Long-Awaited Copyright Law." *China Business Review* 17, no. 5 (Sept.–Oct. 1990): 24–28.

Schwartz, Benjamin. *The World of Thought in Ancient China*. Cambridge, Mass.: Harvard University Press, 1985.

Seng Tan-ju. "Film and Video Piracy—The Need for a Taiwan Solution." In National Anti-Counterfeiting Committee, *Intellectual Property Rights Enforcement Seminar*. Taipei: National Anti-Counterfeiting Committee, 1987.

Sesser, Stan. "Opium War Redux." *New Yorker*, Sept. 13, 1993.

"Shangbiao guanli tiaoli" (The Regulations on the Control of Trademarks).

Effective from Apr. 10, 1963. *Zhonghua renmin gongheguo fagui huibian* (The Collected Laws and Regulations of the People's Republic of China), 13 (Jan. 1962–Dec. 1963): 162–64. Beijing: Falü chuban she, 1964.

"Shangbiao juce zanxing tiaoli" (The Provisional Regulations on Trademark Registration). Promulgated on Aug. 28, 1950. In *Zhongyang renmin zhengfu faling huibian* (The Laws and Decrees of the Central People's Government) (1949–50): 528–31, Beijing: Renmin chuban she, 1952.

"Shangbiaofa" (The Trademark Law). In Tao Baichuan, Wang Zijian, Liu Zongrong, and Ge Kechang, eds., *Liu fa quanshu* (The Complete Book of the Six Laws). Taipei: Sanmin chuban she, 1992.

"Shangbiaofa tiaowen xiuzheng caoan zongshuoming" (The Complete Explanation of the Draft Revised Trademark Law Provisions). Taipei: Lifayuan, [1985]. Mimeo.

"Shangbiaofa tiaowen xiuzheng caoan zongshuoming" (The Complete Explanation of the Draft Revised Trademark Law Provisions). Taipei: Lifayuan, [1989]. Mimeo.

Shao Chiung-hui. "The Internationalization of Copyright Protection in Taiwan." L. L. M. paper, Harvard Law School, 1994.

Shattuck, John. "Public Attitudes and the Enforceability of Law." Paper prepared for the U.S. Office of Technology Assessment, 1985.

Shen Jungui. "Protection of Trademark Right by Criminal Proceedings in China." *China Patents & Trademarks*, no. 3 (1992): 60–62.

Shen Ren'gan. " 'Copyright' and 'Author's Right' as They Are Understood in China." *China Patents & Trademarks*, no. 1 (1990): 54–56.

Shen Ren'gan and Zhong Yingke. *Banquanfa qiantan* (A Review of Copyright Law). Beijing: Falü chuban she, 1982.

Shen Ren'gan et al. *Zhonghua renmin gongheguo zhuzuoquanfa jianghua* (Talks on the Copyright Law of the People's Republic of China). Beijing: Falü chuban she, 1991.

Shen Yuanyuan. "To Copy or Copyright: China's International Copyright Relations." LL.M. thesis, Harvard University, 1989.

———. *Faming yu faxian quan* (Invention and Discovery Rights). Beijing: Falü chuban she, 1986.

"Shenghuo yongpin jiamao shi li." *Zhongguo xiaofeizhe bao* (China Consumers' Newspaper), Oct. 15, 1987.

"Shenqing zhongguo zhuanli xingzhi" (Guide to Filing Patent Applications in China). Original Chinese and English translation reprinted in *China Patents & Trademarks*, no. 1 (1993): 98–99.

Sheridan, James. *China in Disintegration, 1912–1949*. New York: Free Press, 1975.

Sherwood, Robert. *Intellectual Property and Economic Development*. Boulder, Colo.: Westview Press, 1990.

Shi Wengao. *Guoji zhuzuoquanfa zhi xilun* (A Review of International Copyright Law). Taipei: Sanmin chuban she, 1985.

————. *Zhuzuoquanfa zhi yuanlun* (An Overview of Copyright Law). Taipei: Shangwu chuban she, 1985.

Shirk, Susan. *Competitive Comrades: Career Incentives and Student Strategies in China.* Berkeley and Los Angeles: University of California Press, 1980.

"Shishi guoji zhuzuoquan tiaoyue de guiding" (Regulations on the Implementation of International Copyright Treaties). Effective from Sept. 30, 1992. Original Chinese and English translation reprinted in *China Patents and Trademarks*, no. 2 (1993): 84–90.

"Shuji gaofei shixing guiding" (The Trial Regulations on Basic Payments for Books). Effective from Dec. 1, 1984.

Sidel, Mark. "Copyright, Trademark and Patent Laws in the People's Republic of China." *Texas International Law Journal* 21, no. 2 (1986): 259–89.

————. "The Legal Protection of Copyright and the Rights of Authors in the People's Republic of China, 1949–1984: Prelude to the Chinese Copyright Law." *Columbia Journal of Art and the Law* 9, no. 4 (1985): 477–508.

Silk, Mitchell. "Legal Efforts of the United States and the Republic of China on Taiwan at Controlling the Transnational Flow of Commercial Counterfeit Goods." *Chinese Yearbook of International Law* 5 (1985–86): 90–149.

Simon, Denis, and Merle Goldman, eds. *Science and Technology in Post-Mao China.* Cambridge, Mass.: Council on East Asian Studies, Harvard University, 1989.

Simon, Denis, and Michael Y. M. Kau, eds. *Taiwan: Beyond the Economic Miracle.* Armonk, N.Y.: M. E. Sharpe, 1992.

Simone, Joseph. "Copyright Law Enters into Effect." *IP ASIA* 1991, no. 6: 18–21.

————. "Copyright-MOU." *IP ASIA* 1992, no. 2: 14–15.

————. "Protection of American Copyright in Books on Taiwan." *Journal of the Copyright Society of the U.S.A.* 35, no. 2 (1988): 115–57.

Singer, Isaac Bashevis. *The Magician of Lublin.* Beijing: n.d.

Smith, Douglas, and Donald McFetridge. "Patents, Prospects and Economic Surplus: A Comment." *Journal of Law & Economics* 23, no. 1 (1980): 197–203.

Smith, Eric. "Trade-Based Approaches to Copyright Protection." In *Contemporary Copyright and Proprietary Rights Issues* (1987).

Smith, Richard. *China's Cultural Heritage.* Boulder, Colo.: Westview Press, 1984.

Solinger, Dorothy. *Chinese Business Under Socialism: The Politics of Domestic*

Commerce, 1949–1980. Berkeley and Los Angeles: University of California Press, 1985.

Spence, Jonathan. "Opium Smoking in Ch'ing China." In Frederick Wakeman, Jr., and Carolyn Grant, eds., *Conflict and Control in Late Imperial China*. Berkeley and Los Angeles: University of California Press, 1975.

Stewart, Stephen. *International Copyright and Neighbouring Rights*. 2d ed. London: Butterworth, 1989.

Stone, Andrew. "Legal Aspects of Copyright Protection Between the United States and the Republic of China." *Chinese Yearbook of International Law and Affairs* 9 (1989–90): 179–223.

Stross, Randall. *Bulls in the China Shop and Other Sino-American Business Encounters*. New York: Pantheon Books, 1990.

Swanson, James. *Scientific Discoveries and Soviet Law: A Sociohistorical Analysis*. Gainesville: University of Florida Press, 1984.

Syron, Kathleen. "The Year of the Mouse." *China Business Review* 14, no. 6 (Nov.–Dec. 1987): 5.

"Taiwan's Brazen Pirates." *Newsweek*, Nov. 15, 1982.

Tang Yongchun. "Foreign Trademarks in Chinese Characters." *China Patents & Trademarks*, no. 3 (1987): 36 (9 pp.).

Tang Zongshun. "Protection of Intellectual Property." In Rui Mu and Wang Guiguo, eds., *China's Foreign Economic Law*, ch. 5, 1–49. Washington, D.C.: International Law Institute, 1990.

Tang Tsou. *America's Failure in China, 1941–1950*. Chicago: University of Chicago Press, 1963.

Tao Baichuan and Wang Zijian, eds. *Liu fa quanshu* (The Complete Book of the Six Laws). Taipei: Sanmin shu ju, 1983.

Tao Baichuan, Wang Zijian, Liu Zongrong, and Ge Kechang, eds. *Liu fa quanshu* (The Complete Book of the Six Laws). Taipei: Sanmin chuban she, 1992.

Temple, Robert. *The Genius of China: 3.000 Years of Science, Discovery, and Invention*. New York: Simon & Schuster, 1986.

Teng Ssu-yü. "Chinese Influence on the Western Examination System." *Harvard Journal of Asiatic Studies* 7, no. 4 (1943): 267–312.

Tian Ying. "Trademark Controls Are Taking Effect." *China Daily Business Weekly*, Jan. 19, 1992, 4.

Thurston, Anne. *Enemies of the People: The Ordeal of the Intellectuals in China's Great Cultural Revolution*. Cambridge, Mass.: Harvard University Press, 1988.

Ting Lee-hsia. *Government Control of the Press in Modern China, 1900–1949*. Cambridge, Mass.: Council on East Asian Studies, Harvard University. 1974.

"Trademark Regulations." Reprinted in *Foreign Relations of the United States*

(1906), pt. 1, item no. 1681, pp. 237–39 (Aug. 15, 1904). Washington, D.C.: Government Printing Office, 1906.

"Treaty of Friendship, Commerce, and Navigation Between the United States of America and the Republic of China" (Nov. 4, 1946). Treaties and Other International Acts Series, no. 1871.

Trubek, David, and Marc Galanter. "Scholars in Self-Estrangement: Some Reflections on the Crisis in Law and Development Studies in the United States." *Wisconsin Law Review* 1974, no. 4: 1062–1102.

Tseng-Ch'en Ming-ruu. *Zhuanli shangbiaofa xuanlun* (Selected Essays on Patent and Trademark Law). 3d ed. Taipei: Guoli Taiwan daxue, 1988.

Tu Wei-ming. *Centrality and Commonality: An Essay on Confucian Religiousness.* Albany: State University of New York, 1989.

Twitchett, Denis. *Printing and Publishing in Medieval China.* New York: Frederick C. Beil, 1983.

"Understanding Between the American Institute in Taiwan and the Coordination Council for North American Affairs." Signed on June 5, 1992, in Washington, D.C.

U.S. Congress. House of Representatives. Subcommittee on Oversight and Investigation of the Committee on Energy and Commerce. *Unfair Foreign Trade Practices Stealing American Intellectual Property: Imitation Is Not Flattery.* 98th Cong., 2d sess., Feb. 1984.

U.S. Department of State. *1991 Human Rights Reports–China.* Feb. 1992.

U.S. International Trade Commission. *The Effect of Foreign Product Counterfeiting on U.S. Industry.* USITC Publication no. 1479. 1984.

———. *Foreign Protection of Intellectual Property Rights and the Effect on U.S. Industry and Trade*, Report to the U.S. Trade Representative, Invest. no. 332–245. USITC Publication no. 2065. 1988.

U.S. Office of Technology Assessment. *Intellectual Property Rights in an Age of Electronics and Information.* Washington, D.C.: Government Printing Office, 1986.

U.S. Trade Representative, Office of the. "Fact Sheet on AIT–CCNAA Understanding Regarding IPR Protection in Taiwan." Washington, D.C., 1992. Mimeo.

Vogel, Ezra. *The Four Little Dragons: The Spread of Industrialization in East Asia.* Cambridge, Mass.: Harvard University Press, 1991.

"Waiguoren huo waiguoqiye shenqing shangbiao juce daili banfa" (Measures Concerning Agents for Foreign Individuals or Foreign Enterprises Applying to Register a Trademark). In *Zhongguo shewai jingji fagui huibian* (The Collected Laws and Regulations of the People's Republic of China with Respect to Foreign Economic Matters), 1949–85: 1162–63. Beijing: Renmin chuban she, 1986.

Walder, Andrew. *Communist Neo-Traditionalism: Work and Authority in Chinese Industry.* Berkeley and Los Angeles: University of California Press, 1986.

Waley, Arthur, trans. *The Analects of Confucius.* London: Allen & Unwin, 1938.

Wang, Francis, and Laura Young. "Taiwan's New Copyright Regime: Improved Protection for American Authors and Copyright Holders." *International Lawyer* 27, no. 4 (1993): 1111–21.

Wang Guang. "Taiwan yu dalu zhuzuoquanfa bijiao" (A Comparison of Taiwan and Mainland Laws on Copyright). *Faxue yanjiu* (Research on Legal Studies) 75, no. 4 (1991): 68–72.

Wang Jiafu. "Shilun zhuanlifa de zhiding" (An Examination of the Formulation of the Patent Law). *Faxue yanjiu* (Research on Legal Studies) 16, no. 5 (1981): 27–32.

Wang Jiafu and Xia Shuhua. *Zhuanlifa jianlun* (A Brief Discussion of Patent Law). Beijing: Falü chuban she, 1984.

Wang Jie. "Symposium on Intellectual Property Systems Held in Beijing." *China Patents & Trademarks,* no. 3 (1992): 107–9.

Wang Ke. "Essence of Escalation of Sino–U.S. Trade Frictions." *Zu Qing,* Jan. 5, 1992, pp. 43–45. Translated and reprinted in *Foreign Broadcast Information Service* CHI-92-0009, Jan. 14, 1992, pp. 9–12.

Wang Liwei. "China's Patent Law and the Economic Reform Today." *UCLA Pacific Basin Law Journal* 9, nos. 1–2 (1991): 254–75.

Wang, Y. C. *Chinese Intellectuals and the West, 1872–1949.* Chapel Hill: University of North Carolina Press, 1966.

Wang Yonghong. "Deeper Crackdown Urged on Faked Goods." *China Daily,* Sept. 15, 1993, 3.

Wang Yujie. "Zhongguo tese de shehuizhuyi zhuanlifa" (A Socialist Patent Law with Chinese Characteristics). *Minzhu yu fazhi* (Democracy and Legal System) 57, no. 4 (1984): 20–22.

Wang Zhengfa. "Administrative Resolution of Intellectual Property Infringement in China." *China Patents & Trademarks,* no. 3 (1992): 10–14.

———. "The Chinese Intellectual Property System at the Turning Point." *China Patents & Trademarks,* no. 1 (1992): 19–28.

———. "Proliferation of Fake and Inferior Pharmaceuticals in China Should Be Tackled Comprehensively." *China Patents & Trademarks,* no. 1 (1991): 40–45.

———. "Technology Transfer—China's Outlook and Future Needs." *China Patents & Trademarks,* no. 2 (1987): 48–57.

Wasserstrom, Jeffrey, and Elizabeth Perry, eds. *Popular Protest and Political Culture in Modern China: Learning from 1989.* Boulder, Colo.: Westview Press, 1992.

Watson, Alan. *Legal Transplants*. Philadelphia: University of Pennsylvania Press, 1977.

Watson, Burton. *Ssu-ma Ch'ien: Grand Historian of China*. New York: Columbia University Press, 1958.

Watt, John. *The District Magistrate in Late Imperial China*. New York: Columbia University Press, 1972.

Weinreb, Lloyd. "Fair's Fair: A Comment on the Fair Use Doctrine." *Harvard Law Review* 103, no. 5 (1990): 1137–61.

Wen Fong. "The Problem of Forgeries in Chinese Painting." *Artibus Asiae* 25, nos. 2–3 (1962): 95–140.

Wen Xikai. "Chinese Patent System Further Amplified as Reform Goes in Depth." *China Patents & Trademarks*, no. 3 (1992): 24–27.

Willoughby, Westel. *Foreign Rights and Interests in China*. Baltimore: Johns Hopkins Press, 1920.

Winkler, Robin. "Intellectual Property Laws: Legislative Update." *IP ASIA* 1992, no. 2.

———. "Taiwan." *IP ASIA* 1991, no. 9.

———. "US–ROC Trade Talks on Copyright." *IP ASIA* 1990, no. 7.

———. "US Taiwan Trade Talks." *IP ASIA* 1990, no. 8.

Woodmansee, Martha. "The Genius and the Copyright: Economic and Legal Conditions of the Emergence of the 'Author.'" *Eighteenth-Century Studies* 17, no. 4 (1984): 425–48.

Wu Kuang-ch'ing. "Ming Printers and Printing." *Harvard Journal of Asiatic Studies* 7, no. 3 (1942–43): 203–60.

Wu Naitao. "Copyright Comes Under Legal Protection." *Beijing Review* 34, no. 37 (1991): 19–21.

Wu Wen-ya. "The Board of Foreign Trade Export Trademark Approval Procedure." In National Anti-Counterfeiting Committee, *Intellectual Property Rights Enforcement Seminar*. Taipei: National Anti-Counterfeiting Committee, 1987.

Xia Shuhua. *Zhuanlifa gaiyao* (The Essence of Patent Law). Beijing: Jingjixue chuban she, 1987.

Xiao Xionglin. *Zhongmei zhuzuoquan tanpan quanji* (Complete Papers on Sino-American Copyright Negotiations). Taipei: Sanmin shu ju, 1989.

Xie Xiang and Guo Jiakuan. "Sounds of History's Footsteps: Written on the Eve of the Implementation of the Copyright Law." *Zhongguo qingnian bao* (China Youth Newspaper), May 29, 1991, 4. Translated in *Foreign Broadcast Information Service* CHI-91-114 (June 13, 1991).

Xing'an huilan (Conspectus of Penal Cases). Shanghai: Dushu jicheng chuban she, 1986.

Xue Yunsheng. *Duli cunyi* (Thoughts About Certain Matters Gleaned While

Perusing the Substatutes). T. H. Huang, ed. Reprint. Taipei: Chengwen chuban she, 1970.

Yang Lien-sheng. *Studies in Chinese Institutional History*. Cambridge, Mass.: Harvard University Press, 1961.

Yang, Xiaobing. "Protecting Trademark Rights." *Beijing Review* 34, no. 27 (July 8, 1991): 37–39.

Yankelovich, Skelly, and White, the Policy Planning Group. "Public Perceptions of the Intellectual Property Rights Issue." Paper prepared for the U.S. Office of Technology Assessment, 1985. Mimeo.

Yao Yuxiang, ed. *Da Qing lü li huitong xinsuan* (The Comprehensive New Edition of the Code of the Great Qing Dynasty). Reprint. Taipei: Wenhai chuban she, 1964.

Ye Dehui. *Shulin qinghua* (Quiet Words in a Forest of Books). 1920. Reprint. Beijing: Zhonghua shu ju, 1957.

Ye Yuqi. "Shangbiaofa xiuzheng de yingxiang" (Influences on the Revision of the Trademark Law). *Shibao zhoukan* (Times Weekly), Dec. 11, 1985.

Ying Ming. "The System of Software Copyright Registration in China." *China Patents & Trademarks*, no. 4 (1992): 77–78.

Yu Jianyang. "Review of Patent Infringement Litigation." *Journal of Chinese Law* 5 (1991): 297–347.

Yu, Susan. "U.S. Retaliation Fear Hits Taiwan: Time Running Out?" *Free China Journal* 10, no. 28 (1993): 1–2.

Yuan Yi. "Zhongguo gudai banquan shi kaolüe" (A Consideration of the History of Copyright in Classical China). *Faxue zazhi* (Legal Studies Magazine), 30, no. 3 (1985): 40–42.

———. "Zhongguo jindai banquan de yanbian shiqi" (The Period of Development of Modern Chinese Copyright). *Faxue zazhi* (Legal Studies Magazine), 33, no. 6 (1985): 46 (3 pp.).

Zelin, Madeline. "Merchant Dispute Mediation in Twentieth-Century Zigong, Sichuan." In Kathryn Bernhardt and Philip Huang, eds., *Civil Law in Qing and Republican China*. Stanford: Stanford University Press, 1994.

Zhang Jing. "Dalu chubanpin falü wenti tantao" (A Frank Discussion of Legal Problems with Mainland Publications). *Wenhua chuban* (Cultural Publishing). Taipei, 1991.

Zhang Jinglu. *Zhongguo jindai chuban shiliao* (Historical Materials on Chinese Publishing in Recent Times). 2 vols. Shanghai: Renmin chuban she, 1954–58.

———. *Zhongguo xiandai chuban shiliao* (Materials on Chinese Publishing in Modern Times). Shanghai: Zhonghua shuju gufeng youxian gongsi, 1954.

Zhang Xujiu. *Shangbiaofa jiaocheng* (A Course of Study on Trademark Law). Beijing: Falü chuban she, 1986.

Zhang Youyu. "Xu" (Preface). In *Zhongguo falü nianjian* (The Law Yearbook of China), 1–5. Beijing: Falü chuban she, 1987.

Zhao Xiuwen. *Zhuzuoquan* (Copyright). Beijing: Falü chuban she, 1987.

Zhao Zelu. "Zhuanli quan" (Patent Rights). In *Minfa tongze jiangzuo* (A Course of Lectures on the General Principles of the Civil Law). Beijing, 1986.

Zheng Chengsi. *Banquanfa* (Copyright Law). Beijing: Renmin daxue chuban she, 1990.

———. *Banquan gongyue, banquan baohu, yu banquan maoyi* (Copyright Treaties, Copyright Protection, and Copyright Trade). Beijing: Renmin daxue chuban she, 1992.

———. *Chinese Intellectual Property and Technology Transfer Law*. Hong Kong: Butterworth, 1987.

———. "The Future Chinese Copyright System and Its Context." *International Review of Industrial Property and Copyright Law* 15 (1984): 141–68.

———. "Printing and Publishing in China and Foreign Countries and the Evolution of Copyright (I)." *China Patents & Trademarks*, no. 4 (1987): 39–43.

———. "Printing and Publishing in China and Foreign Countries and the Evolution of Copyright (II)." *China Patents & Trademarks*, no. 1 (1988): 44–51.

———. "Trade Marks in China: The First Specific Law in the Field of Chinese Intellectual Property." *European Intellectual Property Review* 4, no. 10 (1982): 278–84.

Zheng Chengsi and Michael Pendleton. *Copyright Law in China*. North Ryde, NSW, Australia: CCH International, 1991.

———. "A Response to United States Government Criticisms of the Chinese Copyright Law." *European Intellectual Property Review* 13, no. 10 (1991): 257–66.

Zheng Songyu. "Interview." *IP ASIA* 1992, no. 9: 30–32.

———. "Sum Up the Past, Look Forward to the Future and Render Better Service to the Industrial Property Undertaking in China." *China Patents & Trademarks*, no. 3 (1991): 3–10.

"Zhengwuyuan guanyu jiangli youguan shengchang de faming, jishu gaijin ji helihua jianyi de jueding" (Decision Encouraging Inventions, Technical Improvements, and Rationalization Proposals Concerning Production). Issued August 16, 1950. In *Zhongyang renmin zhengfu faling huibian* (The Collected Laws and Decrees of the Central People's Government), 357–58. Beijing: Renmin chuban she, 1952.

Zhongguo falü nianjian she, ed. *Zhongguo falü nianjian* (The Law Yearbook of China). Beijing: Zhongguo falü nianjian she, 1992.

Zhongguo gaoji faguan peixun zhongxin and Zhongguo renmin daxue faxueyuan, eds. *Zhongguo shenpan anli yaolan* (The Compendium of Judicial Decisions of China). Beijing: Zhongguo renmin gongan daxue chuban she, 1992.

"Zhongguo renmin zhengzhi xieshang huiyi de gongtong gangling" (Common Program of the Chinese People's Political Consultative Conference). Passed at the 1st Plenary Session of the CPPCC, Sept. 29, 1949. In *Zhonghua renmin gongheguo faling huibian* (The Collected Laws and Regulations of the People's Republic of China), 1 (1949–50): 16–25. Beijing: Renmin chuban she, 1952.

"Zhongguo zhishichanquan baohu zhuangkuang" (The State of China's Intellectual Property Protection). *Renmin ribao (haiwaiban)* (People's Daily [Overseas Edition]) June 17, 1994, 3.

Zhongguo zhuanli bao (China Patent Newspaper). Beijing, 1991–93.

Zhonghua renmin gongheguo, Guojia tongji ju. *Zhongguo tongji nianjian* (The Yearbook of Chinese Statistics). Beijing: Zhongguo tongji chuban she, 1988–91.

Zhonghua renmin gongheguo guowuyuan gongbao (The Gazette of the State Council of the People's Republic of China). Beijing: Zhonghua renmin gongheguo guowuyuan bangongting, 1986–92.

"Zhonghua renmin gongheguo minfa tongze" (The General Principles of the Civil Law of the People's Republic of China). Promulgated on Apr. 12, 1986, and effective from March 1, 1987. In *Zhonghua renmin gongheguo fagui huibian* (The Collected Laws and Regulations of the People's Republic of China), Jan.–Dec. 1986: 1–34. Beijing: Falü chuban she, 1987. English translation available in *The Laws of the People's Republic of China, 1983–86*, 225–50. Beijing: Foreign Languages Press, 1987.

"Zhonghua renmin gongheguo shangbiaofa" (The Trademark Law of the People's Republic of China). Promulgated on Aug. 23, 1982, and effective from March 1, 1983. In *Zhonghua renmin gongheguo fagui huibian* (The Collected Laws and Regulations of the People's Republic of China), Jan.–Dec. 1982: 519–27. Beijing: Falü chuban she, 1986. English translation available in *The Laws of the People's Republic of China, 1979–82*, 305–13. Beijing: Foreign Languages Press, 1987.

"Zhonghua renmin gongheguo shangbiaofa (1993 nian xiuding ben)" (The Trademark Law of the People's Republic of China [1993 Revised Version]). Adopted Feb. 22, 1993. Original Chinese and English translation reprinted in *China Patents and Trademarks*, no. 2 (1993): 84–90.

"Zhonghua renmin gongheguo shangbiaofa shishi xize" (The Implementing Regulations of the Trademark Law of the People's Republic of China).

Promulgated on Jan. 3, 1988, and effective from Jan. 13, 1988. In *Zhonghua renmin gongheguo fagui huibian* (The Collected Laws and Regulations of the People's Republic of China), Jan.–Dec. 1988: 887–99. Beijing: Falü chuban she, 1990. English translation published as a pamphlet. Beijing: Foreign Languages Press, 1986.

"Zhonghua renmin gongheguo xianfa" (The Constitution of the People's Republic of China). Promulgated on and effective from Sept. 20, 1954. In *Zhonghua renmin gongheguo fagui huibian* (The Collected Laws and Regulations of the People's Republic of China), Sept. 1954–June 1955: 4–31. Beijing: Falü chuban she, 1956. English translation available in Albert Blaustein, ed. *Fundamental Legal Documents of Communist China*. South Hackensack, N.J.: E. B. Rothman, 1962.

"Zhonghua renmin gongheguo xianfa" (The Constitution of the People's Republic of China). Promulgated on and effective from Dec. 4, 1982. In *Zhonghua renmin gongheguo fagui huibian* (The Collected Laws and Regulations of the People's Republic of China), Jan.–Dec. 1986: 1–42. Beijing: Falü chuban she, 1986. English translation available in *The Laws of the People's Republic of China, 1979–82*, 1–34. Beijing: Foreign Languages Press, 1987.

Zhongguo xiaofeizhe bao (China Consumers' Newspaper). 1987–93.

"Zhonghua renmin gongheguo xingfa" (The Criminal Law of the People's Republic of China). Promulgated on July 6, 1979, and effective from Jan. 1, 1980. In *Zhonghua renmin gongheguo fagui huibian* (The Collected Laws and Regulations of the People's Republic of China), Jan.–Dec. 1979: 48–86. Beijing: Falü chuban she, 1986. English translation available in *The Laws of the People's Republic of China, 1979–82*. Beijing: Foreign Languages Press, 1987.

"Zhonghua renmin gongheguo xingzheng susongfa" (Administrative Litigation Law of the People's Republic of China). *Renmin ribao* Apr. 10, 1989, 2. English translation available in *Chinese Law and Practice* 3, no. 5, 37.

"Zhonghua renmin gongheguo zhuanlifa" (The Patent Law of the People's Republic of China). Promulgated on March 12, 1984, and effective from Apr. 1, 1985. In *Zhonghua renmin gongheguo fagui huibian* (The Collected Laws and Regulations of the People's Republic of China), Jan.–Dec. 1984: 529–43. Beijing: Falü chuban she, 1986. English translation available in *The Laws of the People's Republic of China, 1983–86*, 65–76. Beijing: Foreign Languages Press, 1987.

"Zhonghua renmin gongheguo zhuanlifa (1992 nian xiuding ben)" (The Patent Law of the People's Republic of China [1992 Revised Version]). Adopted Sept. 4, 1992. Original Chinese and English translation reprinted in *China Patents & Trademarks*, no. 4 (Dec. 1992) 93–102.

"Zhonghua renmin gongheguo zhuanlifa shishi xize" (The Implementing Regulations for the Patent Law of the People's Republic of China). Promulgated on Jan. 19, 1985, and effective from Apr. 1, 1985. In *Zhonghua renmin gongheguo fagui huibian* (The Collected Laws and Regulations of the People's Republic of China), Jan.–Dec. 1985: 557–81. Beijing: Falü chuban she, 1986. English translation published as a pamphlet. Beijing: Foreign Languages Press, 1986.

"Zhonghua renmin gongheguo zhuanlifa shishi xize (1992 nian xueding ben)" (The Implementing Regulations for the Patent Law of the People's Republic of China [1992 Revised Version]). Effective from Jan. 1, 1993. Original Chinese and English translation reprinted in *China Patents and Trademarks*, no. 1 (1993): 78–97.

"Zhonghua renmin gongheguo zhuanliju xingzheng fuyi guicheng (shixing)" (The Rules on Administrative Reconsideration of the Patent Office of the People's Republic of China [for Trial Implementation]). Promulgated on Dec. 29, 1991, and effective from Feb. 1, 1992. Original Chinese and English translation reprinted in *China Patents & Trademarks*, no. 3 (1992): 70–74.

"Zhonghua renmin gongheguo zhuanli ju gonggao. Di ershiliu hao" (Announcement No. 26 of the Patent Office of the People's Republic of China). Nov. 20, 1989. Original Chinese and English translation in *China Patents & Trademarks*, no. 2 (1990): 74–75.

"Zhonghua renmin gongheguo zhuanli ju gonggao. Di ershiqi hao" (Announcement No. 27 of the Patent Office of the People's Republic of China). Dec. 11, 1989. Original Chinese and English translation in *China Patents & Trademarks*, no. 2 (1990): 74–75.

"Zhonghua renmin gongheguo zhuzuoquanfa" (The Copyright Law of the People's Republic of China). Promulgated on Sept. 7, 1990, and effective from June 1, 1991. In *Zhonghua renmin gongheguo fagui huibian* (The Collected Laws and Regulations of the People's Republic of China), Jan.–Dec. 1990: 755–70. Beijing: Falü chuban she, 1991. English translation in *China Patents and Trademarks*, no. 1 (1991): 61–64.

"Zhonghua renmin gongheguo zhuzuoquanfa shishi tiaoli" (The Implementing Regulations for the Copyright Law of the People's Republic of China). Effective from June 1, 1991. Original Chinese and English translation reprinted in *China Patents and Trademarks*, no. 1 (1991): 61–69.

"Zhonghua quanguo zhuanli daibiaoren xiehui zhangcheng." (The Rules Governing Branches of the All-China Association of Patent Agents). In *Zhuanli fagui huibian* (The Collected Laws and Regulations Concerning Patent Matters), 1984–90. Beijing: Zhuanli wenxian chuban she, 1991.

Zhu Wenqing. "Shilun zhuanlifa de renwu" (An Examination of the Mission of Patent Law). *Fudan faxue* (Fudan Legal Studies), 1985.

Zhu Xisen. *Shangbiao yu shangbiaofa* (Trademark and Trademark Law). Beijing: Gongren chuban she, 1986.

"Zhuanlifa" (Patent Law). In Tao Baichuan, Wang Zijian, Liu Zongrong, and Ge Kechang, eds., *Liu fa quanshu* (The Complete Book of the Six Laws). Taipei: Sanmin shu ju, 1992.

"Zhuanlifa daili zanxing guiding" (The Provisional Regulations Regarding Patent Agents). Promulgated on and effective from Sept. 12, 1985. In *Zhonghua renmin gongheguo fagui huibian* (The Collected Laws and Regulations of the People's Republic of China), Jan.–Dec. 1985: 582–85. Beijing: Falü chuban she, 1986.

"Zhuanlifa tiaowen xiuzheng caoan zongshuoming" (The Complete Explanation of the Draft Revised Patent Law Provisions). Taipei: Lifayuan, [1990]. Mimeo.

"Zhuanli guanli jiguan chuli zhuanli jiufen banfa" (The Patent Administrative Authorities' Measures for the Adjudication of Patent Disputes). Promulgated on Dec. 4, 1989. Original Chinese and English translation reprinted in *Chinese Law and Practice*, 4, no. 4 (1990): 40–48.

Zhuanli shangbiao nianbao (Patent and Trademark Yearbook). Taipei: Ministry of Economic Affairs, 1989.

"Zhuzuoquanfa" (The Copyright Law). In Tao Baichuan, Wang Zijian, Liu Zongrong, and Ge Kechang, eds., *Liu fa quanshu* (The Complete Book of the Six Laws). Taipei: Sanmin shu ju, 1992.

"Zhuzuoquanfa tiaowen xiuzheng caoan zongshuoming" (The Complete Explanation of the Draft Revised Copyright Law Provisions). Taipei: Lifayuan, [1985]. Mimeo.

"Zhuzuoquanfa tiaowen xiuzheng caoan zongshuoming" (The Complete Explanation of the Draft Revised Copyright Law Provisions). Taipei: Lifayuan, [1986]. Mimeo.

"Zhuzuoquanfa tiaowen xiuzheng caoan zongshuoming" (The Complete Explanation of the Draft Revised Copyright Law Provisions). Taipei: Lifayuan, [1990]. Mimeo.

Zongtong fu gongbao (The Gazette of the President's Office). Taipei, 1989–92.

Zou Shencheng. "Baohu banquan shi yu he shi heguo?" (The Protection of Copyright Started When and in What Country?) *Faxue yanjiu* (Research on Legal Studies) 63, no. 2 (1984): 63.

"Zuigao renmin fayuan guanyu kaizhan zhuanli shenpan gongzuo de jige wenti de tongzhi" (The Circular of the Supreme People's Court Addressing Several Questions Involved in Rendering Judgement in Patent Cases). Promulgated on Feb. 16, 1985. *Zhonghua renmin gongheguo zuigao renmin fayuan gongbao* (The Gazette of the Supreme People's Court of the People's Republic of China) 4, no. 1 (1985): 16–18. Beijing: Zhonghua renmin gongheguo zuigao renmin fayuan bangongting, 1985.

"Zuigao renmin fayuan guanyu shenli zhuanli jiufen anjian ruogan wenti de jiehui" (Answers of the Supreme People's Court to Several Questions on Resolution of Patent Disputes). *Zhonghua renmin gongheguo zuigao renmin fayuan gongbao* (The Gazette of the Supreme People's Court of the People's Republic of China), no. 1 (1993): 26–27. Beijing: Zhonghua renmin gongheguo zuigao renmin fayuan bangongting, 1993.

"Zuigao renmin fayuan guanyu shenli zhuanli shenqing quan jiufen anjian ruogan wenti de tongzhi" (The Circular of the Supreme People's Court Addressing Several Questions Concerning Cases Involving Disputes over the Right to Apply for a Patent). Promulgated on Oct. 19, 1987. *Zhonghua renmin gongheguo zuigao renmin fayuan gongbao* (The Gazette of the Supreme People's Court of the People's Republic of China) 6, no. 4 (1987): 8. Beijing: Zhonghua renmin gongheguo zuigao renmin fayuan bangongting, 1987.

"Zuigao renmin fayuan guanyu zhuanli qinquan jiufen anjian diyu guanxia wenti de tongzhi" (The Circular of the Supreme People's Court Addressing the Question of Territorial Jurisdiction in Cases Involving Disputes over Patent Infringement). Promulgated on June 29, 1987. *Zhonghua renmin gongheguo zuigao renmin fayuan gongbao* (The Gazette of the Supreme People's Court of the People's Republic of China) 6, no. 3 (1987): 13. Beijing: Zhonghua renmin gongheguo zuigao renmin fayuan bangongting, 1987.

Glossary

baihua　白話

banquan　版權

baozheng　保證

buchong guiding　補充規定

cao yaoshu yaoyan　抄妖書妖言

dacheng　大成

danwei　單位

dao　道

daotai　道臺

daode　道德

de　德

dian　典

doujiang　豆漿

fa　法

fabiao　發表

fang　方

faren　法人

fen　分

fugu　复古

fumu guan　父母官

fuxun yiqing　俯順夷情

gaofei　稿費

gongan　公安

guofu　國父

guojia jiguan　國家機關

guozijian　國子監

hang zhang　行章

hanjian　漢奸

hong　行

huawairen　化外人

jia cheng　家程

jianhou　監候

li　里

li　禮

liang　兩

likin　厘金

neibu　內部

ruanjian　軟件

san xian　三限

shangbiao　商標

shi　詩

shi e　十惡

shixing　試行

shuhao　書號

songgon　訟棍

taijian　太監

tangguo　糖果

tianli　天理

tianming　天命

tie fan wan　鐵飯碗

tou shu shi ya zui　偷書是雅罪

waiyi　外夷

wancheng　完成

wei zhixing gongwu　為執行公務

wen　文

wenren　文人

xian　縣

xiang yue　鄉約

xixu　習俗

yamen　衙門

yiwei　意味

Yuan　院

yuan　元

yundong　運動

zanxing　暫行

zheng shi　正史

zhengming　正名

zhuanli　專利

zhuzuoquan　著作權

ziran　自然

Index

In this index an "f" after a number indicates a separate reference on the next page, and an "ff" indicates separate references on the next two pages. A continuous discussion over two or more pages is indicated by a span of page numbers, e.g., "57–59." *Passim* is used for a cluster of references in close but not consecutive sequence.

Library of Congress Cataloging-in-Publication Data
Alford, William P.
To steal a book is an elegant offense : intellectual property law in Chinese
civilization / William P. Alford
    p.   cm. — (Studies in East Asian law)
Includes bibliographical references and index.
ISBN 0-8047-2270-6 (cloth : acid-free paper)
1. Intellectual property—China—History.   I. Title.   II. Series.
KNN1155.A958   1995
346.5104′8—dc20
[345.10648]   94-15742   CIP

∞ This book is printed on acid-free, recycled paper.